IS SOUTHEASTERN EUROPE DOOMED TO INSTABILITY?

A REGIONAL PERSPECTIVE

Editors

Dimitri A. Sotiropoulos and Thanos Veremis

FRANK CASS

LONDON • PORTLAND, OR

First published in 2002 in Great Britain by
FRANK CASS PUBLISHERS
Crown House, 47 Chase Side, Southgate
London, N14 5BP, England

and in the United States of America by
FRANK CASS PUBLISHERS
c/o ISBS, 5824 N.E. Hassalo Street
Portland, Oregon 97213-3644

Website: http://www.frankcass.com

British Library Cataloguing in Publication Data

Is Southeastern Europe doomed to instability? : a regional
perspective
1. Democratization – Balkan Peninsula 2. Human rights –
Balkan Peninsula 3. Internal security – Balkan Peninsula
4. Balkan Peninsula – Politics and government – 1989–
I. Veremis, Thanos II. Sotiropoulos, Dimitri A.
320.9'496'09049
ISBN 0 7146 5289 X (cloth)
ISBN 0 7146 8256 X (paper)

Library of Congress Cataloging-in-Publication Data

Is southeastern Europe doomed to instability? : a regional perspective /
editors, Thanos Veremis and Dimitri A. Sotiropoulos.
    p. cm.
This collection first appeared as a special issue of the Journal of
southeast European and Black Sea studies, 2/1 (January 2002).
Includes bibliographical references and index.
✓   ISBN 0-7146-5289-X (cloth : alk. paper) — ISBN 0-7146-8256-X (pbk. :
alk. paper)
    1. Balkan Peninsula—Politics and government—1989- I. Veremães,
Thanos. II. Såotåeropoulos, Dåemåetråes A., 1960- III. Journal of
southeast European and Black Sea studies.
    DR48.6 .I8 2002
    320.9496—dc21   2002001276

This group of studies first appeared as 'Is Southeastern Europe Doomed to
Instability? A Regional Perspective', a special issue of *The Journal of Southeast
European and Black Sea Studies*, 2/1 (January 2002)
ISSN 1468-3857, published by Frank Cass and Co. Ltd.

Printed in Great Britain by
Antony Rowe Ltd., Chippenham, Wilts

Contents

Introduction

DIMITRI A. SOTIROPOULOS
AND THANOS VEREMIS

THE PURPOSE OF THIS VOLUME

The greatest peril of the states of Southeastern Europe (SEE) – states that are now more numerous and individually less important to the West than during the Cold War – lies in their being neglected and isolated. To avoid political isolation and to enhance their chances to attain economic stability and social cohesion, Southeast European states need to re-structure and re-focus their policies in order to address the problems of the region. This entails their political and economic integration, albeit in a gradual fashion, into the European Union. It also calls for their cooperation on a regional basis in order to overcome the twin dangers of being perceived as endemically unstable and of being excluded from the European and Euro-Atlantic processes.

If the principal objective of local SEE actors is to formulate strategies and tactics, which will serve the above aims, aid from and interaction with extra-regional actors is irreplaceable. However, a less obvious point is that local perspectives must also be voiced and offered to an international audience for consideration. The purpose of this collected volume is to air concerns of experts and intellectuals coming from the region of SEE. Such a concerted effort includes both an analysis of recent developments and a presentation of findings and recommendations that international observers and policy makers may find useful. There is, after all, 'local knowledge' – in the anthropological sense of the term – of and about SEE that governments and civil society organizations involved in the area may want to consider seriously. The point is to take into account political and scholarly work that is already being done in the region and to build on it by providing a Southeast European perspective.

At a time when Western values and methods are questioned as a result of NATO's involvement in Kosovo, of the simmering tensions in FYR of Macedonia (FYROM) and of the dangers posed to the integrity of Bosnia and Herzegovina several years after the Dayton and Paris accords, it is important to pause and re-think the role of the international community and its major institutions as well as the role of regional and local actors.

The idea is not to counter-pose the international to the regional actors, but to underline the role of the latter in limiting any reticence in SEE societies towards accepting Western-inspired notions of democracy and civil society, as well as standards of employment conditions, income and welfare provision. We try to apply such notions and standards in SEE in the next section of this introduction, emphasizing the interplay of international and regional actors.

ENDURING COMMONALITIES OF SOUTHEAST EUROPEAN STATES

The peaceful and democratic political transition in the Federal Republic of Yugoslavia (FRY) in the autumn and winter of 2000, the ethnic tensions in FYROM at the beginning of 2001, the rivalries that surfaced again in Bosnia and Herzegovina in the early spring of 2001, and the peaceful first elections in Kosovo in autumn 2001, show that there are both positive developments and recurrent sources of instability in SEE.

It is obvious that changes at the national level are often integrally linked with developments at the level of international and foreign policy. This is particularly true in the case of FRY, where the new political leadership, which emerged in late 2000, has to deal with the usual problems of transition from authoritarian role and simultaneously meet the challenges of the ongoing process of Yugoslavia's disintegration. Clearly, domestic changes in FRY affect and are affected by developments in Montenegro, FYROM and Kosovo. Furthermore, other states in the region will have to take into account the emergence of FRY from almost a ten-year-long political and economic isolation – a trend that may influence their bilateral actions as well as their strategies towards the international community.

One way to sort out the complexities of the situation in SEE may be to highlight the commonalities that Southeast European states and societies share. Five such commonalties stand out as most important.

First, the structural problems of today are the legacy of the region's authoritarian past, which require high-cost solutions. These may entail radical changes in economic policies, the reform of political and social institutions (for example, government, parliament, the judiciary system, education, public administration, the media), and even long-term efforts to alter perceptions of identity and of the international community.

Second, policy formulation in the contemporary SEE is only the first step towards the tortuous process of actual social and political change. However, while the social problems in SEE, often locked in a downward spiral, are similar, the co-ordination of policy-formulation is not facilitated at all by the fact that some states in the area are very fragile, while other states, which already have secure borders and some internal stability, are very ineffective in actually implementing public policies.

Third, some security problems, such as external threats and internal ethnic conflict (hard security) as well as the problem of organized crime and the provision of the most basic amenities to the population (soft security) cannot be solved simultaneously, as citizens would have wished and politicians may have promised. In fact, problems often seem to follow different paces of evolution, or may not be solved at all for a long time. Fourth, in view of the above, the new democratic regimes of SEE have undergone, or perhaps may undergo in the future, a crisis of legitimacy. We know from the experience of other transitions from authoritarian rule that the path to democracy, economic prosperity and social cohesion may not be continuous and uninterrupted. Stability in all these respects is hard to attain and, once achieved, may be harder to preserve. A possible stagnation of political and economic development in SEE, or even a reversal of promising processes that have already started in individual countries, cannot be precluded. Yet, this volume hopefully shows that there is ground for optimism.

In the SEE, aspects of modernity co-exist with traditional aspects, such as divided and segmented communities and the personification of political feuds. Such aspects do not represent unchangeable traditions, since they constitute only the outcomes of particular historical periods. Instability in SEE is not 'innate'. Particularly in the Western Balkans, it is probably a historically specific phenomenon, the result of the interplay of national and international factors in an extended period of time.

WESTERN POLICY IN THE WESTERN BALKANS

Any strategy for salvaging SEE from strife, underdevelopment and criminal networks, must consider the mercurial nature of Western policy in the region. Components of that policy include a superpower that is without peer in making and implementing military decisions and the EU members who are nowhere near a common foreign and security consensus. Whereas the Americans have little incentive to prolong their involvement in SEE, Europe has every reason to prevent its Southeastern neighbourhood from becoming a permanent source of illegal migration and criminality.

Past history does not give Europeans high marks for their role in the region. Although it is becoming increasingly clear that the region would have been better off if Yugoslavia had not split into so many mutually hostile and economically problematic fragments, the Western powers are still unwittingly contributing to the process of dissolution and separation of ethnicities. From the early unqualified recognition of Slovenia and Croatia, to its synergy in creating segregated and ethnically cleansed protectorates, such as Bosnia-Herzegovina and Kosovo, the West has been sidetracked from its original intentions. In meting-out punishment to the culprits of the fratricidal wars, NATO has targeted Serbia exclusively, although some of the blame for the atrocities committed is shared by others. The massive 1999 bombings have undermined the FRY's economy to such an extent that it will take that state and its smaller neighbours a long time to overcome their devastation.

The West still fails to see the long-term dangers of structural underdevelopment that threaten the area. The danger does not arise from shortcomings in its multicultural and free-market developments, but from the inability of the states in the region to impose law and order after the collapse of their administrative mechanisms. In failed states, the West should help to construct new mechanisms and legal systems. Kosovo, which is rapidly becoming a haven of organized crime, does not need the presence of KFOR as much as it needs a force to control crime and, of course, the establishment and application of a legal system. In short, Kosovo needs laws, police, judges and prisons, as well as democratic legislation. At the moment criminality reigns supreme and is being exported to neighbouring areas, which offer fertile ground for its worth. Still, the electoral failure of extreme nationalist Kosovar parties in autumn 2001 is a good sign.

In spite of the ray of hope provided by the political change in Belgrade, the Western Balkan scene is still fraught with difficulties. It is not enough that Milosevic has been replaced by Kostunica; economic support for FRY is vital for its survival as a viable state. Unless the economic structures are repaired, the Yugoslavs, like the Albanians before them, will search for a better future in Western Europe and Greece. Furthermore, Montenegro's possible breakaway from the Federation serves no practical purpose other than to make President Juganovic the undisputed master of his realm, although this may create another weak state for the West to look after. Greece, which will be one of the first countries to face the new waves of immigrants, should embark on a serious campaign to prop up the Federation.

But the economy is not the only problem facing the region. In 2001, UCK continued its destabilizing activities in the western FYROM and the Kosovo triangle. Continued bombing incidents, directed against the remaining Serb population in Kosovo, should have spurred languid public opinion in the West into action. Unfortunately, the West is not particularly interested in the region; perhaps because it does not realize that the local problems are exportable and it sees only the region's paucity in resources and lack of strategic significance. Ultimately, this indifference is the reason why the West has failed so many times in SEE. The principle of humanitarian intevention has revolutionized international relations. Since the international system after the Second World War was based on state sovereignty, NATO's newly acquired vocation as an instrument of punishing human rights transgressors, even if it must violate state sovereignty in the process, has antagonized the UN in its own mission. NATO must continue to apply its resources to such missions of retribution, or reduce the significance of its 1999 operation against FRY into an act of selective justice. The events of 11 September 2001 have made this dilemma more acute. If the Republican administration in Washington DC chooses to practise a unilateralist foreign policy and desists from the multilateralism of its predecessor, then Western policy in the region may be left to the initiative of the Europeans.

The Stability Pact has been the major European response to the current problem of inertia in SEE. According to its Director, Bodo Hombach, this institution is a two-way street. It establishes conditionality between reforms and regional cooperation on the one hand, and outside assistance to these efforts and an EU perspective on the other. Thus, it draws on the two success stories of post-War Europe: European unification and the Helsinki Process. 'Like the Helsinki Process it created a triple track approach: Democratization and Human Rights–Economic Development–a Sustainable Security Environment. In short, there will be no peace and security without democracy and economic development'.[1] Although the Stability Pact contributed to the demise of the Milosevic regime by supporting the opposition through city partnerships and aid to the free media (the Szeged Process), current assets allocated for the reconstruction of FRY and its virtual province, Kosovo, are hardly adequate. If the West fails to acknowledge and rectify the devastation caused by the protracted embargo and the 1999 war on Serbia, Europe will reap the harvest of its errors and its insouciance in the form of criminality and migration seeping into Western cities from the Southeast. Instead of being miscast as the proverbial powder keg, SEE might yet become the stagnant backwater of Europe.

THE CHAPTERS OF THE VOLUME

The regional perspective taken in this collected volume acknowledges the sober endurance of the aforementioned domestic commonalties and international complexities. It tries to combine, in each individual contribution to the volume, contentions about historical, longer-term developments with specific policy recommendations useful for those interested in averting instability in the region. The individual chapters of the volume fall in the subject areas of institutional reform, security, democratization, regional cooperation and international relations. Particular case studies are also included. Let us look at the contents of the volume, starting from our last point in the previous section, that is, from a look at the Stability Pact.

Governments and non-governmental actors have been involved in the Pact. An example of the rapprochement between the West and SEE through the mobilization of such collective actors is given in the chapter by the Greek expert Haralambos Kondonis on the Stability Pact and non-govermental organizations (NGOs). Examining the involvement of international and local NGOs in each of the three 'Tables' of the Pact, he assesses the successful and the problematic aspects of those actors and of the Pact itself. The author registers successes and failures and suggests some solutions.

Part of the problem of engaging international and local civic associations in SEE is that the state mechanisms of the region's countries are not accustomed to initiatives emanating from sources other than statal ones. As one of the editors, Dimitri A. Sotiropoulos, claims in his chapter on public administration reform in SEE, modernizing the state apparatus in former one-party states of the region is a long process that remains at an incipient stage. While attention has been mostly paid to the pace and the breadth of privatization, the most important hurdles to reform, which include heavy and sprawling bureaucratic structures and inadequately trained or completely untrained personnel, remain to be overcome.

The issues addressed by the Albanian media experts Remzi Lani and Frrok Cupi in their chapter on mass media in SEE are not very different from the above. While television and radio channels as well as journalists themselves have been freed from constraints that the deposed communist regimes used to impose on them, they have not yet reached the status of an independent and consequential institution. The pluralism of commentary appearing in the printed and the electronic media sometimes conceals the power of private vested interests, while, in other instances, this pluralism is not taken into account by the decision-makers.

If the authorities in SEE can still afford to by-pass, in certain respects, the power of the media, they are reluctant to give up the power to influence young citizens through schooling. As the Romanian analyst Mirela-Luminiţa Murgescu shows in her chapter on school textbooks in SEE countries, few, if any, tolerant and self-critical ideas are diffused through such books, which offer to young citizens national self-images and images of the 'other'.

Many of the aforementioned issues reveal some of the enduring commonalities in the SEE, which we have noted in this introduction. Behind several of the issues noted above, such as the malfunctioning of the public administration, the uneasy relations between media organizations and political elites and even behind the old-fashioned ideas diffused through the mechanisms of education, the landscape of state–society relations looms large. As in most the cases of systemic political and social change, those relations have been fluid, that is, evolving, since the downfall of the socialist regimes in SEE in 1989–90. An expression of this fluidity is the growth of corruption that characterizes contemporary SEE. While an undetermined part of corruption has been found in various sectors of the underground economy, where corruption prevails, there is a feeling that parts of the government and the administration of several SEE countries are heavily involved in the expansion of corruption – and that at all possible hierarchical levels, from the lowest to the highest. The problem is discussed in a chapter written by a Bulgarian expert, Ognyan Minchev, who looks at corruption from a theoretical viewpoint, namely as a function of wider social change.

Corruption does not affect only the extent to which basic principles of modern states, such as the rule of law and equality before the law, are applied. Given the uncontrollable flow of arms, drugs and other smuggled goods throughout SEE, corruption has started affecting the daily life of the region's inhabitants. That is to say, corruption has impinged on the 'soft security' of the region, which is a rising new concern, given that 'hard security' has been attained mostly in the Eastern Balkans (Bulgaria, Romania) and in parts of the Western Balkans (Slovenia, Croatia). For the rest, that is, for the still fragile states that have come out the disintegration of the FRY as well as for Albania, 'hard security' is a goal to be reached. Radovan Vukadinovic shows what are the prospects for security in the region by placing the issue in the context of European security architecture. The Croatian expert analyses related concepts and applies them to the case of SEE.

Others are more sceptical about the ability of Western Europe to offer a protective shell to the emerging unstable new small states and state-like units of SEE. Kosovo is the prime example studied by two Greek experts. Evangelos Kofos offers a view of the area 'from above', from the perspective of someone who analyses the wider Albanian ambitions – ambitions that perhaps may underlie the official Albanian stance on the problem. The author suggests a way out of the current impasse by placing Kosovo under a UN Trustship. Alexandros Yannis presents a view of the same problem 'from below', that is, on the basis of the experience

8   IS SOUTHEASTERN EUROPE DOOMED TO INSTABILITY?

of international community (UNMIK, KFOR, NGOs) on the ground. A different but also 'down to earth' view is given by Veton Surroi, a Kosovar journalist, who argues for a gradual acquisition of more and more autonomy for his land of origin. His chapter, which combines personal memories with the vision of a new society, is the first of several case studies that we have included in this volume in order to make the discussion on stability more concrete.

In this vein, the Bulgarian analyst Ivan Krastev marshals a wealth of data to show that corruption can be controlled in Bulgaria through extensive reform of the state. Predrag Simic, who comes from FRY, focuses on the question of the survival of what has remained of the 'Third Yugoslavia'. He looks at the difficult co-existence of Serbia and Montenegro. The interlinkages of the prospects of Kosovo, Bosnia-Herzegovina and Montenegro are evident: If the latter secedes from FRY, Kosovo would like to follow suit, while the constituent parts of Bosnia-Herzegovina may become even more detached from each other than they already are.

For ten years (1991–2001) the prospect of such a 'detachment' had been rather remote for the nationalities that reside in FYROM. As ideas of secession and armed groups have spilled over from Kosovo into South Serbia and Northern Macedonia, the above prospect has become a closer possibility. The Greek international relations expert Aristotle Tziampiris summarizes the same events and takes up an international-relations perspective on the relations between that country and Greece, suggesting that former adversaries may become co-workers in the effort to promote stability in the region.

While the enduring problems of SEE may seen to affect adversely the chances to achieve stability in the region, the analysis of separate dimensions of stability, presented in the chapters of this volume tends to offer a more optimistic view. Indeed, let us note the most positive contributions. As the Turkish experts Şule Kut and N. Asli Şirin show in their chapter, the successes of cooperation of SEE countries tend to be underestimated. There have been instances of bilateral and multilateral activities and commitments among the countries of the region that are worth imitating. Such activities and commitments can be seen in the context of the gradual integration of SEE countries into the European Union (EU), a prospect discussed by the Bulgarian expert Irina Bokova in her contribution to this volume. For the aim of stability, joining the family of EU serves as a vision which is commonly shared by the vast majority of political forces in EU candidate states. Even if this prospect takes a very long time to materialize in the case of countries that lag behind EU standards, still its function as a base for political consensus cannot be overstated. All in all, the alternation of international relations and domestic, political perspectives on SEE constitutes our combined effort to assess the dialectic between external and internal developments. The authors of this multi-ethnic volume come from the region and submit opinions that merge towards the conclusion that SEE is not doomed to instability.

ACKNOWLEDGEMENT

This volume is the result of a research project. Most essays were written at the beginning of 2001. All contributions are accompanied by lists for further reading. The project that appears in this volume was started in early 2000 by ELIAMEP, an independent Greek thinktank, which has sought funding in Europe and the US. The editors, who travelled in SEE in 2000–2001 to collect data and to meet local politicians and analysts, would like to thank the European Science Foundation and the Ford Foundation for making research for this project possible, through encouragement and financial aid. They would also like to thank the individual contributors to this volume and Ms Elizabeth Phocas, deputy director of ELIAMEP, and her staff (in particular Ms Irene Glypti) as well as the publisher, Frank Cass, for their commitment and help with the publication of this project.

NOTES

1. Lecture by Bodo Hombach, 25 April 2001, JFK School, Harvard University.

The Bright Side of Balkan Politics: Cooperation in the Balkans

ŞULE KUT AND N. ASLI ŞIRIN

Since the end of the Cold War, in the minds of the general public and decision-makers alike, the Balkans has readily been associated with blood and tears. The region itself has supplied most of the evidence for this perception: there has been ample amount of tension and open or latent conflict from Bosnia-Herzegovina to Kosovo and Macedonia. There was not a single Balkan state that did not have bilateral disputes with at least one of its neighbours. The conventional thinking has been that the Balkans was doomed to instability because of the ethnic and religious heterogeneity in the region. Moreover, not only the current conflicts were justifying this perception, but historical legacy has also frequently, albeit selectively, been utilized to prove that the Balkans was nothing but an 'apple of discord'.

In this conflictual environment, the international involvement of outside actors who aimed at conflict resolution or prevention has not escaped the world's attention. The list of peacekeeping operations or military interventions in the area has been quite a long one. From UNPROFOR, IFOR and SFOR in Bosnia and KFOR in Kosovo to the NATO interventions in the former Yugoslav area, the direct international military involvement in nationalist wars has given examples of international cooperation for dealing with the actual conflict situations. In addition, the UNPREDEP in the Republic of Macedonia has been registered as the first true peacekeeping mission of the UN with the aim of conflict-prevention. From Dayton to UNMIK, peace-building efforts of the international community need to be coupled with an ongoing crisis management in the Balkans. All of these have necessarily required a high degree of cooperation by international and regional actors.

However, neither the good-neighbourly relations amidst conflictual environment, nor cases of collaboration for regional cooperation could receive half as much attention as did the conflicts and conflict-resolution efforts in the Balkans. This article aims to draw attention to genuine cooperation initiatives in the region and argues that Balkan politics also has a bright side. It is the enhancement of this bright side that may actually ensure stability and security in the region.

COOPERATION IN THE BALKANS: FROM INTERWAR TO POST-COLD WAR YEARS

In the midst of war and conflict, it was not surprising that the genuine cooperation efforts in the Balkans did not gain much attention in the 1990s. However, the Balkans was also one of the regions where a significant number of initiatives for cooperation were put into practice in the post-Cold War era. These were initiated by the countries of the region as well as by outside actors, and almost exclusively in the second half the 1990s. Today, there is a multiplicity of cooperative schemes in the region where bilateral, trilateral and multilateral interaction has become quite a regular practice. Most of these schemes involve both governmental and non-governmental actors; and most of them are multi-dimensional schemes.

Despite the legacy of Balkan Wars and some deeply conflictual relations in the Balkans, examples of good-neighbourliness and cooperation even in the past were not necessarily scarce in the region. The Balkan Conferences that started in 1930 were aiming at a loose federation of Balkan nations in economic, social, cultural, political and intellectual fields. The Balkan Pact of 1934 hence became a partial achievement of the Balkan Conferences since it was solely based on security considerations of the signatory states, Turkey, Greece, Romania and Yugoslavia.[1] The coming of the Second World War swept it away.

During the Cold War era, the Balkan Alliance or the Second Balkan Pact of 1953–54 constituted yet another partial cooperation scheme in the region. It was based on the 'Friendship and Cooperation Agreement' signed by Turkey, Greece and Yugoslavia in Ankara in February 1953. It became effective with the signature of the Pact on 9 August 1954 in Bled, Yugoslavia. With this treaty, the frontiers of the signatory states would be secured against outside aggression. The Balkan Alliance was formed with the help of the US and fitted well into the Cold War context. The US wished to win Yugoslavia over to the Western Bloc by forming an alliance between Yugoslavia and two NATO members in the region. So the basic motive behind the Pact was security concerns of the West rather than an overall cooperation among the states of the region. That is why most of the Balkan states, in other words all the Balkan members of Eastern Bloc, were excluded from the Balkan Alliance.[2]

The Balkan Alliance did not last long. There were two main reasons for its failure. First, the rapprochement between Belgrade and Moscow led to Yugoslavia's adoption of an 'active neutrality' policy based on the belief that states with different economic and political systems could coexist peacefully. Moreover, as Yugoslavia took the leadership of the non-alignment movement in the 1950s, the Balkan Alliance not only lost its significance for Yugoslavia, but also became a contradiction. Second, the emerging dispute between Turkey and Greece over Cyprus in the mid-1950s led to the deterioration of relations between the two other pillars of the Alliance.

The Balkan Alliance, which had already lost its importance because of the divergent interests of its members, was explicitly dissolved in 1960. In any case, the Alliance was hardly a genuine Balkan initiative, not because it was framed by an outside actor, the US, but because it was based almost solely on the security concerns of the Western Bloc rather than having a comprehensive regional economic, political and social outlook.

However, the cooperation efforts in the region continued throughout the second half of 1950s and the 1960s. The plans prepared by Romanian Prime Minister Stoica constituted a noteworthy initiative in this respect. The first plan, prepared in September 1957, was based on a general understanding of cooperation in economic, cultural and social fields. The Plan was all-inclusive, that is, open to all of the six Balkan countries. Although there were unresolved bilateral conflicts between some of the Balkan states, the idea was that these disputes should not constitute an obstacle to cooperation among Balkan nations. Bulgaria, Albania and Yugoslavia accepted the plan with enthusiasm, whereas the two other leading Balkan states, Turkey and Greece, opposed it – not primarily because of their mutual problems, but because the plan was perceived with equal suspicion both in Athens and Ankara as a Soviet-sponsored scheme.

Stoica repeated his call for regional cooperation in June 1959. This time there was also an emphasis on the need for the establishment of a nuclear-free zone in the Balkans. Moreover, the Soviet Union was strongly supporting the plan, which was consequently refused once again by Turkey and Greece. Turkey declared its objections by a direct note to Moscow whereas Greece preferred to communicate with Romania.[3] Stoica had failed to get the support of the two crucial countries of the region and this was no surprise in the Cold War environment.

At the beginning of the 1960s, a Committee of Cooperation and Mutual Understanding in the Balkans was formed as a result of the efforts of Bulgaria, Romania, Yugoslavia and Greece. Ankara refused to participate in the first meeting and it was not invited to subsequent meetings. The work of the Committee was to bear no results.

Relations among most of the Balkan states continued to develop fast in the 1960s, as demonstrated by the rapprochement between Bulgaria and Yugoslavia and the development of relations among Yugoslavia,

Greece and Romania. On the other hand, after the 1963 crisis in Cyprus, Turkey felt the pressing need to develop its own relations with the states of the region in order to form a 'counterweight' against Greece.[4]

Renewed cooperation efforts in the 1970s and 1980s, on the other hand, were a consequence of détente. Various initiatives concentrated, as in the 1930s, on low politics to provide a forum for regional consultation and cooperation at a political and experts level. Like earlier attempts, internal considerations were the driving force.[5]

Towards the end of the 1980s when the whole socialist bloc was about to change drastically, a meeting of foreign ministers of all the Balkan countries was held in Belgrade in February 1988. The participants were Albania, Bulgaria, Greece, Romania, Turkey and Yugoslavia. This meeting paved the way for regional cooperation initiatives in various fields, such as trade, economy, industry, culture, transport, environment and humanitarian issues. The major objective was to contribute to economic, social and intellectual prosperity of the region. Various meetings were held at different levels in order to prepare the ground for rapprochement among the states of the region. These meetings formed the basis of the Balkan Multilateral Cooperation Process. As an observer put it, the Balkan cooperation of 1987–91 period constituted the 'Golden Era'.[6]

By the time the second meeting was held in Tirana in October 1990, the international system had changed drastically. At the Tirana meeting, the states of the region agreed that the establishment of democratic regimes was the first step to integration into Europe. The post-communist transition was coupled with instability and ethnic conflicts in the region. The disintegration of Yugoslavia came shortly after the Tirana meeting, and stability in the Balkans received another serious blow. The crisis in former Yugoslavia became yet another impediment for region-wide cooperation. The third meeting that would be held in December 1991 in Sofia had to be suspended. Balkan Multilateral Cooperation Process had to wait until 1996 to be revived.

The Yugoslav conflict had, in fact, two opposite impacts on cooperation in the Balkans. On the one hand, it delayed the launching of genuine cooperation initiatives during wartime. On the other, it became instrumental in the multiplication of cooperation initiatives later, since it taught a hard lesson to all the states of the region of how costly the conflict can be. Once the Bosnian war ended, both the US and the EU, as well as countries of the region initiated various kinds of successive cooperation schemes in the second half of the 1990s. It is therefore no coincidence that the cooperation initiatives gained momentum immediately after the signing of the Dayton Peace Agreement in late 1995.

Examples of post-Cold War bilateral cooperation in the Balkans are abundant. The cooperation drive that followed the drastic change in Bulgarian–Turkish relations in the early 1990s had ironically come after seriously strained relations in the late 1980s. The cooperative mood accompanying the Greek–Turkish rapprochement that gained momentum following the 1999 earthquakes in both countries is yet another striking example. The fruits of the steady improvement in Greek–Macedonian relations since the signing of the Interim Agreement in 1995, or the early (1992) and the recent (1999) waves of rapprochement between Bulgaria and the Republic of Macedonia cannot be ignored in this respect either. Despite the Albanian Question in the Balkans, the governmental relations between Albania and Macedonia have also been surprisingly mature and correct. The Federal Republic of Yugoslavia and Albania did not lose time in re-establishing diplomatic relations once Milosevic was ousted from power. Albanian–Greek relations have also drastically improved since the second half of the 1990s, leading to cooperation in many fields. Albanian–Turkish relations continued to be well through the 1990s. Bulgarian–Greek relations have already been developing since the end of the Cold War. Romanian–Turkish relations have also developed remarkably again since then, coupled with close economic cooperation. Not only the well-known relations between Bosnia and Turkey, but also the little-known regular meetings of consultation between Croatia and Turkey that began during the war in Bosnia, still continue. Even the relations between Serbia and Turkey have been cool but correct, despite the conflicts in Bosnia and Kosovo. Greece's close relations with Serbia do not come as a surprise despite the latter's involvement in the NATO operation against Yugoslavia. Macedonian–Serbian relations have remarkably been good – falsifying the expectations that the latter's independence would fuel yet another war. Greek–Romanian and Bulgarian–Romanian relations are also as close, as they have always been.

This list of 'good relations' does not preclude the fact that the countries in the region do have bilateral problems. They all have a series of minor or major disputes. Territorial neighbours have more problems, distant ones have fewer. The nature of those problems varies from direct bilateral disputes to their divergent stances in the regional conflicts. However, despite all and while not denying the existence of disputes, most Balkan states have managed to develop their bilateral relations with one another through some sort of cooperation. In other words, engagement in cooperation did not necessarily require the solution of disputes as a precondition. Moreover, in some instances, fruits of cooperation in one field could help to boost the will for the solution of some of the disputes.

Trilateral cooperation was also a distinctive mode of cooperation in the Balkans. Bulgaria and Romania kept meeting with their Greek and Turkish counterparts regularly, albeit separately, since the mid-1990s. In the meeting held between the leaders of Turkey, Bulgaria and Romania in April 1998 the significance of regional security and stability was emphasized. The three countries would cooperate in political, economic and military fields. On the other hand, Bulgaria was equidistant to Turkey and Greece. In October 1997, a meeting in which defence ministers of Southeast European countries participated was held in Sofia. Bulgaria paid special attention to Greece and Turkey's roles to foster cooperation in the military field. Finally, in early 1999, the foreign ministers of Bulgaria, Greece and Turkey joined hands in the most welcome meeting when they visited the border areas together. It was more than a symbolic gesture when they have decided to intensify cross-border cooperation.

Turkey and Greece were the only non-communist countries of the region. The end of communism and the Cold War had opened a whole new world for both in the Balkans. In the meantime, they have been portrayed as the two leaders of the two competing axes in the Balkans. Turkey has established and developed its relations with each of the old and new states in the region from the very start. Greece, which followed a policy of resentment in the first half of the 1990s towards most of the region, drastically switched to a policy of good-neighbourliness in the second half of the decade. Greece and Turkey, henceforth, were designated as two rivals in the Balkans. However, this rivalry had both negative and positive aspects. The negative aspect involved the conflict situations especially in the first half of the 1990s. It was simply a pity that because of the conflicting positions of the two states they could not join in a common action against aggression in Bosnia.[7] The positive aspect involved the cooperative processes and benefited the third parties in the region, hence leading to constructive results. This part of the rivalry, similar to the US–EU rivalry in the region, involved the two powerful parties' competition with one another in leading the region through cooperation. Each has invested in the countries of the region, has become foreign aid donors, and has promoted and participated in various regional cooperation schemes or projects. Hence, Turkish–Greek rivalry in a way has also become instrumental in the increased interaction and cooperation in the Balkans and has contributed to the regional welfare. However, initiation of regional cooperation schemes has not been confined to Turkey and Greece.

Multilateral cooperation schemes in the Balkans are initiated both by the countries of the region and the outside actors. An early example of regional cooperation, Black Sea Economic Cooperation (BSEC), founded in 1992, was a Turkish initiative to bring the countries of the

Black Sea, Caucasus and the Balkans regions together. All the Balkan states except former Yugoslavia became the founding-members of the BSEC.[8] Later examples of schemes initiated by the regional actors include the Balkan Conference of Stability and Cooperation in Southeast Europe (BCSC), which was revived in July 1996 with the Sofia meeting, and the Multinational Peacekeeping Force in Southeast Europe. Other regional cooperation initiatives such as the Royaumont Initiative of the European Union, which was launched in February 1996, the US-supported Southeast European Cooperative Initiative (SECI), which was initiated in December 1996, the Stability Pact that was established in 1999, and the Partnership for Peace project launched by NATO in 1994 are all initiated by outside actors.

The multilateral meeting in Sofia held on 6–7 July 1996 was significant in terms of revitalizing the cooperation efforts among the states of the region after a period of long-lasting conflicts. At the end of the meeting the 'Sofia Declaration on Good-Neighbourly Relations, Stability, Security and Cooperation in the Balkans' was signed by Albania, Bosnia-Herzegovina, Bulgaria, the Federal Republic of Yugoslavia, Greece, Romania and Turkey. With this declaration the participants agreed to launch a comprehensive process of multilateral cooperation in areas such as enhancing good neighbourly relations, cross-border economic cooperation, development of humanitarian, social and cultural contacts, and combating organized crime.[9] The results of the meeting were also significant since the participants pledged to act in accordance with the principles declared in Helsinki Final Act about international relations and confidence-building measures on the one hand; on the other hand, they reiterated their will to contribute to the implementation of the Dayton Peace Agreement.

The foreign ministers of Southeast European countries met in Thessaloniki for the second time in June 1997. This time the scope of cooperation among the states of the region was enlarged. It was decided that informal summits between the heads of the states were necessary in order to enhance cooperation. In this meeting, Republic of Macedonia, participating as FYROM, was among the signatories, and Bosnia-Herzegovina, Croatia and Slovenia were observers. The focus of attention was need for cooperation in the construction of the pan-European transport corridors.

The first Balkan summit was held in Heráklion in Crete in November 1997. At the end of the summit, the leaders issued a joint statement in which the prospects for economic prosperity and political cooperation were listed. In order to create the necessary conditions for economic, social and political prosperity the states of the region should act in cooperation. Another significant aspect of the summit was that the participants agreed on the idea that integration with the European and Euro-Atlantic structures should be the major priority of the Southeast European countries.

The mood and the agenda of the Istanbul meeting of the 'Sofia Process' held in June 1998 was no different from those of the previous meetings. The same ideals including the prospects for regional cooperation were outlined. Although the BCSC was once again suspended by the Kosovo Crisis in 1999, it was to be revived after Kostunica's rise to power in Yugoslavia, coupled with other regional cooperation initiatives.

On the other hand, the Multinational Peace Force for Southeast Europe (MPFSEE) Initiative is another significant regional initiative. The agreement about this force was signed in September 1998, and the parties to the agreement were Albania, Bulgaria, Greece, Italy, Macedonia, Romania and Turkey. The aim was to contribute to security and stability in the region through regional peacekeeping. In this context, a SEE Brigade was established in August 1999 and Plovdiv in Bulgaria was designated as the Brigade's headquarters.

In addition to the initiatives developed by the states of the region, the cooperation efforts initiated by outside actors are also noteworthy. NATO has introduced the Partnership for Peace (PfP) programme in June 1994. The major objective of the PfP programme was to achieve stability and security throughout Europe by enhancing peace-keeping abilities and capabilities through joint planning, training and exercises, and by so doing increasing the interoperability of the partner country's military forces with those of NATO.[10] The invitation for this partnership was accepted by 27 countries. Now there are 26 members of the programme, including the Balkan states Albania, Bulgaria, Romania and the Republic of Macedonia.

Another such initiative was the Royaumont Initiative which came into existence as a result of US and EU efforts to foster cooperation in the region. The initiative came particularly from France and it was based on the Pact on Stability in Europe that was developed by French Prime Minister Balladur. Its major aim was to promote stability and friendly relations among Balkan nations. Hence the Royaumont Process, also known as the Process of Stability and Good-Neighbourliness in SEE, emerged as a French initiative and was soon converted into an EU initiative in February 1996. It assigned crucial importance to the support and interaction of NGOs, and the promotion of projects encouraging the development of a civil society in the region. The initiative supported regional cooperation primarily in the fields of education, culture, communication, institutions and scientific research.[11] The projects within the Initiative were successful, and they were funded or carried out by EU members such as Greece, the UK, Luxembourg, France and the Netherlands. The projects usually focused on interethnic dialogue, academic cooperation and education, cooperation in environmental, cultural and scientific issues.[12]

The Southeast European Cooperative Initiative is another scheme created by outside actors. SECI is primarily a US initiative, and its major aim is to prepare the ground for economic as well as environmental cooperation in the Balkans region. Especially cooperative action in the economic field is required in order to create a regional market that will attract foreign investors to the region. The concept of SECI was developed by the US in late 1995 and subsequent negotiations between the US and the EU led to the establishment of SECI in December 1996. Major points on which SECI would focus were highlighted in the 'Southeast European Cooperative Initiative Final Points of Common EU–US Understanding'.[13] According to the US view, participation in the SECI was a considerably important step for the SEE countries, which are willing to integrate into the European and Euro-Atlantic structures. SECI would also be a forum to discuss issues of common interest to the participating states, and it would provide the necessary conditions for close cooperation among the states of the region. The emphasis was on the development of the private sector. On the other hand, a Business Advisory Council co-chaired by Turkey and Greece was established by a group of businessmen. The SECI would be in close contact with the United Nations Economic Commission for Europe (UNECE). By 1999, seven projects were under way.[14]

Finally, the Stability Pact for Southeastern Europe deserves attention. It was adopted in the aftermath of the Kosovo Crisis of 1999 as a result of the EU's efforts. Its major aim was to contribute to security, stability and prosperity of the region. It is no different from the objectives of the previous initiatives. The Pact is not composed only of states of the region. The EU, the European Commission, the Russian Federation, the US, the OSCE Chairman in Office as well as a representative of the Council of Europe and representatives from other groupings and international organizations such as the UN, OECD, IMF and others are among the participants.

Within the Pact, there is a Southeastern Europe Regional Table that would be responsible for the coordination of the activities carried out by three 'Working Tables' (WT), namely the WT on Democratization and Human Rights, the WT on Economic Reconstruction, Development and Cooperation and the WT on Security Issues. These are specialized agencies to deal with specific issues of common interest to the participants. The Stability Pact is a catalyst for enhanced coordination among international organizations and structures.[15] There are short-, medium- and long-term projects carried out by the Working Tables.

In the first two years relatively successful results were achieved in terms of projects.[16] The participants were enthusiastic about the activities of the Pact. However, this enthusiasm is a necessary but not sufficient condition for the success of the Stability Pact. The major test is how the Stability Pact performs in terms of completion of planned projects.

The issue areas and the scope of cooperation schemes vary, but each has connections to and a spillover effect on other areas. The first area of cooperation is economic, where the schemes usually involve both intraregional trade and outside investment in the region. As pointed out above, Stability Pact, SECI or the RI falls into this group. The second area concerns political relations, where the BCSC is successfully leading the way. The third area of cooperation is military cooperation. The Multilateral Balkan Peacekeeping Force (MPFSEE) is a particular example in this context. The Partnership for Peace programme of NATO is also a valuable scheme as it brings the countries of the region into joint exercises with their neighbours and other NATO members.

The effectiveness of all these different kinds of schemes, processes and initiatives in attaining their goals has long been a matter of concern. Their slowness and inefficiency have long been criticized, and 'cooperation fatigue'[17] is another potential issue facing the participants from within and outside the region. Duplication of projects and lack of coordination are additional deficiencies. Spending money in an uncoordinated way is another problem as are the unfulfilled commitments.

On the other hand, the success of any regional cooperation depends largely on its inclusiveness. The absence of Milosevic's Yugoslavia in these schemes or its exclusion from many of them was unavoidable. However, it was also a fact that the Balkan cooperation without active involvement of the new Yugoslavia would not produce as much stability as the region hoped for. Hence Kostunica's rise to power in Yugoslavia in late 2000 was notable not only for Yugoslavia, but also for the whole region and the regional cooperation processes. The international community's approach towards the country changed drastically as a result of the domestic developments in FRY. This change in attitude could easily be observed in the EU's announcement of lifting sanctions on Yugoslavia. Cooperation in the Balkans started to improve as the political regime has changed in Yugoslavia. With Yugoslavia participating in these initiatives, the cooperation efforts will gain more meaning, and they will be more efficient and effective.

The Balkan countries are trying hard to integrate into the European and Euro-Atlantic structures. Their efforts to become full members of the EU are noteworthy.[18] In this respect, their willingness to participate in the regional cooperative initiatives are significant since these efforts should prepare suitable ground for integration with the West rather than constituting an obstacle as sometimes argued by many from the region. On the other hand, as the foundational years are over, it may safely be argued that the success of the cooperation drive in the Balkans depends on various factors, the most important of which are first, the full commitment of both the outside and regional parties, second, non-exclusionary character of the scheme and third, the availability and good-management of financial resources.

CONCLUSION

The Balkans is not a region doomed to instability. Conflict in Yugoslavia has taught a hard lesson to all the states in the region. It may safely be expected that the Balkan states will not resort to force for the solution of disputes or for matters of hard security, and they will increase their cooperation especially in the areas of soft security in the coming years. This expectation is also justified by the experience of the region at large even during the most conflictual period between 1990 and 1995 in the Balkans.

First of all, the third Balkan War did not erupt. Contrary to the expectations of many, war was restricted to certain territories of former Yugoslavia. It did not spill over into the other parts of the Balkans. Secondly, the Balkans in the 1990s did not become a theatre for religious wars. Not only did the states in the so-called Orthodox-Muslim axes not fight with one another, but in many instances they have cooperated for stability in the region. Moreover, this was already a dubious expectation in the presence of, for instance, 'Muslim' Turkey's relations with Catholic Croatia and Orthodox Bulgaria, or 'Orthodox' Greece's involvement in the NATO operation against Yugoslavia. Thirdly, except for the former Yugoslav federation, there was not a single territorial change in the region. Even the international boundaries of the newly independent states of the former Yugoslavia were the same as the internal borders during the socialist federation. Not a single other state in the Balkans attempted to change the borders. Despite the rise of nationalism in the region as elsewhere, the governments in the Balkans did respect the territorial integrity of their neighbours, and the separatist calls of certain minorities were more or less managed by these states.

Cooperation in the Balkans involved both governmental and non-governmental actors. The enormous non-governmental interaction between the think tanks, intellectuals, businessmen and other civic groups in the region since the end of communism is a sign that the people of the Balkans prefer cooperation to conflict. Cooperation is the precondition for stability in any region and the Balkan experience in cooperation is no less striking than the region's legacy of conflict. The fact that cooperation does exist in the Balkans has largely and unfairly been undermined. However, it deserves to be underlined together with the success stories of good-neighbourly relations in the region.

NOTES

1. For more about the Balkan Pact of 1934, see Kerner, Robert J. and Harry N. Howard (1936); Geshkoff, Theodore I. (1940); Jankovic, Branimir M. (1988); Winrow, Gareth (1993); Türkeş, Mustafa (1994).
2. For more information about the Balkan Alliance of 1953, see Bilman, Levent (1998); Sander, Oral (1969) pp.83–125.
3. For more information about the Stoica plans , see Sander (1969) pp.148–58.
4. For more information about the bilateral relations between Balkan states, see Sander (1969) pp.163–76.
5. See Clément, Sophia (2000) p.78.
6. See Kondonis, Haralambos (1998).
7. See Kut, Şule (1995) pp.314–15.
8. Initially former Yugoslavia was also invited to become a member, but the invitation was not pushed forward when the war broke out in Slovenia and Croatia.
9. Cited from the Sofia Declaration in Bilman (1998) p.73.
10. See *The NATO Handbook* (1998–1999) pp. 86–7.
11. See Dwan, Renata, ed. (1999) p.246.
12. For more information about the Royaumont Process, see Dwan (1999) pp.245–7; Bilman (1998), pp.70–72; the Initiative's web-site http://royaumont.lrf.gr/
13. For the Final Points, see Schifter, Robert (1998) pp.4–5.
14. For more about SECI , see Schifter (1998) pp. 1–13; Dwan (1999) pp.249–52; Bilman (1998) pp.74–5; the Initiative's web-site http://www.unece.org/seci
15. Report on the Achievements of the Stability Pact, http://www.balcanica.org/content/RS/sou16.doc
16. For more about the Stability Pact and its projects see Pierre, Andrew J. (1999); Stability Pact for South Eastern Europe; The Pact's web-site http://www.stabilitypact.org ; Ladika, Susan (1999).
17. Bilman (1998) p.81.
18. For more information about efforts of the Balkan states, see Pierre, Andrew J. (1999).

REFERENCES

Alp, Ali Hikmet (2000): 'The South-East Europe Co-Operation Process: An Unspectacular, Indigenous Regional Co-Operation Scheme', *Perceptions*, V, 3, September–November 2000, pp.39–48.
Bilman, Levent (1998): 'The Regional Cooperation Initiatives in Southeast Europe and the Turkish Foreign Policy', *Perceptions*, III, 3, September–November 1998, pp.58–81.

Clément, Sophia (2000): 'Subregionalism in South Eastern Europe', in, Stephen C. Calleya, ed., *Regionalism in the Post-Cold War World*, UK and USA: Ashgate Publishing Ltd, pp.71–98.

Çeviköz, Ünal (1998): 'European Integration and Regional Co-Operation in Southeast Europe', *Perceptions*, III, 4, December 1997–February 1998, pp.143–53.

Dwan, Renata, ed (1999): *Building Security in Europe's New Borderlands: Subregional Cooperation in the Wider Europe*, New York: EastWest Institute.

Geshkoff, Theodore I. (1940): *Balkan Union: A Road to Peace in Southeastern Europe*, New York: Columbia University Press.

Hombach, Bodo (2000): 'Stability Pact for South-Eastern Europe: A New Perspective for the Region', *Perceptions*, V, 3, September–November 2000, pp.5–21.

Jankovic, Branimir M. (1988): *The Balkans in International Relations*, Basingstoke and London: Macmillan.

Kerner, Robert J. and Harry N. Howard (1936): *The Balkan Conferences and the Balkan Entente 1930–1935: A Study in the Recent History of the Balkan and Near Eastern Peoples*, Berkeley, California: University of California Press.

Kondonis, Haralambos (1998): 'Prospects for Balkan Cooperation After the Disintegration of Yugoslavia', *East European Quarterly*, 32, 3, http://www.epnet.com.

Kut, Şule (1995): 'Turkish Diplomatic Initiatives for Bosnia-Hercegovina', in, Günay G. Özdoğan and Kemali Saybaşılı, eds., *Balkans: A Mirror of International Order*, Ýstanbul: Eren Yayıncılık, pp.295–315.

Ladika, Susan (1999): 'The Balkan Stability Pact', *Europe*, 391, November 1999, http://www.epnet.com.

The NATO Handbook (1998–1999): (Second Reprint) 50th Anniversary Edition, Belgium: Office of Information and Press.

Pierre, Andrew J. (1999): *De-Balkanizing the Balkans: Security and Stability in Southeastern Europe*, United States Institute of Peace (Special Report), http://www.usip.org/oc/sr/sr990920/sr990920.

'Report on the Achievements of the Stability Pact www.balcanica.org/content/RS/sou16.doc.

Sander, Oral (1966): 'The Balkan Cooperation in Perspective', *Milletlerarası Münasebetler Türk Yıllığı*, 7, pp.104–20.

—— (1969): *Balkan Gelişmeleri ve Türkiye (1945–1965)*, Ankara: A.Ü. S.B.F. Yayınları.

Schifter, Robert (1998): 'The Southeast European Cooperative Initiative: Its Origins and Its Development', *Mediterranean Quarterly*, 9,4, Fall 1998, pp.1–13.

'Stability Pact for South Eastern Europe' http://www.stabilitypact.org/pact.htm

Türkeş, Mustafa (1994): 'The Balkan Pact and its Immediate Implications for the Balkan States, 1930–34', *Middle Eastern Studies*, 30, 1, pp.123–44.

Winrow, Gareth (1993): 'The Balkans in International Politics: An Examination of the Inter-War Period', in *İki Dünya Savaşı Arasında Avrupa ve Balkanlar: İdeolojiler ve Uluslararası Politika Sempozyumu*, İstanbul: Aybay Yayınları.

Zorlu, Hilmi Akýn (2000): 'The Role of the South-Eastern Europe Brigade (SEEBRIG) for Military Cooperation in the Region and the Multinational Peace Force South-Eastern Europe (MPFSEE) Initiative's Potential for Crisis Management', presented at PfP Planning Symposium 2000: Partnership, An Alliance Fundamental Security Task http://www.isn.ethz.ch/pfpdc/documents/2000/Planning_Symposium_Oberammergau/Zorlu/Word.htm

Integrating Southeastern Europe into the European Mainstream

IRINA BOKOVA

THE CURRENT STATE OF AFFAIRS

Since 1999 the political landscape in Southeastern Europe has been dramatically and positively transformed. Refugees have returned to Kosovo and the internationally buttressed regime there functions, albeit with difficulty. There has even been an outbreak of moderation in the Kosovo local election results. The Stability Pact process as a long-term regional initiative has begun a new quality of Europe taking responsibility. Albania and Macedonia have not been destabilized as was feared by some. Bulgaria, Romania and Turkey have been boosted by the Helsinki decisions on EU enlargement. Bosnia is improving slowly. In Croatia the passing of the Tudjman regime exceeded the most optimistic scenarios. In Serbia the democratic election of Vojislav Kostunica to replace Milosevic has finalized a period of uncertainty, ethnic hatred and wars.[1]

All this has been a truly remarkable performance, the most decisive steps having been taken through the democratic choices of the populations of the region. The European part of the story has also been important. 'Europeanization' – integration into modern Europe – is manifestly the reference, anchor and motivation for the region. In the circumstances it is very important to have a sincere intellectual debate about what happened, why it happened, what has been achieved, and finally, where we are now.

For most of the last ten years following the democratic changes in the East, Southeastern Europe has been left outside the European mainstream. What we witnessed and still witness are sometimes developments and tendencies that run counter to the very purpose of the changes themselves – instead of democracy and stability we see dictatorship and conflict, instead of economic prosperity and technological advance, we see poverty and social instability, instead of moves towards integration, we see disintegration and fragmentation. It is not the task of this article to dwell upon the causes, which are both of internal and external nature. But it is very important now in the aftermath of the conflict in Kosovo, after several wars in former Yugoslavia and after the toppling of the Milosevic regime to make a clear and sincere assessment of the responses to the events in order to pursue policies with long-term goals and visions.

WESTERN RESPONSES

It is hardly disputed now that the Western response to and attitude towards the region for most of the time has been one of neglect, of contradictory and mixed signals. The policy of 'wait and see', which was in fact an inert policy of 'containment', without committing any resources, brought about in some cases paralysis, in others a polarization of the situation and in yet others chaos and discontent.

The Yugoslav wars and the Western response is a case in point. As one knowledgeable researcher in the area, Dr Dimitris Keridis, rightfully points out in his paper 'The Balkan Crisis: Causes, Consequences, Western Response and the Way Ahead' (1999):

> The West embarked on an incremental policy of reactive rather than proactive response to developments on the ground. Thus it allowed itself to be drawn deeper and deeper into the conflict without a clear vision of what should be achieved and without a clear exit strategy.[2]

The European Union has made an immense contribution to the transition in Central and Eastern Europe by offering assistance and an accession perspective. Conversely, after ten years the EU has a much poorer record in dealing with state disintegration, ethnic conflict and humanitarian catastrophes in the Balkans. Prior to the Kosovo war, Europe's engagement in the region was neither consistent, nor unified, nor decisive.[3] This was the asssessment of the The Club of Three, an informal network of British, French and German leaders in government, business, the media and academia at their 'special session' on the 'Balkans and the New European Responsibilities', held on 29–30 June 2000 in Brussels. In the Report of the Meeting it was pointed out that 'The breakdown of the Berlin Wall erased the East–West dividing line, but eventually created a new division, between Europe and the Balkans'.[4]

The truth is that the West never developed a vital strategic interest in the region. If it had one before the 1990s, and that was reflected in its favourable and on the whole supportive attitude towards former Yugoslavia, now after the fall of the Berlin Wall the West lost interest in this country and the region as a whole. For a very long period of time, apart from the Greek–Turkish détente, there was hardly anything that could keep its interest on a long-term basis. The prevalence of the military and security reasoning over the economic and political ones, caused mainly by a distorted and rather biased understanding of the causes and consequences of the past and current problems, brought about wrong and often counterproductive policies.

Even the conflict in Kosovo, or rather because of the conflict in Kosovo, the West was and to some extent still is more than ever confused about its response to the region. The highly controversial bombing of Yugoslavia did not bring about the results expected by many. As the liberal opposition in Yugoslavia argued during the conflict, it was one of the reasons for prolonging the agony called Slobodan Milosevic regime, an agony both for the Serb people as well as for their neighbours. Isolating Serbia has proven to be detrimental – it hit the liberal opposition and strengthened Milosevic and his supporters,[5] not to mention its repercussions on the economic development of the region as a whole.

Now that Milosevic is no longer in power, the Balkans have every reason to believe that prospects for a new beginning are ahead. It is the first time since the beginning of the 1990s that countries in the region have the opportunity to freely discuss problems and seek solutions. It is the first time since the beginning of the 1990s that all countries in the region declare that they share common values and common goals with a view to integrating the whole region into the European and Euro-Atlantic structures. If the 1990s marked a new beginning for most of the countries in the region after the dismantling the old communist regimes, transformation was often distorted and was hampered to a great extent because of the developments next door.

The Kostunica government's priorities are clear, namely Yugoslavia's rapid integration into the international community, reconciliation and development of relations in the region. At the informal European Union's Council, held on 13–14 October 2000 in Biarritz during the French Presidency, Kostunica made clear that his long-term goal for Yugoslavia is membership of the European Union.

THE CHALLENGES

It took two wars, military conflicts and economic hardships to understand that the Balkans pose one of the greatest challenges to Euro-Atlantic security and stability. It is also one of the greatest challenges in terms of the ability of the EU and of NATO as the main European and

Euro-Atlantic structures and institutions to implement their new role in Europe – to bring about stability and security and to help accelerate the political and economic change in SEE.

In other words, the greatest challenge is the integration of SEE into the European mainstream. It is both a challenge and a solution. Integration is the key word for both Balkan security and conflict-resolution as well as for economic prosperity and for growth, European integration is crucial and vital for the countries in the region; it is a powerful incentive to change and to accept the values of liberal democracies or what is rightfully called the 'Europeanization' of the Balkans.

As simple as it may sound this is a challenge of immense historic proportions that will finalize the overcoming of the division of Europe that goes beyond the twentieth century's ideologies and dilemmas. There are serious policy hazards to be resolved, including the ordering of relations between Serbia, Montenegro and Kosovo and to some extent Bosnia. Also EU policies face dilemmas.

Milosevic and Tudjman permitted Europe to evade the issue of how really to integrate the Balkans into Europe. This can no longer be evaded. The issues extend in a seamless web from immediate and local issues on what Serbia's new leadership does next, through to wider Southeast European policy, on into EU enlargement policy, which then links to the whole widening-deepening dilemma of the EU itself.

From that point of view the main challenges in this process are as follows: first, to extend the European democratic space with its liberal standards of democratic political process, freedom of expression and treatment of minorities to SEE. A very important challenge is to avoid double standards and prejudices and to be consistent in the comrehension of what a true democratic process, values and standards are. In that sense the most difficult and important challenge still remains the problem of how to democratize multi-ethnic societies with all the implications that entails.

Among the most interesting and stimulating cases and experiences is that of Bulgaria. The tension in the multi-ethnic relations and the policy of persecution of the Turks with the name-change 'campaign' that started in 1985 and reached its peak in 1989 was one of the most serious factors that brought about the downfall of the communist regime. The Bulgarian ethnic model that emerged at the beginning of the 1990s amidst fears, mistrust, anxieties and concerns, is a mixture of constitutional and legislative provisions, of already considerable experience of political behaviour, and of a history of parliamentary process.

Bulgaria has often been criticized for the specific provision in its new constitution, adopted in 1991, prohibiting the formation of political parties on an ethnic basis. At the same time the organization that is basically viewed as 'the' political party of the Bulgarian Turks, that is, the Movement of the Rights and Freedoms, has participated in all the democratic elections since then, and alone or in coalition with other political parties, it has had a constant and visible political and parliamentary presence. This 'dualism' of the definitions and political practice is the result of a tacit political consensus that emerged among the Bulgarian political class some ten years ago, that started a process of involvement, interaction and dialogue as an inherent part of the Bulgarian political model.

EUROPEAN VALUES AND THE POLITICAL ROLE OF THE STATE

A common feature of the countries in the region is that at the beginning of the transformations domestic policies were the main factor for the retarded development of the reform process. The wars in former Yugoslavia with its implications for the whole region just increased the risks and demonstrated three obvious 'absences' – lack of institutions, lack of rule of law, lack of competitive economies.

In most Balkan countries the state remains the main instrument to achieve the fundamentals of democratization and to accomplish the economic transformation (such as privatization, restitution). Balkan state authorities perform the bulk of the work in this regard, which is quite inevitable, but at the same time increases bureaucracy and prevents stimulation of cooperation with the civil society. There is another side of the problem. The assumption by the state of major functions regulating the transition is a positive phenomenon if the public authorities are at the disposal of everyone, preserve their autonomy, and remain impartial to economic and private interests. This is the issue of the distinction between the private and public spheres – the main characteristics of the European political model.

'Europe' continues to be regarded as a civilized model and as a general value system assessed in quite broad categories. This model and its choice are still contemplated irrationally. In this regard the European Union as a political and economic project needs to be adopted in full by societies in the region. That is why the requirements of the project are 'less known' among the Balkan people, compared with Europe in principle. It is much easier to de-clare adherence to 'European values' than to follow 'European procedures'.

Quite often the state is an instrument of private, group or party-biased interest.[6] Private considerations are dominating the public interest. This phenomenon, reinforced by the introduced and accepted understanding that democracy means less statehood, limits the potential of the authorities to preserve the public interest and to guarantee accordingly law and order. Generally, this tendency compromises the state legitimacy.

1. The issue of corruption as illegitimate 'privatization' constitutes one of the main obstacles in the transitional period;
2. the weakening of the state authority has favoured the expansion of the activities of organized crime and has endangered the respect for fundamental human rights;
3. throughout the transitional period the state authorities have been victims of party struggles and influences, compromising their effectiveness and impartiality to private interests.

As a whole these developments are extremely dangerous as they compromise the European model of a democratic state. The general trend in Europe towards 'less statehood', often confused with the classical liberal idea of limited statehood, which is opposed to the mighty state of the communist doctrine, has led to the dangerous limitation of the powers of the public authorities. The withdrawal of the state from the classical positions of a public power in many cases is negotiated in favour of a number of groups, which exist in the margin between the public and the private. In this case the main responsibilities of the state in a democratic society are under question – its responsibility for the integrity of the society, for the integration of the different social groups as well as its responsibilities for the human rights and mostly for the guarantees of people's life and property.

Throughout the debate on the Bulgarian transitional period the question of the 'optimal state' is not a nostalgia for the 'communist statehood', but a position asserting the overall responsibilities of the state towards society, democracy and human rights.

Throughout the Balkans there is a widespread concern that states are not democratic, but rather corrupt. Not only are favours sold, but laws are passed that serve special interests rather than the public as a whole.[7] In most cases corruption generates the establishment of 'clientele' networks based on informal relations through appointments of 'loyals' at the different levels of the governmental–party–economic–non-governmental structures or through an exchange of mutual favours that make it difficult to investigate and prosecute law violators. Such a mechanism has an enormous negative corruption potential since 'clientelism' is just another, more 'soft' and more obscure type of corruption. The more this kind of relations penetrate the state authorities, the more corruption turns into a rule of life and leads to the alienation of the political system and the country from the European values.

We are witnessing a real paradox: 'clientele' relations of the political system are presented as the price of the consolidation of the state, and the consolidation of the state is considered to be the necessary condition for the further Europeanization of the political system. The outcome is that Europeanization of the political system is carried out through its 'clientelism'.[8]

ECONOMIC REFORM AND TRANSITION

The second biggest challenge is how to modernize economies on a market basis with a view to their participation in the new globalized world economy. This is a complex task, as it entails change and transformation that cannot be done in isolation and without counting the external factors. Of course, the most important factors in this process are internal and they relate to the capacity of the political elites to grasp the necessity of carrying out inclusive economic policies which from a long-term perspective bring about better living standards for the majority of the people.

This is a problem to be solved by all economies in the region albeit with different priorities and policy instruments. The most advanced among them, Bulgaria and Romania, which have passed a difficult and painful road towards starting negotiations for membership with the EU, are ardously fighting to keep the momentum going. The biggest challenge for both countries is how to combine strategies for integration with strategies for development, which go along in their main features and goals, but do not entirely coincide.

Another important factor that determines the process of integration of the region within the European mainstream is the fact that countries in Southeastern Europe have different and quite uneven stages of economic development, which makes them depend not so much on regional economic cooperation for their economic growth, but rather on external exchange, support and investment. They all have high budget and trade deficits, low rate of investment and high unemployment (Appendix 1).

Except for Slovenia and Croatia, the living standards in the other countries are significantly below those in Central Europe. The integral index – GDP per capita – does not exceed US$2000. The ranging of the countries by indexes for human development puts Bulgaria at 63rd place,

Romania at 68th place, Macedonia at 70th place and Albania only at 100th place.

Countries in the region still do not have big trade flows among themselves. More than 60 per cent of the trade from the region is with countries from the EU and CEFTA. On one hand, this is the legacy of the past – countries in the region belonged to different economic, political and security entities, which was the reason for lack of interest, lack of infrastructure (a case in point is still the lack of railroad between Sofia and Skopje), lack of cooperation between companies in the different sectors that still persists. On the other, this is the result of scarce domestic resources, hence the need for constant inflow of foreign investment drawn from outside the region. The only exception to this trend is the increasing exchange of Bulgaria and Romania with Greece and Turkey. Such a tendency is mainly due to the overall increase in the trade since Bulgaria and Romania are countries enjoying liberalized trade relations with Greece as an EU member-state, and with Turkey on the basis of free-trade agreements.[9]

The wars and embargoes, with all the implications for infrastructure, have hurt even this modest exchange and might lead to chronic trade deficits in many countries in the region. This development eliminates the few competitive advantages of the region that have emerged in some sectors of the economy. In this situation it is difficult to count on endogenous factors for regional development and growth. 'Centrifugal' forces still dominate. The countries quite naturally are oriented towards interregional formations and centres for development.

The level of intraregional trade confirms this statement. In countries such as Romania in 1998 it did not exceed 3 per cent of the export and 1.5 per cent of the import. The republics of the former Yugoslavia were an exception. Obviously a significant segment of the intra-Yugoslavian trade has been transformed into intraregional. The information about the foreign trade of the Balkans with selected EU countries shows the existence of orientation of foreign trade flows towards countries such as Germany, Italy, Austria and Greece, which, because of their geographical position, are active in the south and southeastern part of the continent (Appendix 2).[10]

The analysis of foreign trade by goods groups would show the lack of opportunities for more intensive intraregional exchange. Most of the countries have identical or near-identical export lists, which deprives them of a potential for regional cooperation.

The Balkans as a whole attract an insignificant part of the foreign direct investments in CEE after the fall of communism – only about 8 per cent of all investments. This is somewhat less than 10 per cent of the investments in Central Europe and only twice as much as the investments in the Baltic. The impression is that Slovenia and Croatia attract over one-third of all investments in the Balkan region.

POSSIBLE SOLUTIONS

The Yugoslav conflict and especially the war in Kosovo have increased the significance of the external factor to the extent that nowadays the West plays a crucial role in the economic recovery or rather the reconstruction of the region. In fact this is one of the reasons for the re-emergence of ideas of some new type of assistance, that is, some kind of a Marshall Plan for the Balkans, a phenomenon that we did not see ten years ago, at the beginning of the changes. A whole series of questions that may lead to possible solutions are on the agenda of the public debate: do we need a new Marshall Plan and is that feasible in the present day realities? And if so, what kind of Marshall Plan do we want so that we reach long-term stability and economic growth for the benefit of vast majority of people? Is the Stability Pact the most efficient and working plan to reconstruct the region? Do we need other instruments as well for boosting investment and growth? Is the Stability Pact a substitute for the integration efforts of the countries in the region, to 'contain' their striving to become members of a united Europe? Is the new division of the Balkans into Western and Eastern Balkans reflecting a real difference in political and economic maturity of the countries or is it a new dividing line hurting the quest for overcoming the differences and finding the common interest? Since autumn 2000, after the change of regime in Belgrade, should there be new priorities and new debate over the future of the region? Is regional cooperation adequately responding to the changing political environment?

What should be taken into account is the different understanding of the Marshall Plan type of arrangement that is held by politicians inside and outside the region. To be more precise, there were calls for a Marshall Plan for Eastern Europe at the beginning of the 1990s, but they were quickly dropped after understanding that situations as well as the underlying reasoning for such a plan were very different. To the East the rather vague expectation was for a big amount of financial resources that should be spent for investment and growth. To the West it meant and it means mainly a political arrangement for building democracies, rule of law and institutions. The analogies with Western Europe after the Second World War are both proper and erroneous.

Indeed the outcome of the Marshall Plan for Europe was both political and economic. To the extent that the enormous devastation of the Second World War was overcome more quickly (it does not mean that it would not have been overcome anyway and that it was rather a matter of speed and of common arrangement), the Marshall Plan was a successful economic endeavour and help. Equally true is the assessment that the Marshall Plan speeded up the establishment of stable democratic institutions and, what is more important, it helped the emergence of bold political ideas that brought about the creation of institutions such as NATO, the Council of Europe, the OECD, and finally the European Economic Community. In such a way the Marshall Plan achieved one of its main goals – to stop the influence of communist ideas in the West and to establish a strong Euro-Atlantic relationship that is the pillar of present-day security arrangement in the continent.

The list of questions may be prolonged and they are all valid. Oddly enough they reflect both a relief as well as an anxiety and fear that the new situation might slow down the support for the integration efforts for some countries (Bulgaria and Romania) or that it may 'draw back' to the region countries who have chosen to stay outside regional cooperation (Slovenia and Croatia).

'WESTERN BALKANS' – DO WE NEED NEW DIVISION LINES?

There are several important points to be made when talking about possible solutions and about bringing SEE into the European mainstream.

First, let us turn our attention to the term 'Western Balkans', introduced into Eurospeak at the 1998 Vienna European Council. The discussion on the relevance of this term or rather on whether it is appropriate has brought about contradictory opinions on the matter. The initial reaction from all parts was highly negative, owing to the simple fact that it added another division to the already fragmented Balkans. Other arguments emerged later on, which sometimes coincided in its support or rejection but from entirely different points of view.

The most persuasive among them, elaborated during the Meeting of the Club of Three on 29–30 June 2000 in Brussels, stated that 'it (the term Western Balkans) suggests that structural problems like economic underdevelopment and ethnic nationalism are now reduced to this shrinking region on the European periphery. Discursively, it places these contries outside Europe, while contsructing a region againts indigenous realities and perceptions'.[11] In the Report of the Meeting of the Three it was strongly pointed out that 'use of the term "Southeastern Europe" rather than "Western Balkans" would imply recognition of the fact that the region already is part of Europe, that its problems are European problems and that any viable solution has to be a European solution, involving both the deepening and the widening of the Union ...' Thus the Union is *de facto* dividing a region with the left hand, while promoting multilateral cooperation among the states of the same region with the right hand.[12]

new division

Indeed the countries from the so-called 'Western Balkans' have posed a real threat to the security and stability of the region and of Europe as a whole. They are in most cases weak, failing states unable to follow sustainable reform policy. The EU dilemma was either to continue encouraging reform and stability through external support measures and without much involvement, that is, follow the previous policy 'containment' of the region; or to give them a clear long-term European perspective. The EU opted for the second. In 1999 it opened a long-term accession perspective for these countries with the Stabilization and Association Process. This was an important shift of EU policy that demonstrated enhanced awareness of the strategic and political dimension of enlargement.

SAA

The individual reaction of the different players in the region is a case in point. Slovenia, which is one of the front runners for membership in the EU, has practically alienated itself from the Balkan problems. Bulgaria and Romania, having as their strategic priority membership in the EU, have been for most of the time suspicious of all schemes of regional cooperation that do not have a European or transatlantic component. Their main fear is, and rightfully so, that regional cooperation and integration may be considered a precondition for EU accession, which will be a setback for their EU ambitions. Having in mind the socio-economic heterogenity of the region and its long tradition of mistrust and non-cooperation, it is more than obvious that intraregional integration as a stand-alone strategy for economic reform is not viable. Economic cooperation in the region, trade and infrastructure alone cannot bring about the necessary element of a take-off strategy for sustainable reform.

The fears of Bulgaria and Romania are linked also to another consequence of the developments in Yugoslavia, especially after the democratic opposition in Yugoslavia won the presidential elections in November 2000 and Milosevic stepped down. The paradox lies in the fact that both countries showed solidarity with the West in the efforts to oust Milosevic from power and to end the Kosovo crisis. They have repeatedly emphasized the negative impact of sanctions on their economies and they both were eager to end the conflict. After it was over, their concern was that the 'Western Balkans' became the main focus of EU interest in the area and that Bulgaria and Romania will be 'neglected' or dragged into some regional schemes, which will slow down their accesion process.

Both countries followed closely the debate in the EU on the possible 'breakthrough' decisions, solving the problems of the Western Balkans and the region with one all-out effort in the framework of the EU enlargement process, introducing some kind of 'new associated or partial membership' or 'membership light' for the Balkans. The ideas that envisage priority for economic rather than political or civil-society incentives and EU acceptance of compromises in the adoption of the acquis were perceived by Bulgaria and Romania as a threat to their integration efforts, turning them into hostages of the structural deadlock of the region. The support, including financial, and the focus was not on Bulgaria and Romania as future prospective members of the Union in the region but on the 'Western Balkans', which brought about some form of dissapointment and open doubt as to the objectives of EU policies in the region.

'REGIONALITY' AND 'EUROPEANIZATION'

The dilemma between the 'regionality' and 'Europeanization' as seen by some governments in the region is both real and illusionary. Regional cooperation and constant regional interaction at different levels – political, economic, institutional, cultural, civil society, cross-border cooperation, trade and infrastructure, is of vital importance for the region. A critical mass of exchange and interaction is still needed in order to reach a stage where common institutions will appear and common solutions will be found. This mass will create the necessary framework for the long due change in mentality, in attitudes and in relations apart from the obvious positive political and eventually economic impact. Regional cooperation is bringing new political culture in the region at times when political and ethnic divisions in some parts look deeper than ever.

During the last 5–6 years various initiatives emerged both on the part of the international community such as the Royaumont initiative of the EU or SECI initiative of the US, as well as from the region itself. In 1996 the first Meeting of Ministers of Foreign Affairs of the Balkan countries took place in Sofia, which unleashed a whole series of meetings at different levels and in different formats – a development that was unthinkable only a few years ago. This is an extremely dynamic and positive process that should be intensified and enriched with new ideas and should cover new areas.

What was lacking for a long time – a comprehensive proactive policy of the West – started with the Stability Pact, an initiative of the German Presidency of the European Union in the aftermath of the Kosovo crisis. The Stability Pact, adopted on 10 June 2000, lays down a framework for cooperation between the EU, the European Commission, the US, Russia, Japan, the Balkan countries, Turkey and other countries, plus regional and international organizations and international financial institutions. The aim is to bring peace, stability and economic development to the region. The Pact sets out principles and areas of action with a view to a common approach. It specifies the role played by each party, that of the EU being to focus on the development of programmes to underpin democracy, stimulate the economy and foster contractual relations within the region. The Pact was the much-needed Western involvement in the solution of problems of the region and it is viewed as such. Of course, one might hear conflicting views on its merits and possible accomplishments but the most valuable aspect of the Stability Pact no doubt is its comprehensiveness and strive to combine political interest with economic activity, including the attraction of private investment to the region.

On the other hand, the Stability Pact still has to prove its effectiveness and vitality. There should be some tangible results in economic terms if we want it to be supported by public opinion in the countries of the region. As a comprehensive long-term structural project, it is under tremendous pressure of time and expectations (from donors and recipients) to produce accountable and sustainable results in the short term.[13]

Another aspect is the firm commitment of the West in terms of strategic interest both to the security and to the economic development of the region. There is a fear, and rightfully so, that the Stability Pact might serve as some kind of a substitute to the integration efforts of the countries in the regions and especially those of Bulgaria and Romania. At worst, it risks being *ersatz* real policy. Its problem is that it has no real power as substitute for EU integration – the main instruments of policy initiative (aid, trade and institutional integration) are those of the EU.[14]

The decision of the Helsinki Council to start negotiations for membership with Bulgaria and Romania no doubt was a historic one and definitely a move in the right direction from the point of view of stability and security in the region as a whole. It was exactly the long-expected political message to both countries that was much needed in order to speed up reform and political stability.

Let me immediately point out that the political reasoning of such a decision is more than obvious and there should not be any illusion if we want to make the right and realistic decisions further on. In rough economic terms Bulgaria and Romania are far from ready in the short-term complying with the Copenhagen criteria for competitive economies that might stand the pressures of the Internal Market of the Union. Such was the conclusion contained in the Regular Report of the European Commission on the Progress towards Accession issued in November 2000.[15] Both countries have made efforts in attaining macroeconomic stability, which compared with the situation in other countries of the region is a positive development but needs to be turned into an irreversible tendency of economic life.

However, structural reforms still need to be taken further and enterprise restructuring needs to be advanced in both countries. Financial intermediation continues to be weak, and much remains to be done in areas such as the functioning of the land market and the enforcement of bankruptcy cases. Measures to address weaknesses in the implementation and enforcement of the legal and regulatory framework need to be taken to improve the business climate. Bureaucratic barriers to foreign and local enterprise creation must be eliminated. A sustained implementation of the existing reform programme and higher levels of investment are key requirements for continued growth, developing the enterprise sector, and building up competitiveness. The main statistical indicators for Bulgaria and Romania compared with the other candidate countries from Central and Eastern Europe show that in some areas both countries are lagging behind the others (Appendix 3).

The reasons for this development are manifold and some of them have been addressed in this chapter. Figures matter but something more is at stake – the political will of the West not only to encourage change, but to take over the responsibility for its making. Europe has taken such bold steps in the past. In the 1950s, the project of European integration was a political idea, followed by economic measures. The Marshall Plan aimed at both political and economic goals.

The Stability Pact and the European integration efforts by the countries in the region should go in parallel and should not be a substitute for one another. While the Stability Pact creates an important framework for mobilizing political support for private investment initiatives, the integration efforts bring about profound domestic change and alignment with European standards and norms. I would go further and argue that the integration efforts are a constant strife to assert European values and for that matter they are of profound importance.

All this analysis demonstrates that the Stability Pact and the EU integration efforts should go hand in hand. It is equally important that this understanding is shared by both players – countries in the region and their partners from the EU. No one should distance himself from this approach as it is of vital importance to keep the momentum of what has been achieved. The European Union should avoid the impression that it makes a step forward and then steps back in hesitance and in inability to act. Having in mind the complex situation in Southeastern Europe and the importance of a clear and persistent political message, Europe should not disengage once again from the problems in the region, including enlargement towards the Southeast. Adopting new formulas for enlargement, the so-called 10+2, leaving the two associated countries – Bulgaria and Romania for some next round of enlargement, does not testify to the visionary long-term policy of stability and prosperity of Southeast Europe.

The most fragile of the post-Communist regimes of Central and Eastern Europe need the support of a strong EU integration trajectory now, not in 10 years time. Otherwise there will at best be a stagnating transition, at worst a relapse into chaos, repression and violence.

In order to sum up – European integration is the key word for the solution of the problems in the region. It does not mean, of course, that problems will be solved by themselves. We know too well that integration will not by itself bring growth, and that it is up to the national governments to make the right political and economic choices. But it is equally true that European integration mobilizes support and resources, and that is a powerful incentive for change and for preventing 'cleptocracies' from dominating economies in the region. The West should be more visionary and should stay deeply involved in Balkan politics through its institutions – NATO and the European Union. There is a historic chance to start making a change in this part of the world – maybe slowly at the beginning, but it should be pursued without hesitation and with much more boldness and imagination.

APPENDIX 1

The main economic indexes characterizing the development of the Balkan countries are presented in the table below.[16]

TABLE 1
MAIN INDEXES

	Albania	Bulgaria	Romania	Bosnia and Herzegovina	Croatia	Macedonia	Yugoslavia	Slovenia
Capital	Tirana	Sofia	Bucharest	Sarajevo	Zagreb	Skopje	Belgrade	Ljubljana
Currency	lek	lev	leu	Marka konvertibilna	kuna	denar	dinar	tolar
Exchange rate to 1 US$, 18 July 2000	139.20	2.04	21573	2.19	8.1	65.1	11.6	221.53
Territory, km2	28750	110910	237500	51100	56530	25710	102173	20250
Population, in 000s, 1998	3315	8283	22526	3294	4668	2003	10614	1985
Village population, %, 1997	62	31	43	–	43	39	–	48
Natural growth of the population, ‰, 1997	15.6	–6.9	–1.8	5.0	0.8	6.6	2.0	–0.3
Life expectancy (1997)								
– men	68.5	67.2	65.2	69.5	67.1	69.6	69.9	71.0
– women	74.3	74.4	73.0	75.1	75.7	74.0	74.6	78.6
GDP in 1999 compared with 1989, %	95.7	70.7	75.8	–	77.9	76.8	41.6	105.3
GDP per capita	926.8	1315	1695	3039	4820	1548	–	9779
GDP per capita compared with EU, %	–	24	23	–	–	–	–	59
Private sector, % of GDP	75	65	60	–	55	60	–	50
Foreign trade, % of GDP	17.3	40.8	25.2	41.5	30.6	49.2	–	48.5
Average salary in dollars at the end of 1999	–	124	97	176	415	164	144	936
Indexes for human development								
– value	0.699	0.758	0.752	–	0.733	0.746	–	0.845
– rank	100	63	68	–	55	73	–	33

Source: WB, PNUD, European commission for Europe, UNICEF, EBRD, The Economist Intellegence Unit. Quoted from *Le Courrier des Pays de l'Est*, No. 1006, 2000, pp.216–17.

APPENDIX 2

TABLE 2
FOREIGN TRADE OF BALKAN COUNTRIES (1998, %)

	Export		Import	
	EU	Balkans	EU	Balkans
Albania	87.4	8.4	83.8	7.1
Bulgaria	43.2	7.0	37.0	2.7
Croatia	49.1	29.5	59.0	10.3
Macedonia	37.8	37.5	37.5	28.9
Romania	56.5	3.0	75.6	1.5
Slovenia	63.6	16.6	66.3	6.1
Yugoslavia	36.0	35.4	51.1	17.5

Source: WB, PNUD, European Commission, UNICEF, EBRD, The Economist Intellegence Unit.

TABLE 3
FOREIGN TRADE OF BALKAN COUNTRIES WITH SELECTED EU COUNTRIES
(%, 1998)

	Export				Import			
	Germany	Italy	Austria	Greece	Germany	Italy	Austria	Greece
Albania	6.9	49.4	1.5	20.5	4.2	46.5	1.5	26.6
Bulgaria	9.5	11.7	1.1	8.2	11.8	7.2	2.4	4.2
Croatia	17.9	18.9	5.3	0.4	20.2	18.7	7.8	0.2
Macedonia	16.2	3.6	–	8.1	13.4	5.5	–	7.3
Romania	16.8	19.5	2.1	2.1	16.4	15.8	2.7	1.7
Slovenia	39.4	14.9	6.8	0.4	20.7	16.7	8.4	0.1
Yugoslavia	9.2	11.5	1.6	4.9	13.4	10.1	3.3	3.8

Source: WB, PNUD, European Commission, UNICEF, EBRD, The Economist Intellegence Unit.

APPENDIX 3

TABLE 4
CANDIDATE COUNTRIES MAIN STATISTICAL INDICATORS (1999)

	Area 1000 km²	Population Million inhabitants	Density Inhabitants /km²	%	Agriculture % gross added value	% employment
Bulgaria	111	8.3	75	2.4	17.3	26.6
Cyprus	9	0.7	78	4.5	4.2	9.3
Czech Rep.	79	10.3	130	-0.2	3.7	5.2
Estonia	45	1.4	32	-1.1	5.7	8.8
Hungary	93	10.1	109	4.5	5.5	7.1
Latvia	65	2.4	37	0.1	4.0	15.3
Lithuania	65	3.7	57	-4.1	8.8	20.2
Malta	0.3	0.4	1333	4.2	2.5	1.8
Poland	313	38.7	124	4.2	3.8	18.1
Romania	238	22.5	94	-3.2	15.5	41.7
Slovakia	49	5.4	110	1.9	4.5	7.4
Slovenia	20	2.0	100	4.9	3.6	10.2
Turkey	775	64.3	83	-5.0	14.3	41.3

Sources: Eurostat, from national sources.

TABLE 5

	Inflation rate	Unemployment rate	General government spending	External trade			Current account	Foreign direct investment[1]	
	Annual average	International labour organization definition % active population	Balance in GDP%	Trade balance exports /imports, %	Exports EU, % total exports	Imports EU, % total imports	Balance % GDP	Stock per capita	Net inflow % GDP
Bulgaria	2.6	17.0	0.2	72.5	52.6	48.6	-5.3	256	6.1
Cyprus	1.3	3.6	n.a.	13.2	50.7	57.3	-2.6	28602	2.1[2]
Czech Rep.	2.0	8.7	-1.6	93.0	69.2	64.0	-2.0	1357	9.1
Estonia	4.6	11.7	-4.6	68.3	72.7	65.0	-6.2	1052	4.6
Hungary	10.0	7.0	-3.7	89.3	76.2	64.4	-4.3	1654	2.9
Latvia	2.4	14.5	3.9	58.4	62.5	54.5	-10.6	825	5.8
Lithuania	0.8	14.1	n.a.	62.1	50.1	49.7	-11.2	511	4.5
Malta	2.1	5.3	n.a.	69.6	48.7	65.4	-3.5	3465[2]	3.4[2]
Poland	7.2	15.3	-2.7	59.6	70.5	64.9	-7.5	485	4.3
Romania	45.8	6.8	n.a.	81.8	65.5	60.4	3.8	220	2.4
Slovakia	10.6	16.2	-0.6	90.2	59.4	51.7	-5.9	366	3.7
Slovenia	6.1	7.6	-0.6	85.8	66.0	68.6	-2.9	532	0.2
Turkey	64.9	7.6	n.a.	65.3	52.6	53.9	-0.7	1042	0.4[2]

Notes: [1]Source: Transition Report EBRD
[2]1998 source: UNCTAD

Sources: Eurostat, from national sources.

NOTES

1. Emerson (2000).
2. Keridis (1999) p.3.
3. Club of Three (2000) p.5.
4. Ibid. p.5.
5. Ibid. p.6.
6. Todorov and Ivanov (2000) pp.26–7.
7. Gligorov ed. (2000).
8. Todorov and Ivanov (2000) p.30.
9. Stanchev (1999) p.7.
10. Mintchev (2000).
11. Club of Three (2000) p.15.
12. Ibid.
13. Ibid. p.18.
14. Emerson (2000).
15. European Commission (2000).
16. Mintchev (2000).

REFERENCES

Boudier-Benbasaa, Fabienne, and Yorgos Rizopoulos (1999): 'Tendences et Caracteristiques des Investissments Directs Etrangers dans les Pays Balkaniques', *Revue d'Etudes Comparatives Est-Ouest*, No. 4.

Center for the Study of Democracy (2000): 'Stability Pact and Integration of SEE in the European Economy', Working Paper, Sofia.

Club of Three (2000): 'The Balkans and New European Responsibilities', Special Meeting of the Club of Three, Brussels, 29–30 June 2000, p.15. The Club of Three is a an informal network of British, French and German leaders in government, business, the media and academia, meeting at twice-annual intervals or organizing 'special sessions'.

Emerson, Michael (2000): CEPS, Brussels, *Europa South-East Monitor*, No. 16, November 2000.

European Commission (2000): 'Enlargement Strategy Paper, Report on Progress Towards Accession by Each of the Candidate Countries', Brussels, 8 November 2000.

Gligorov, Vladimir, ed. (2000): *Balkan Reconstruction: Economic Aspects*, Vienna: Vienna Institute for International Economic Studies.

Heimerl, Daniela, Yorgos Rizopoulos and Neboisa Vucadinovic (1999): 'Contradictions et Limites des Politiques de Reconstruction dans les Balkans', *Revues d'Etudes Comparatives Est-Ouest*, No. 4.

Keridis, Dimitris (1999): *The Balkan Crisis: Causes, Consequences, Western Responses and the Way Ahead*, The Kokkalis Program on Southeastern and East-Central Europe and the John F. Kennedy School of Government, Harvard University.

Mintchev, Vesselin (2000): 'Is Visegrad a Viable Cooperation Pattern to be Studied and Implemented by South Eastern Europe?', Eger, Hungary, 13–15 November 2000, European Policy Forum, Sofia.

Stanchev, Krassen (1999): 'The Balkans in 2010: Economic Scenarios', Sofia: Institute for Market Economy.

Todorov, Antony and Andrei Ivanov (2000): 'Monitoring of Bulgaria's EU Accession Process', Sofia, November 2000.

Civil Society and Multilateral Cooperative Models: The Role of Non-Governmental Organizations in the Stability Pact for Southeastern Europe

HARALAMBOS KONDONIS

INTRODUCTION

At the outset of the 1990s, the international community, in trying to assist and secure the transition process in Eastern Europe, decided to cooperate only at a governmental level with the new post-communist independent states. It took some time to be realized that building a sound economic environment and a new democratic society is something more complicated and more actors must be involved. Very often, development assistance or even humanitarian aid vanished in the hands of corrupt or incapable governments and administrations. Huge development projects and funds ended up strengthening legal or illegal economic elites, widening the social and economic gaps in the transition societies with crucial side-effects. It is undeniable that the needs of democratic institution building and fighting of corruption and organized crime were clearly underestimated. Issues of human rights and the complexity of interethnic relations, the democratic structure of the judiciary, public administration, the army and the police, the importance of education and equality were issues that were shadowed by the axiomatic importance of economic development.

The issues of economic liberalization, privatization and political stability were understandably a priority. The question is: can we achieve these on a long-term basis, without a simultaneous democratization process? The active participation of civil society in building new democratic institutions, new norms and socio-political behaviour; in creating a viable state where the rule of law will guarantee civil human and minority rights; in promoting respect, tolerance and understanding among different political, social and ethnic groups, is more than essential

for a balanced development and a European direction for the countries
of Southeastern Europe.

In a region characterized by new independent states, entities and
international protectorates, fragile borders and strong nationalisms, grey
and illegal economies, high unemployment and marginalized social and
ethnic minorities, the problems are more or less the same. Therefore, a
regional approach is needed on all levels. The prospects for regional
development must be based on regional cooperative networks and
initiatives, at the political, economic and social levels. Civil society, non-
governmental organizations (NGOs) and groups, research centres and
universities, mayoralties and municipalities, can play a vital role in
activating the civic energies, which were and still are passively
entrapped, smouldering below authoritarian regimes and old
undemocratic attitudes.

THE UNIQUENESS OF THE STABILITY PACT

All the initiatives during and immediately after the war in Kosovo
demonstrated the need for a new cooperative structure. It was obvious
that the new initiative had to combine and coordinate: international
institutions (IOs), such as the European Union, the Organization for
Security and Cooperation in Europe (OSCE), and the United Nations,
which provide political directions and human rights standards;
international financial institutions (IFIs), such as the World Bank, the
International Monetary Fund (IMF), and the European Investment Bank
(EIB), which provide the mechanisms, the experience and the
possibilities for funding; and regional initiatives by the countries of the
region, which are aware of the real priorities and needs both at the state
and non-governmental level.

As a consequence, the Stability Pact (SP) for Southeastern Europe
was signed on 10 June 1999, in Cologne, as a European Union initiative
under the auspices of the OSCE. Regardless of the final results and the
justifiable criticism regarding the effectiveness, the delays and the
transparency of the Stability Pact structure, it is undeniable that the
Stability Pact is a unique and unprecedented multilateral cooperation
model because:

- the international community has a determined 'regional approach'
  for the reconstruction issues in Southeast Europe;
- both international organizations with significant political gravity and
  international financial institutions with the appropriate financial
  mechanisms participate actively in the SP structure and activities;

- the existence of the three Working Tables (WTs) is an effort to combine the economic reconstruction, the building of stable democratic institutions in a secure social and international environment, creating the necessary preconditions for a sustainable development in the region;
- the priorities of development policy are defined by both the donor and the recipient countries, by creating the necessary mechanisms and a combined structure for the selection, control and evaluation of the proposed projects;
- it has underlined the significance not only of international organizations and member-states of the SP, but also of the private sector, the non-governmental organizations (NGOs), and all forms of the civil society.[1]

More than ten years after the end of the Cold War, it is undeniable that the development and eventual integration of transition countries into the European structures requires a balanced economic and social development in a secure environment. The active participation of civil society, especially of NGOs with relevant experience, has proved to be essential in order to re-create coherent and democratic societies. It is the first time that the international community understands in practical terms that a parallel democratic transition of society on all levels must be directly linked to any economic development process.

THE CIVIL SOCIETY IN SOUTHEASTERN EUROPE

After 45 years of communism, the civil society sector and NGOs in Southeastern Europe are lacking experience, economic funds, know-how and the appropriate mechanisms. The meaning of civil society and the need, the role and the function of real independent NGOs is difficult even to understand. Unfortunately, many NGOs in Southeastern Europe are connected with governmental (or ex-governmental) officials, having a close political affiliation, promoting specific political interests. In addition, they are interested exclusively in funding, lacking long-term strategy. Funding often is secured by good connections with people in the government or international organizations. Furthermore, local NGOs are lacking experience and know-how. As a result, they are dependent on strong international NGOs, and their effectiveness is limited.

It is characteristic of the influence of the communist regime on the civil society sector that the only country that has an active, experienced and well-structured NGO mechanism is FR Yugoslavia, where the authoritarian regime for decades was not openly against civil activities.

Similarly, NGOs in the region still function in a transition society, with some remaining undemocratic structures and attitudes.[2] Violation of human rights, marginalization of social groups and undemocratic state behaviour are considered as 'normal' by the majority of the people. NGOs have the difficult task to impregnate the values of civil rights into societies, which were lacking real democratic education and practice.

Furthermore, NGOs in Southeastern Europe have to function in an environment full of uncertainty and interethnic conflicts. Nationalism, irredentism, ethnic hate and lack of tolerance and understanding still devastate the region. Sound economic development is undermined by numerous illegal activities, corruption, trafficking in human beings, etc. The difficulties that the NGOs have to overcome trying to address all these problems are obvious, and in many cases NGO activists have to face discrimination and persecution from the state, extremist groups or even mafias, whose interests can be jeopardized by a democratic and just society.

Operating in an unfriendly climate and because of the many shortcomings regarding access to the international funds, ineffective mechanisms and lack of experience, regional NGOs are looking for international partners and sponsors. As a result, firstly regional cooperation on the civil-society level remains limited and, secondly, local NGOs tend to be dependent on powerful and well-organized international NGOs. On the other hand, the international community has realized the need to create regional networks and to promote regional and interboundary cooperation. One of the criteria for project funding is that the proposed programme must promote and include civil society actors from more than two Southeast European countries, underlining the regional approach of the Stability Pact.

On the other hand, dependency on and consequent control by international NGOs can create many problems for the sound development of the NGO sector in the region. On a long-term basis, the possible creation of a huge NGO international 'industry' with regional branches, can prove to be fatal for the significant role that civil society has to play for the democratic development of the regional countries. Such an outcome is against the real meaning and the values of an independent and fruitful participation of local NGOs.

THE PARTICIPATION OF CIVIL SOCIETY IN THE STRUCTURE OF THE STABILITY PACT

Examining the Stability Pact members, it is noticeable that multi-collectivism is one of the basic characteristics of the Pact. Beyond its core, which is the recipient countries of Southeastern Europe, there is an amalgam of states, international organizations and regional interstate initiatives with significant differences.[3] These differences are reflected also on the civil society level.

It is obvious that the main differentiation within the Stability Pact structure is that of donor countries and international organizations on the one hand and recipient Southeast European countries on the other. The latter are Albania, Bosnia-Herzegovina, Bulgaria, Croatia, Former Yugoslav Republic of Macedonia (FYROM) and Romania. Since 26 October 2000, FR of Yugoslavia has become also officially a member state of the Stability Pact, after the electoral victory of the democratic opposition at the end of September.[4]

In addition, the Royaumont Process, the EU regional cooperation initiative in Southeastern Europe, ended in 2000, and it is no longer considered a member of the Stability Pact. Similar discussions have already started for the US-sponsored Southeast European Cooperation Initiative (SECI). The role of the above-mentioned initiatives regarding civil society is significant, since many NGOs, research centres and universities were involved in regional projects, within their structure.

The basic structure of the Stability Pact is based on the Secretariat of the Special Coordinator, the Regional Table and more importantly the three Working Tables and the relevant Sub-Tables or Task Forces, where in fact the civil-society sector is active. Because of its subject area, the 1st Working Table on Democratization and Human Rights is the natural location for NGOs activities, although in other cross-table initiatives, such as anti-corruption, trafficking in human beings, gender, education, environment, etc., and in initiatives of the 2nd and 3rd Working Tables, NGOs' participation is vital for their success.

Before presenting in detail the actual participation and contribution of the international and local NGOs in the Stability Pact projects, we have to underline that in many instances projects, which are funded by governments, especially in the case of the 1st Working Table, are implemented by NGOs. This is quite difficult to show in the detailed project tables of the Stability Pact Secretariat. As a consequence, the role of NGOs is sometimes underestimated by researchers, who are not aware of the actual involvement of the NGO sector in those projects.

TABLE 1
IMPLEMENTING AGENCIES
(PROJECTS IN EUROS; LEADING COUNTRY OR ORGANIZATION IN PARENTHESES)

Implementing agencies/task forces	States	International organizations	International NGOs	Southeast European NGOs[1]	Total
Human rights & minorities: (Slovenia/CoE)	1,260,000	3,024,000	2,222,000	828,000	7,334,000
Good governance: (CoE)	50,000	4,693,500	3,020,000	248,000	8,011,500
Gender issues: (OSCE)	–	270,000	1,653,000	210,000	2,133,000
Media: Mr Moisy (French Journalist)	2,912,500	7,315,000	9,925,500	2,013,500	22,166,500
Education (Austria)	4,352,000	2,417,500	9,215,500	2,091,000	18,076,000
Parliamentary cooperation: (International Institute for Democracy)	–	–	3,590,500	–	3,590,500
Return of refugees: (UNHCR)	1,250,000	235,220,500	14,438,000	–	250,908,500
Szeged process[2]: (Hungary)	2,846,000	–	–	–	2,846,000
Total	12,670,500	252,939,500	44,063,000	5,390,000	315,066,000

Notes: [1]In this study we consider Slovenian and Greek NGOs as part of the regional Civil Society, although Greece and Slovenia participate in the Stability pact as donor countries.

[2]Szeged is a Hungarian town near the Hungarian–Yugoslav border. The Szeged Process encouraged the creation of networks between Yugoslav mayoralties and municipalities controlled by the democratic opposition and local authorities from Stability Pact member states.

Source: Office of the Special Coordinator of the Stability Pact (OSCSP), Quick Start Package, Working Table I, Progress Report, March 2001

Therefore, the following tables are concerned with the implementation agency of the projects. On that level, the contribution of international and local NGOs and other civil society actors in every Working Table can be seen in a more analytical way.

It is also characteristic that international NGOs have the responsibility of implementing the projects, but this process involves many local NGOs, in order to strengthen the regional cooperation at the civil-society level creating regional networks. Therefore, projects that have been included in the international NGOs category most times include also Southeast European NGOs. In addition, many different

FIGURE 1
IMPLEMENTING AGENCIES
TASK FORCES OF WORKING TABLE 1

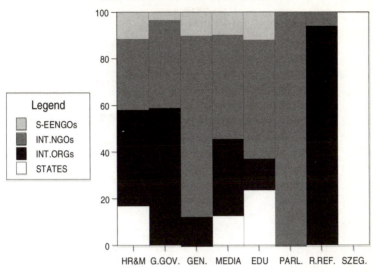

Source: see Table 1.

FIGURE 2
PARTICIPATION OF SOUTHEAST EUROPEAN NGOs

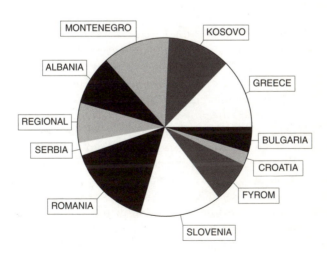

Source: see Table 2.

FIGURE 3
IMPLEMENTING AGENCIES WORKING TABLE 1

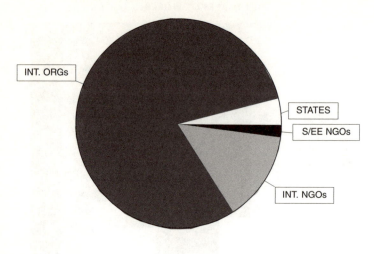

Source: see Table 3.

actors are involved in the implementation process, such as states, international organizations and NGOs, which makes the effort of categorizing them even more difficult.[5]

Human Rights and Democratization

As far as the 1st Working Table is concerned, the role of both international and local NGOs is significant. They have the responsibility of implementing projects of a total value €49.45m, meaning 15.7 per cent of the whole amount pledged during the Donors Conference in Brussels in March 2000 for projects of the Quick Start Package (QSP) of the 1st Working Table. On the other hand, we have to point out that international NGOs are much more involved implementing 14 per cent (€44m) of the project funds, compared with the relative 1.7 per cent (€5.4m) of the local NGOs. This unbalance can create dependencies and side effects, such as discouragement of the local civil-society sector to participate in Stability Pact projects and difficulty to initiate independent and regionally based projects.[6]

Local NGOs are very active in the Education and Youth, Media, Good Governance Task Forces. In particular, in the 'Human Rights and Minorities' Task Force, Southeast European NGOs implement 11.28 per cent of the project funds, and for Gender issues almost 10 per cent. On the contrary, Parliamentary Cooperation projects are dominated by international NGOs and Return of Refugees projects by international organizations, whereas the Szeged Process for the democratization of Serbia was carried out by countries, mainly Hungary and the US.[7] It is also noteworthy that in the Human Rights and Minorities, Media and Education Task Forces there is a characteristic balance among the implementing agencies. In addition, we have to consider that projects that officially are implemented by international organizations and NGOs often involve local actors from the civil society, who in fact undertake the implementation of projects, while international actors play an advisory and supervisory role.

It is noteworthy that even at the regional level, NGOs from Greece and Slovenia, which in fact are donor countries within the Stability Pact, implement 27.6 per cent (€1.5m) of the total project funds for the local NGOs. This shows that donor countries tend to fund their own NGOs. Also, Slovenia and Romania, co-chair countries for the 1st Working Table in the July 2000–June 2001 period, by having specific persons in decision-making posts have attracted more than 30 per cent of the project funds. Another trend is that because of the embargo in Serbia, NGOs from other Yugoslav provinces, such as Montenegro and Kosovo, received a relatively high percentage, 24.3 per cent, of the project funds. It is undeniable that the participation of Bulgarian and Croatian NGOs must be encouraged, since they are limited to less than 5 per cent of the project funds.

TABLE 2
PARTICIPATION OF SOUTHEAST EUROPEAN NGOs

Country or province of implementing NGO	Projects in euros	%
Romania	868,642	15.7
Slovenia	842,600	15.3
Montenegro	694,700	12.6
Greece	680,000	12.3
Kosovo	645,100	11.7
Albania	511,250	9.3
FYROM	408,950	7.4
regional projects	400,000	7.2
Bulgaria	231,000	4.2
Croatia	131,500	2.4
Serbia	111,100	2.0
Total	5,524,842	100.00

Source: Office of the Special Coordinator of the Stability Pact (OSCSP), Quick Start Package, Working Table I, Progress Report, March 2001

TABLE 3
IMPLEMENTING AGENCIES (PROJECTS IN EUROS)

Lead and implementing agencies/sectors	States	International organisations	International NGOs	Bilateral development agencies	Total
Trade	78,600	–	–	641,100	719,700
Infrastructure	15,000,000	1,311,980,000	–	–	1,326,980,000
Infrastructure studies	8,850,000	12,300,000	–	–	21,150,000
Investment compact	142,500	142,5001	–	–	285,000
Economic reforms & business development	–	278,400,000	–	800,000	279,200,000
Environment	–	13,800,000	–	–	13,800,000
Social dimension	2,500,000	28,700,000	14,438,000	–	45,638,000
Total	105,092,500	1,645,322,500	14,438,000	1,441,100	1,766,294,100

Note: 'Investment Compact' is a common project of the Organization for European Cooperation and Development (OECD) and the UK.

Source: Office of the Special Coordinator of the Stability Pact (OSCSP), Quick Start Package, Working Table II, Progress Report, February 2001.

The role of regional NGOs and civic initiatives was officially acknowledged by the Stability Pact Declaration on NGO–Government Partnership in Southeastern Europe, approved by the Regional Table in Bucharest on 27 October 2000.[8] The declaration, which was an initiative of the Chairman of the 1st Working Table, P. Roumeliotis, underlined the significance of civil society in democratization, peace-building, promotion and protection of human rights, development of cross-border cooperation and generally in promoting the spirit and values of the Stability Pact. It is accepted that NGOs bring enormous value to society, complementing the state and the market, with their voluntary and community activity, which is fundamental to the development of a democratic, socially inclusive society. Therefore, the Stability Pact encourages the governments of the region to promote greater NGO.

Economic Reconstruction, Development and Cooperation

It is rather normal that NGOs are not involved in the 2nd Working Table on Economic Reconstruction, Development and Cooperation, where International Financial Institutions have the leading role. The only case is the Friedrich Ebert Foundation, based in Germany, whose project on Social Security and Human Development, is fully funded by the German government and it is implemented in all target/recipient countries of Southeastern Europe. International NGOs are involved only in the Social Dimension Sector, implementing projects worth €14.4m, which in fact is a considerable percentage, 31.6 per cent, of the total amount for this specific sector. The latter and the relevant 'Initiative for Social Cohesion' focus on social protection, health, housing, employment, vocational training and the strengthening of small and medium-sized enterprises (SMEs). The dominant sector of Working Table II is 'Infrastructure', where international organizations, such as the World Bank, the European Union and the European Investment Bank, are leading agencies. It is important to note that more than €1.3bn have been pledged for infrastructure projects, which is 75 per cent of the total amount pledged for Working Table II.

Security Issues

Defence Reform and Economics and Humanitarian De-mining Task Forces dominate the funds pledges for Working Table III (86.8 per cent of the total funds), whereas participation of the civil society is limited to the Judiciary Sector. International NGOs implement 34.3 per cent of the project funds (€800,000) of this sector. In fact, civil society is involved in Justice and Home Affairs activities, more than it is shown in Table 4, beyond the Stability Pact structures. Many international and local NGOs have already started or even completed projects in Southeastern Europe on a bilateral basis, which sometimes can function rapidly, avoiding the bureaucratic delays of the Stability Pact. Especially on Humanitarian De-mining, Democratization of Army and Police, Anti-Corruption Initiative, Legislative and Judicial Reforms, Independence of Judiciary and so on, the civil-society sector must be encouraged to participate in future Stability Pact programmes.

PROBLEMS AND LIMITATIONS

It is a fact that despite the high expectations that the Stability Pact has created, it has to overcome a significant number of structural problems and limitations regarding the actual situation in Southeastern Europe. Firstly, the multi-collectivism regarding the membership of the Stability Pact has resulted in a complex bureaucratic structure, which is inflexible and unable to face the quick political and economic changes in the region and to overcome its own structural weaknesses. As a consequence it is extremely difficult for the Secretariat to coordinate numerous members, Working Tables and Sub-Tables, and their respective chairmanships. Conflicting interests and visions regarding cooperation and development

TABLE 4
IMPLEMENTING AGENCIES (PROJECTS IN EUROS)

Implementing agencies/task forces	States	International organisations	International NGOs	Total
Sub-Table A: Defence and security				
Defence reform and economics (UK)	17,500,000	9,000,000	–	26,500,000
Arms control, non-proliferation & military contacts	1,595,500 + 4 projects funded by Switzerland	30,000	–	1,625,000 + 4 projects funded by Switzerland
Small arms & light weapons	1 project implemented by Norway	–	–	1 project implemented by Norway
Humanitarian de-mining	–	32,347,500	–	32,347,500
Sub-Table B: Justice and home affairs				
Anti-corruption & organized crime	80,000	1,910,000	–	1,990,000
Judiciary, police & border police	3,186,500	1,340,000	800,000	2,326,500
TOTAL	22,362,000 + 5 projects	44,627,500 + 5 projects	800,000	67,789,500

Source: Office of the Special Coordinator of the Stability Pact (OSCSP), Quick Start Package, Working Table III, Progress Report, November 2000

in Southeastern Europe, different needs and priorities are functioning ineffectively within the chaotic mechanism of the Stability Pact. In that huge structure, NGOs are being squashed between bureaucracies and state interests.

In addition, the staffing and the functional structure both of the Secretariat and the offices of the National Coordinators remain problematic, with considerable lack of coordination and a long-term development strategy. It is crucial to note the lack of political will of member states and organizations to staff and financially support departments and directorates that are responsible for the Stability Pact. Therefore, the civil-society sector cannot easily understand the directions and the decisions both at national and Stability Pact level. As a result actions between government and NGOs are difficult to coordinate in an effective way.

Undeniably, at the outset both the donor countries and even more the recipient countries did not have the appropriate mechanisms in order to coordinate actions and initiatives and to plan the whole structure for the selection, the control and the evaluation of the proposed programmes.

The difficulty of defining specific priorities for each country on the basis of regional development is still obvious.

Moreover, in Southeastern Europe, the state administration and its attitude were and in many cases still are negative to the NGO involvement in the planning and implementation of a long-term development strategy. Because of the authoritarian regimes in Eastern Europe during the Cold War, the NGO sector was either underdeveloped or totally controlled. Similarly, on the western side of the 'Iron Curtain' in the Balkans, countries such as Greece and Turkey, being influenced by the Cold War climate and also having authoritarian social structures for a long time, have had a negative approach to civil society. Any NGO involvement and activity used to face state scepticism. Ten years after the end of the Cold War, civil society tends to find its real role in the new democracies of Southeastern Europe despite the many shortcomings.

One of these shortcomings is that the state does not have an overall and advanced view of development and the significant participating and consultative role that the civil-society actors can play. The state development agencies and ministries of the countries of Southeastern Europe are inexperienced and have small budgets and ineffective mechanisms, being unable to exploit the activity and the knowledge of the NGOs.

In addition, there is a lack of a criteria list for the approval and final funding of programmes. It is undeniable that member states and the Stability Pact itself have not informed not only NGOs, but also the private sector, for the priorities, the criteria and the process of a Stability Pact project. Since there is not a defined process, it is totally unclear to the NGOs who is actually responsible for the approval and the final evaluation of a proposed project. Is it the Secretariat, the donor country or the chair of the Sub-Table/task force?

Certainly both the Secretariat and the National Coordinators have not informed in an appropriate way the actors of the private sector and the civil society who are interested in playing an active role in the reconstruction and democratization process. As a result, Stability Pact projects are approachable only by few private companies and NGOs, mainly with good connections both in the donor and in the recipient countries. The exclusion of the majority of the civil-society associations from Stability Pact projects, mainly because of lack of information caused either by inability and lack of the appropriate information mechanisms or specific individual or even political interests, jeopardizes the whole philosophy of the Stability Pact and civil society.

As we have noted above, the multi-collectivism of the Stability Pact has created a rough polyphony and has imported the competition among states and organizations within its structure. As a consequence, competition and conflicting interests have slowed down or cancelled some development projects. This phenomenon has occurred both on the level of donor countries, regarding their control and influence in areas and sectors of specific interest, and on the level of recipient countries regarding their competition for the 'slice' of the international development aid.

Similarly, competition among NGOs, both international and local, has created delays and problems on the field, especially in areas with high 'NGO concentration' levels, such as Bosnia with more than 400 NGOs and Kosovo with about 250 NGOs. Therefore, international organizations such as the European Community Humanitarian Office (ECHO) or the United Nations Development Programme (UNDP), have to play a coordinating role, setting the priorities and selecting reliable and experienced NGOs for carrying out specific important projects, avoiding overlapping and vacuum of responsibilities.

THE NEED FOR DIRECT ACTIONS AND THE ROLE OF NON-GOVERNMENTAL ORGANIZATIONS

The above-mentioned limitations and problems in the function and the effectiveness of the Stability Pact do not reduce its significance. It is pertinent that it offers an unprecedented and important multilateral cooperation model for development and security in Southeastern Europe. In addition, it is a fact that most of the problems have been understood by all members involved. What is needed is the definition and materialization of direct actions and the political will for the exploitation of the many positive aspects of the Stability Pact. Furthermore, it is noteworthy that both donor and recipient countries have improved their mechanisms for the realization of the proposed and funded projects. Since the establishment of the Stability Pact, all parts involved have gained considerable experience in order to coordinate their respective mechanisms and structures. For both the practical and undeniably necessary improvement of Stability Pact effectiveness and the greater NGO involvement in its projects some direct actions are needed!

The Secretariat and the National Coordinators of all member-states have to launch an information campaign in order to inform the public and all the parties involved regarding the structure, the mechanisms and the goals of the Stability Pact. It is necessary to explain what Quick Start

Package (QSP)[9] means, and how long it takes for the funding and the implementation of a programme, so that misunderstandings and unjustified high expectations can be avoided. In addition, it has to be underlined that recipient countries are responsible for the creation of the necessary mechanisms to set the priorities and to implement the projects within their borders.

Furthermore, better communication between states and NGOs will strengthen transparency of the administration and the legislative process, increasing citizens' confidence in the activities of public institutions and eliminating bureaucratic sources of corruption and access to funds by only a few groups and NGOs close to administrative and governmental centres of power.

In addition, the role of local NGOs must be strengthened. The participation of NGOs from Southeastern Europe is still limited because of lack of experience and know-how, in contrast with some well-structured and well-funded NGOs from the developed countries, which almost monopolize the Stability Pact projects on a non-governmental level. As mentioned above in the 1st Working Table, international NGOs implement projects of €44m total worth, compared with €5.4m for local NGOs. It is important that the creation of an NGO-industry is avoided, which will recycle big amounts of funding and therefore will control the newly established and comparatively smaller NGOs from the region. Therefore, the fixing of specific quotas for participation of Southeastern European NGOs in Stability Pact projects can be a solution.

Furthermore, state–civil society relationships in Southeast European countries are based on scepticism and lack of trust. Therefore, a partnership must be promoted and an engagement and consultation mechanism must be institutionalized on a sustained and systematic basis in areas where NGOs have experience. Such mechanisms will respect the diversity of opinions of both sides, ensure openness of communication and can be based on agreed ground rules of engagement. In a developed democratic country, the state itself has to facilitate and promote NGO activities and ensure that civil-society involvement remains unrestricted, creating a receptive environment for NGOs.[10]

Therefore, the importance of civil society for all three Working Tables must be underlined. Beyond the 1st Working Table on Democratization and Human Rights, in which the participation of the civil society sector is axiomatic, NGOs can play a vital role also in task forces, sectors and specific issues of the 2nd and 3rd Working Tables, such as environment, social cohesion, judiciary, anti-corruption initiative, migration, trafficking in human beings, etc., proving once more the significance of civil society on all aspects of economic and social development. The state administration also has to mobilize all the governmental and non-governmental powers for the successful materialization of the Stability Pact development projects. Governments must facilitate access to funds for NGOs, easing their participation in these multilateral projects. In addition, possible tax benefits can lower considerably the functional cost, especially of a small to medium sized NGO. Generally, states must ensure access to funding for NGOs and line up their legislation with the internationally recognized standards.

Additionally, the speeding up of the funding process is necessary. It is noteworthy that both recipient and donor countries and NGOs do not have the appropriate mechanisms and sometimes the legislation for the quick funding of projects. The whole process is very slow, starting from the approval of a project until the moment that the recipient gets the funds. It is a fact that relative experience has been gained by all parties, but still it is necessary that the mechanisms be improved, being always in line with the relative national legislation.

Communication and coordination within the Stability Pact structure has also to be improved. Inadequate exchange of information and overlapping or gaps in duties and actions influence dramatically the effectiveness and the credibility of the Stability Pact and participation of civil-society actors. Closer cooperation among the Task Forces and the Working Tables is needed. Similarly, both the donors and NGO networks have to meet regularly in order to coordinate their actions and their specific interests. The use of new technologies and especially the Internet can be extremely helpful in improving the level of information and coordination of all parts involved.

Furthermore, the evaluation of the Quick Start Package (QSP) has to be completed. Actually only a low percentage of the 200 approved projects has already been implemented, although a majority of them has already started. It is noticeable also that many sectors and problems can not be dealt with only by specific Working Tables or Task Forces. A horizontal approach and flexibility regarding cross-table projects are needed involving different Working Tables and Task Forces. Cases such as the anti-corruption initiative, gender issues, education and new technologies, need cooperation and coordination among the chairmen and the relative mechanisms of the involved sectors. NGOs can assist considerably since they have the necessary understanding of complex social issues and the flexibility to move and act on different social levels. The Secretariat has to supervise and to prevent any overlapping of actions and possible competitive tendencies.

Beyond the structure itself, the Secretariat has to define and present a specific list of regional criteria: this will be very helpful to Task Force leaders and National Coordinators in their cooperation both with the Secretariat and the actors interested in taking part, coming either from the private sector or civil society. As a result, specific directions and principles based on a long-term development strategy will define the priorities and the projects needed in the near future, making the consultation, participation and active involvement of the NGOs possible. NGOs have to line up with principles and to propose projects that meet those specific criteria, such as the 'regional dimension', which characterizes the whole philosophy of the Stability Pact, involving civil society actors from as many countries of the region as possible. In addition, the criterion of 'added value' has to be defined and implemented, meaning that a project (even after the end of the initial funding) has to find a way of creating a follow-up process, a productive action either in economic or social terms. The continuation of the programme possibly with alternative funding and partners, even on similar or different sectors, proves its viability and must be a basic selection criterion for Stability Pact programmes.

Similar to the above-mentioned criterion of 'added value' is that of 'regional transferability'. A project must have the ability of regional inclusiveness, transforming itself from local or inter-boundary to regional, creating a network in all Southeast European countries and being in line with the whole logic of the Stability Pact. Furthermore, Task Forces and sub-Working Tables must focus on specific sectors and projects, gaining visibility and effectiveness of the programmes and control of the whole process. In that way the function of the Stability Pact structure will be improved and simultaneously the public will see and understand its significance, its adopted development projects and the important role of civil society. In addition, all actors involved will be more active and willing to participate in the reconstruction and democratization process.

In order for specific strategies and policies to be implemented, the wording of a clearly defined Priority Agenda can prove to be very useful. Multi-collectivism and different priorities of Stability Pact members, despite the many advantages, can lead to postponements and considerable delays. In addition, the strategic planning of every Working Table and Sub-Table or Task Force must be reflected in relative Action Plans, which will include specific directions for the mid- and long-term goals. The fulfilment of those goals and the project realization process must be examined by the Secretariat, the Regional Table and the Chairman of the relative Working Table, at least every six months.

CONCLUSIONS

Ideally, civil society and NGOs, in a receptive environment for them, having the encouragement of the state, provided with a long-term strategy, must be in a position to propose specific projects, to receive funds, to implement their programmes and finally to accept the control and evaluation of their action by their sponsors, in this case the Stability Pact mechanisms, but most of all by the people who can judge directly regarding the effectiveness, usefulness and durability of the implemented project.

Unfortunately, neither civil society in Southeastern Europe, nor the Stability Pact as a multilateral cooperative model are experienced and effective in order for this ideal scenario to materialize. Local NGOs, still in a rather embryonic state, lacking in know-how, funding, professional mechanisms and long-term strategy, are trying to find their way in a region characterized by ethnic conflicts and competing national interests, where the culture of civil society is still underdeveloped. Furthermore, the state still understands the role of civil society as a tool to promote its own policy, not as something genuine that develops society in a multi-level way, freeing productive and independent powers.

The Stability Pact has come to promote economic development based on democratic structures in a secure environment, to coordinate actions and to strengthen regional cooperation. As far as civil society is concerned, the Stability Pact supported it with declarations and NGO-promoting statements, but failed, up to now, to provide the appropriate mechanisms and the necessary political will in order to develop an independent and sound civil society in Southeastern Europe. Bureaucratic and rather chaotic mechanisms, lack of specific priorities and long-term development strategy and competition among the members have created an inappropriate cooperative developmental model for fruitful participation of local NGOs. Civil society in Southeastern Europe participates in the Stability Pact in a spasmodic and dependent way: it is dependent on both state policies and strong multinational/international NGOs.

Despite all this, the Stability Pact is an unprecedented model on regional cooperation history. Fortunately, its shortcomings have been understood by all parties involved rather quickly. It remains to be seen if there is the political will from the international community to overcome these problems and to promote a balanced regional development process, in which the citizens of Southeastern Europe, participating in all aspects of social life, will experience economic prosperity and democratic institutions in a secure and just environment.

NOTES

1. Stability Pact for Southeast Europe, Official Text, Article III.10.
2. For the international principles of freedom of association, see Article 11 of the European Convention on Human Rights; Article 22 of the International Covenant on Civil and Political Rights; Article 20 of the Universal Declaration on Human Rights; and similar UN and OSCE Declarations.
3. It is not the aim of this article to describe the structure of the Stability Pact. For a detailed view, see http://www.stabilitypact.org
4. The Republic of Montenegro, according to its declaration of 26 October 2000, considers that the FRY delegation represents only the Republic of Serbia until the two republics reach an agreement on their future relations.
5. Data from the Quick Start Package Progress Report, Office of the Special Coordinator of the Stability Pact (OSCSP), February 2001. It is characteristic that data presented by OSCSP and donor or recipient countries are often different. Only the author is responsible for categorizing the following tables and graphics.
6. See relative tables and graphics.
7. In March 2001, the Stability Pact Special Coordinator decided that the Szeged Process has to further its initiatives to the whole region, since democratic forces have come to power in Serbia after the September 2000 election victory.
8. Stability Pact Declaration on NGO–Government Partnership in Southeastern Europe, Regional Table, Bucharest on 27 October 2000.
9. The Quick Start Package (QSP) was adopted in March 2000 in Brussels during the Donors' Conference. It includes more than 200 projects with a total value of 1.8 billion euros, although donor countries enthusiastically pledged more than 2.4 billion euros!
10. Based on the Stability Pact Declaration on NGO–Government Partnership in Southeastern Europe, Bucharest, 27 October 2000.

REFERENCES

Atwood, B. (1996): 'Our Biggest Challenge: To Deal in a Much More Realistic Way with Humanitarian Needs', *ECHO News*, December, No. 132.
Bakker, A.F.P. (1996): *International Financial Institutions*, London: Longman.
Culperer, R. (ed.) (1997): *Global Development Fifty Years after Bretton Woods*, London: MacMillan Press.
Griffin, K. (1991): 'Foreign Aid after the End of the Cold War', *Development and Change*, No. 4.
Hoffman, G. (1972): *Regional Development Strategy in Southeastern Europe: A Comparative Analysis*, New York: Praeger.
Houliaras, A. (1998): *International Development Aid in the 21st Century*, Athens: Exantas (in Greek).
Jelic, V. (1988): 'Continuing Balkan Cooperation', *Review of International Affairs*, No. 922.
Jorgensen, K.E. (1997): *European Approaches to Crisis Management*, The Hague: Kluwer Law Int.
Kondonis, H. (1998): 'Prospects for Balkan Cooperation after the Disintegration of Yugoslavia', *East European Quarterly*, 32, No 3.
Moore, P. (1990): 'Balkan Cooperation Revisited', *Report on Eastern Europe*, Vol. 1, No. 12, March.
Rieff, D. (1995/6): 'The Humanitarian Trap', *World Policy Journal*, Vol.12, No. 4, winter.

Serageldin, I. (1994): *Development Partners: Aid and Cooperation in the 1990s*, Stockholm: SIDA.

Stokke, O. (ed) (1995): *Aid and Political Conditionality*, London: Frank Cass.

Svolopoulos, K. (1982): 'Multilateral Cooperation in the Balkans', *Dikeo ke Politiki*, No. 2, Athens (in Greek).

Walden, S. (1994): *Balkan Cooperation and European Integration*, Athens: Papazisis (in Greek).

Weiss, T.G. (1996): 'Non-Governmental Organisations and Internal Conflict', in Brown, M.E. (ed), *The International Dimension of Internal Conflict*, Cambridge, Mass: MIT Press.

From an Omnipresent and Strong to a Big and Weak State: Democratization and State Reform in Southeastern Europe[1]

DIMITRI A. SOTIROPOULOS

INTRODUCTION

Traditionally, throughout the nineteenth and the early twentieth centuries, the state in Southeastern Europe has been simultaneously overpowering and distant. It has been overpowering in the sense that it has frequently required the participation of citizens in military endeavours, it has helped suppress revolts 'from below' against the upper classes and the oligarchic political elites and it has controlled economic activity to some extent, steering or impeding the flow of banking and industrial capital. Despite the fact that various collective actors, such as the military or the large land-owners, enjoyed influence, the state as an institution in Southeastern Europe was strong even before it became a socialist state. At the same time, the state was distant in the sense that, first, it excluded whole regions from recurrent attempts at modernization, letting them continue a life without basic infrastructure and, secondly, it neglected the needs of the less well-off citizens by providing inchoate and very unequal welfare services.

The latter aspects were taken care of by the public administrations of the socialist regimes that emerged after the end of the Second World War. In addition to the authoritarian or totalitarian aspects that characterized such regimes in Southeastern Europe, there appeared, in each of the relevant countries, what Zygmunt Bauman calls a 'caring patronage state' (Bauman 1993: 20 and 22). In these countries in the post-war period, while there was improvement in terms of infrastructural modernization and social welfare, the price paid was too high. It included the restriction of political freedoms and the unaccountability of governments. Moreover, with the advent of socialist regimes the state ceased to be distant. It became omnipresent, penetrating the political and economic, if not also the social life of the citizens, while it remained strong compared with any other organizations or associations.

One area in which the state's double identity as overpowering and strong is particularly felt is the area of public administration. In the one-party states built in Southeastern Europe in the post-war period, the powerful role of the secret police, the army and a very politicized higher civil service dominated by the communist party, cannot be overstressed. At the same time, bureaucratism, that is, bureaucracy not as an administrative tool of modern societies but as a pathological set of structures and processes, alienated and kept citizens of the former socialist states under control, while curtailing any political and cultural pluralism (at least in the totalitarian regimes of Albania and Romania).

This type of state administration may have had positive results in providing the population with educational, health and other social welfare services, regardless of income, in the context of a command economy. On the other hand, it has also had negative effects associated with the prolonged presence of the same political elite in power and the lack of accountability of the public administration to any political institutions other than the governing party organs. Elster *et al.* summarize the issue here: 'The administrative apparatus was centralized and used to a top-down style of governance under the new regime. Those administrative structures are likely to constrain the design and implementation of reforms at the start of transition' (Elster *et al.* 1998: 61–2).

Why is this so? We may argue that while many things changed dramatically after the fall of socialist rule, the state apparatus has been transformed only to some extent, that is, it has become weak but remains big. In the words of Eyal *et al.*, 'In terms of their institutional arrangements, post-communist societies are likely to be characterized by big, weak states'. Writing mainly about Hungary and Poland, those authors go on to say that 'The Central European State is not necessarily strong, but it is very big. It is ironic that after the fall of state socialism, the anti-statist post-communist bureaucracy continues to grow, often in the shape of 'privatization' bureaucracies. Indeed, some economists have suggested that the incomes from privatization are about as high as the cost of administering privatization – this is a good example of what we mean by a big, weak state' (Eyal *et al.* 2000: 190 and 190–93).

In the same vein, it can be argued that public administration in 'existing socialism' is different from public administration in post-socialist democracies in its functions, if not in its structures. During transition to and consolidation of democracy, while some, if not most, of administrative structures remain intact (and thus big), there are changes in personnel and in the orientation of the public administration. The administration must now learn to serve alternative masters, owing to government turnover, and to work by the rules of a new democratic constitution, which is usually promulgated early in the transition process.

The onset of democratization usually calls for the cleansing of the highest ranks of the civil service and the radical restructuring, if not the complete abolition, of administrative departments that have been the pillars of the deposed non-democratic regime, such as the secret police and committees of censorship, among many other tasks. Most importantly, there is an effort to 'de-couple' party bureaucracy from state bureaucracy. These tasks are not easy to accomplish since some resistance and inertia on the part of the bureaucracy combine with the practical necessity of continuity of the basic mechanisms of the state (for example, ministries, state-run enterprises for transport and communications, etc.) under different political regimes. In transitional periods, there is also a scarcity of qualified personnel, since experts and experienced officials have often collaborated with the old political regime, and it is difficult to find new ones to employ under the new regime. On the whole, large structures and old-fashioned personnel render post-socialist administration weak and, more concretely, unable to steer the transition to the market system.

Democratization in Southeastern Europe has coincided with a worldwide tendency towards the shrinkage of state intervention in the economy. Southeast European administration, influenced by international organizations and programmes (such as the PHARE programme), has attempted to face both democratization and liberalization of the economy. As Joachim Jens Hesse puts it 'Public administration is losing some of its former tasks as the state is partly withdrawing from the economy by means of liberalization, deregulation and privatization' (Hesse 1997: 132). In addition, as Elster *et al.* write, '... the submission of the state apparatus to the rule of law, its disengagement from broad areas of social life which it used to control under communism, and the introduction of local government are indispensable ingredients of the democratic character of the new regimes' (Elster *et al.* 2000: 110–11). Most of these challenges have been met with little success in the prolonged process of transition to democracy, to the market system and to a modern public administration in Southeastern Europe, as the examples of Bulgaria, Yugoslavia and Kosovo, discussed below, may show. The discussion of the three cases is followed at the end of the article by considerations of further administrative reform and of the set-up of new democratic political institutions in Southeastern Europe.

THE CASE OF BULGARIA

The Bulgarian civil service has a long tradition of partisanship, even before the installation of the socialist regime. Before the Second World War the civil service was partisan in the sense that it was too 'sensitive' to governmental changes. Appointments, promotions and dismissals of civil servants were frequent, depending on who held power. Soon after the end of the War the situation was stabilized at the cost of strict political control of the administration exercised 'from above', that is, by the ruling Bulgarian Communist Party. This meant that purely political criteria were used for the selection and promotion of administrative personnel, while real power rested in party organs rather than in administrative bodies. It was anyway difficult to disentangle the two. Yet, in the above context, ministries had some autonomy from each other, as there was a lack of coordination among ministries (Verheijen 1999b: 94).

Extensive politicization does not mean that merit was totally disregarded, as every regime needs not only loyalty but also competence in order to survive. Perhaps this was one of the reasons why after 1990, when Todor Zhivkov had fallen from power, there was such a slow effort at administrative reform. Civil servants who were loyal to the previous regime have been useful to the post-socialist one, particularly since in various countries in the beginning of the transition the routines of civil service work were not altered. Other reasons included the imminence of acute economic problems, which has sidetracked attention from administrative reform, and the prolonged stay of former communist elites in power, which, using the vehicle of the Bulgarian Socialist Party (to which the Communist Party was renamed) won the elections and ruled in 1990–91 and again in 1994–7.

Between 1990 and 1998 various plans for reform were initiated by alternating governments but none reached the stage of full implementation. The practice of reversing the administrative policy of the previous government – as soon as a new government was sworn in – was common. This was accompanied with a high turnover of civil service personnel. For instance, the short-lived, interim government of Renata Indzhova, which stayed in power for only two months in 1994, managed to replace approximately 3000 civil servants. A Department for Administrative Reform was created by the Videnov government in 1995, only to be abolished by the short-lived Sofianski government in 1997 (Verheijen 1999b: 97 and 113–14). However, today (in early 2001), there is a Minister of Public Administration, responsible for the corresponding reform.

In the meantime, since early 1995 there has been a re-orientation of plans for administrative reform, 'in line with … the contemporary

European standards of institution-building' (OECD January 1999). This turn was the result of the effort of Bulgaria to change its economic performance and administrative structures in order to meet the criteria set by the EU for new candidate member-states. Still, administrative reform is understood as the passage of a series of bills, submitted to the national assembly (for example, the Law on the Organization of Administration, a Civil Service Law, etc.). The need for a new legal framework notwithstanding, the main problem of reform in Bulgaria and in comparable countries has been a problem of implementation of new laws. The Bulgarian administration is an inchoate set of ministries and semi-independent public agencies, schools, hospitals and even *ad hoc* committees, which are difficult to coordinate. The government of Kostov (1997–2001) considered administrative reform a top priority, expressed in the programme 'Bulgaria 2001' and adopted specific strategies for its implementation. It is too early to say whether the new government which came out of the elections of the early summer of 2001, consisting of the party of the former king Symeon has followed this pattern.

THE CASE OF THE FEDERAL REPUBLIC OF YUGOSLAVIA AND KOSOVO

The contemporary Yugoslav public administration bears the typical characteristics of a West European bureaucracy, at least at the formal level of analysis. The constitution provides for a separation of powers, and the public administration is made up of ministries, entrusted with the formation of policy and the application of laws. A series of laws provide for the meritocratic recruitment and remuneration of civil servants. Importantly, Yugoslavia still is a federal state, consisting of different federal units or republics, and there is legal provision about the repartition of federal civil service senior posts among the republics (an equal number of senior posts is assigned to each republic). There are federal ministries and also ministries at the level of the republics. In practice, of course, the administration of Montenegro has recently taken pains to separate itself completely from the Serbian administration.

In the period before the Second World War and even under the socialist regime, the Yugoslav civil service enjoyed the reputation of being professional and fairly de-politicized, even though it remained very traditional in its outlook and slow in its procedures. Obviously, since under Tito, Yugoslavia became a federal state made up of different republics, there were differences in the institutional set-up and performance of the civil service from one republic to another. The differences remain to this day. For example, speaking of the 1990s, it has been argued that the civil service in Montenegro has been more dependent on political power, while the Serbian civil service has retained its relative autonomy from the government at least through 1998; that local public administration is more effective than central public administration; and that, owing to local indifference and/or resistance in certain regions, such as Kosovo, the public administration has wholly failed (Sevic and Rabrenovic 1999: 70–71).

The protracted financial problems and the long process of disintegration of Yugoslavia, which started in 1991, in combination with the long presence of one party, the Socialist Party, with its autocratic leader, Slobodan Milosevic, in power between December 1990 and October 2000, have had its impact on the Yugoslav civil service. The purchasing capacity of Yugoslav civil servants has deteriorated and, apparently, instances of corruption have multiplied. The traditionally rigid functioning of the public administration has resulted in slow and inefficient services to the public.

According to local experts (Sevic and Rabrenovic 1999:79), 'in the last 160 years or so, the civil service (of Yugoslavia) has retained an enviable level of independence and professional ability'. While the senior posts of the civil service have always been filled with officials who supported the regime, in the second half of the 1990s politicization expanded to lower ranks (ibid). It is also claimed that the Yugoslav civil service is comparatively impartial (Kotchegura 1999:12). Despite such claims, it is hard to believe that before the mid-1990s the Yugoslav civil service was relatively autonomous from the centres of political power, professional in its conduct and immune to politicization 'from above', that is, earlier on by the League of Yugoslav Communists and later by the Socialist Party of Serbia. The older, Titoist elite of this party ruled the country in the post-war period and followed the well-known socialist model of public administration that entails a fusion of political and administrative officials in the top, if not also in the middle ranks of the state mechanism. As in other one-party states, party bureaucrats worked hand in hand with civil servants and occupied the most crucial posts. Slobodan Milosevic had acquired firm control of the party since 1987, changed its name and, after winning the elections of December 1990, probably extended his control to the administration as a whole, including the state-run mass media, the police and the universities (Ash 1999, Thomas 1999). Administrative reform had not been attempted for a period of ten years.

As a consequence, administrative reform in Yugoslavia during transition to democracy, which really started in the autumn of 2000, is not only a technical issue but may also have political qualities. The civil service must be de-politicized, made accountable and responsive to democratically elected governments and to the needs of the citizens rather than the wishes of any elite. The professionalization of the civil service is another aim, which will require training in new management methods and the use of new technologies. Finally, for any reform to be meaningful, the improvement of the income of civil servants is required, if corruption is to be combated.

The political change of October 2000, with the rise of Vojislav Kostunica to the Federal Presidency, has not produced immediate tangible solutions to the above problems, but it has certainly paved the way for a new political climate in the country, conducive to reform. The obvious first administrative and wider political issue is whether Serbia and Montenegro will remain as constituent parts of the same federal state or whether they will part and accordingly re-build their individual public administration systems. This issue is related to the meager chances of re-integrating Kosovo into Yugoslavia. Even if the process of disintegration of Yugoslavia as a state, which has been going on for ten years, was to come to a stop, the Yugoslav public administration would probably evolve towards a set of three very distinct public administrations (the Serbian, Montenegrin and Kosovar administrations).

Under Milosevic, the government of Montenegro had already taken its distance from Belgrade. The federal administrative structure of Yugoslavia has facilitated this endeavour, in the sense that it left the Montenegrin government institutional room for manoeuvre. For instance, the police force of Montenegro has become an independent source of power at the disposal of the governing political elite located in Podgorica rather than in Belgrade. It is claimed (Sevic and Rabrenovic 1999: 57) that, compared with the Serbian ministries, the ministries and generally the public administration of Montenegro are more dependent on the government (of Podgorica).

In the case of Kosovo, as it is widely known, throughout the last ten years there has been a parallel administrative structure. Under the official Serbian-staffed public administration of the region, which served as an instrument of oppression of the Albanian population, there was a rather developed Albanian-speaking administrative structure functioning in the 'underground'. This structure was complete with its own educational and health services, which catered to the needs of Albanian Kosovars. This underground administration also suffered during Nato's war on Kosovo (March–June 1999). After the war, the international administration established under the auspices of the United Nations in the area (UNMIC), has attempted to erect an administrative structure made of nineteen 'departments' (one for each policy area), jointly put together by UN officials and local political party representatives. Care has been taken to allocate four of the departments to Kosovar non-Albanian ethnic groups, such as Serbs and Bosnian Moslems. However, by February 2000 only four of the nineteen departments had been set up, while the Serbs remaining in Kosovo had refused to cooperate in this administrative scheme. In the local government elections of October 2000, the party of Ibrahim Rugova, which in the 1990s had built the parallel, underground administration, prevailed in most municipalities. It is expected that Rugova, who lately also won the national elections of Kosovo, would work both for the national independence of Kosovo and for the rebuilding of the area as a whole.

The administrative needs of Kosovo remain very basic. These are the provision of uninterrupted electricity, the care for safe roads, the control of illegal trade, the support for new, independent mass media and, above all, the collection of guns and ammunition, which are presently in the hands of local paramilitary groups, and the application of rule of law. Thus, administrative needs are to a large extent co-terminus with 'soft security', which the local population is entitled to after so many years of state repression and war. The needs should include the re-integration of all alienated communities, such as the Serb communities of Mitrovica and of a few other enclaves, in the newly emerging state structure. But this aim depends on several changing conditions, that is, on the willingness of local Albanian and Serbs to cooperate, on the stance of the democratic government at Belgrade and on the policy of the international community on this matter.

CONCLUSIONS AND CONSIDERATIONS OF FURTHER REFORM

The Bulgarian and Yugoslav cases are not similar, particularly since the former is a unitary state whereas the latter is a disintegrating federal state. Bulgaria has made some steps towards administrative reform, whereas Yugoslavia has not made any yet. The Bulgarian public administration has known extensive instability, owing to high government turnover and the resulting partisanship, whereas the Yugoslav one has experienced stability, associated with the 'freeze' imposed by the regime of Milosevic on parliamentary democracy.

However, the two countries share some commonalities. Some of the public administration problems of Bulgaria and Yugoslavia are common to most Southeast European countries. To name a few, recruitment is decentralized and each ministry may have more autonomy in selecting new personnel than is desirable for any administration that wishes to function as a cohesive system; salaries vary a lot but are generally very low; and there is a lack of common training available to all civil servants. There are no easy answers to these problems but experience from West European administrations, already transmitted to interested parties through EU, IMF, World Bank and OECD technical assistance, may prove helpful.

To the above, one should add larger questions, specific to the countries of the region, which require even more complicated answers. These are the quest for a new administrative elite, not bound by pre-1989 interests and frames of mind; the re-orientation of middle- and low-ranking civil servants to the needs of ethnic and religious minorities, which exist in most Southeast European countries; the achievement of a balance between attempts at privatization of parts of the public sector, in order to make the economy more competitive in the globalized international environment, and efforts to provide the less well-off categories of the population, struck by war, oppression or prolonged economic hardship, with basic amenities and state subsidies for survival; and the enhancing of the legitimacy of the public administration as an institution and the civil service as a social group by limiting the extent of corruption. This has emerged in Southeastern Europe as the single most demoralizing factor for the wider public. Immediate action is pertinent at the points and sectors where corruption flourishes, namely at borders, ports and airports; in the construction business and particularly in large public works; in taxation services and customs authorities; and in the illegal trade of guns, drugs and female workers throughout the Balkan peninsula. No doubt, the task of administrative reform in Southeastern Europe is daunting.

In addition, if the aim of democratic governments of the area is to construct a modern administration in a twenty-first century European-like democracy, the above more technical issues of administrative reform (and the more substantive issue of limiting corruption) must be addressed in the context of setting-up new political institutions and processes. Such an aim entails decisions about the relative power of the executive branch of government and, thus, of the administrative mechanisms working for it *vis-à-vis* the legislature and the judiciary. While the general tendency in the twentieth century was toward strengthening the executive at the expense of the other two branches of government, in Southeastern Europe such a tendency may prove slippery. Already the cases of the use of executive power by the governments of Sali Berisha in 1992–7 in Albania and of Franjo Tudjman in 1992–2000 in Croatia may serve as counter-examples of democratization that slipped into semi-authoritarianism. Among the many reasons for this situation, from the point of view of this article two stand-out: first, the lack of 'checks and balances' against the peak of the executive and, second, the absence of substantive parliamentary and citizen-based control of the public administration.

On the other hand, in order to survive in the intensifying global antagonism among national economies, societies emerging from state socialism need to adopt efficient and flexible state structures. The democratic control of public administration 'from below', so necessary after several decades of unaccountable governments, may clash with the need to steer economic development 'from above' in order to make a country as a whole more competitive in today's globalized environment. Democratic procedures take time and involve many interested parties (for example, interest groups and associations, social movements, etc.) with variant goals. Those parties are entitled to, and they naturally demand, room for political participation in decision-making. The least they require, at the level of ministerial administration, is to voice their concerns. All these are constituents of modern democracy and must be introduced and implemented in the new democratic regimes of Southeastern Europe, as experience shows that new institutions may be formally adopted but never applied.

However, at the same time, the on-going fluid and problematic 'hard security' and border uncertainty in some countries of the Western Balkans, as well as the fact that the economies of the region are currently much more open than in the past, call for the replacement of the old administrative mechanisms with new slimmer structures, sensitive to changes in the international geopolitical and economic scene. The problem here is that initiators and managers of 'slimmer administrative structures' may regard democratic control and political participation as luxuries. This tension between democracy and efficiency is not new, but acquires acute dimensions in the new democracies coming out of one-party rule. The issue is more important particularly in Southeastern Europe, since the multi-ethnic nature of most societies of the region adds a further demand on public administration, that is, the demand for ethnic representativeness. This aim has been sought in FYR Macedonia during the rule of the Slav Macedonian–Albanian coalition of the VMRO and DP parties. However, as we know from the events of the first half of 2001 in that country, ethnic conflict has not been avoided, and one of the main claims of the Albanian minority has exactly been wider participation in the public administrative structures. This example serves to show that administrative reform itself cannot dispel the image of the big and weak state, so common in Southeastern Europe. The regime may change, but unless administrative reforms are accompanied by society-level consensus building and the expansion of tolerance among ethnic and religious groups, reforms of the kind discussed in this article may look like window-dressing.

In short, administrative reform in itself may leave many things to be desired, in the sense that people are looking for fairness in the functioning of the state. Writing about the perceptions of the Polish citizens who in the past had resisted state socialism, Zygmunt Bauman explains why: '[Under state socialism] blue- and white-collar protesters alike objected to the shabby existence meted out under the auspices of state-administered justice; but what they wished was more justice in state administration, not abdication of state responsibilities' (Bauman 1993: 21).

NOTE

1. Some of the material on Yugoslavia is based on personal visits and non-attributional interviews with officials in Skopje and Albanian Kosovar officials in Prishtina in early 1999 and in early 2000. The author would like to thank Professors Thanos Veremis and Christos Lyrintzis and particularly Mr Theodore Tsekos, an area expert, for their advice and support. The following references also contain materials for further reading.

REFERENCES

Bauman, Zygmunt (1993): 'After the Patronage State: A Model in Search of Class Interests', in Christofer G.A. Bryant and Edmund Mokrzycki, eds, *The New Great Transformation? Change and Continuity in East-Central Europe*, London: Routledge, pp. 14–35.

Dawisha, Karen and Bruce Parrot, eds. (1997): *Politics, Power, and the Struggle for Democracy in Southeast Europe*, Cambridge: Cambridge University Press.

Elster, Jon, Claus Offe and Ulrich K. Preuss (1998): *Institutional Design in Post-Communist Societies: Re-building the Ship at Sea*, Cambridge: Cambridge University Press.

Eyal, Gil, Ivan Szelenyi and Eleanor Townsley (2000): *Making Capitalism Without Capitalists: The New Ruling Elites in Eastern Europe*, London: Verso.

Garton Ash, Timothy (1999): *History of the Present*, Harmondsworth: Penguin.

Government of the Republic of Macedonia (May 1999): 'Strategy on Public Administration Reform in the Republic of Macedonia', unpublished document, Skopje.

Hesse, Jochim Jens (1997): 'Rebuilding the State: Public Sector Reform in Central and Eastern Europe' in Jan-Erik Lane, ed., *Public Sector Reform: Rationale, Trends and Problems*, London: Sage, pp. 114–46.

Klimovski, Savo (2000): *Politics and Institutions*, Taipei: Linking Publishing Co.

Kornai, Janos, Stephan Haggard and Robert R. Kaufman, eds. (2001): *Reforming the State: Fiscal and Welfare Reform in Post-socialist Countries*, Cambridge: Cambridge University Press.

Kotchegura, Alexander (1999): 'A Decade of Transition Over: What is on the Administrative Reform Agenda?' in Tony Verheijen, ed., *Civil Service Systems in Central and Eastern Europe*, Cheltenham: Edward Elgar, pp. 9–14.

Lane, Jan-Erik, ed. (1997): *Public Sector Reform: Rationale, Trends and Problems*, London: Sage.

Linz, Juan J. and Alfred Stepan (1996): *Problems of Democratic Transition and*

Consolidation: Southern Europe, South America, and Post-Communist Europe, Baltimore: The Johns Hopkins University Press.

OECD (January 1999): 'Public Management Profiles for Central and Eastern European Countries: Bulgaria', Paris: Phare Programme-SIGMA.

OECD (June 1999): 'Public Management Profiles for Central and Eastern European Countries: Albania', Paris: Phare Programme-SIGMA.

OECD (August 1999): 'Public Management Profiles for Central and Eastern European Countries: Romania', Paris: Phare Programme-SIGMA.

OECD (September 1999): 'Public Management Profiles for Central and Eastern European Countries: Slovenia', Paris: Phare Programme-SIGMA.

OECD (November 1999): 'European Principles for Public Administration', Sigma Paper No. 27, Paris.

OECD (December 1999): 'Public Management Profiles for Central and Eastern European Countries: Former Yugoslav Republic of Macedonia', Paris: Phare Programme-SIGMA.

Office of the High Representative (OHR) in Bosnia and Herzegovina (2000): 'Information' (The Mandate of the OHR, Offices and Departments of the OHR, Status, Staff and Funding of the OHR), Sarajevo, 6 June 2000.

Sevic, Zeljko and Aleksandra Rabrenovic (1999): 'The Civil Service of Yugoslavia: Tradition vs. Transition' in Tony Verheijen, ed., *Civil Service Systems in Central and Eastern Europe*, Cheltenham: Edward Elgar, pp. 47–82.

Thomas, Robert (1999), *Serbia Under Milosevic: Politics in the 1990s*, London: Hurst and Co.

Verheijen, Tony, ed. (1999a): *Civil Service Systems in Central and Eastern Europe*, Cheltenham: Edward Elgar.

Verheijen, Tony (1999b): 'The Civil Service of Bulgaria: Hope on the Horizon' in Tony Verheijen, ed., *Civil Service Systems in Central and Eastern Europe*, Cheltenham: Edward Elgar, pp. 92–130.

The Difficult Road to the Independent Media: Is the Post-Communist Transition Over?

REMZI LANI AND FRROK CUPI

We do not think anyone in Southeastern Europe would reply to the question in the sub-title affirmatively. Indeed, the question itself would sound more senseless than provocative. Although an integrative theory on the post-communist transition is still lacking, it is already clear that the initial vision of this transition was too festive. Apparently 'the exit from communism' was more difficult and more protracted than was foreseen. 'We have overestimated the rate of the post-communist transition', Brzezinski says (1995: 9) Seemingly, the democratic institutions and free market economy were not as easily exportable and transplantable as a model in the new democracies as had been initially supposed.

In the case of the Balkan Peninsula things got more complicated, especially as a result of the explosion of various sorts of nationalism and wars, initially in Bosnia and then in Kosovo. The transition of the Balkan countries to democracy was a transition threatened by clouds of war. On the other hand, in most countries of the region the transition from dictatorship to democracy has gone through the intermediate phase of a New Authoritarianism. It would be more precise to say that initially the majority of the Balkan peoples did not pass from dictatorship to democracy, but from communist totalitarian regimes to post-communist authoritarian regimes.

The causes of the installation of Balkan *democraduras* should be sought in the poor democratic traditions and the traditional Balkan intolerance; the events in the region which doubtlessly have created factors that impede a normal democratic development; errors of Western policy, which seems to have been unprepared to cope with all the complexities of the problems of democratic development in the peninsula.

Be it as it may, it seems that after a decade, following democratic developments in Croatia and the demise of Milosevic's regime in

Serbia, we are at a turning point, which – let us hope – will be a moment of reflection rather than euphoria. The year 2000 was not an *annus mirabilis*, but a turning point in the history of the peninsula. It was a moment at which the agenda of the post-communist transition and the agenda of the post-war transition were closely intertwined, exercising a perceptible influence on the political, social and economic developments of the countries of the region.

The tortuous and complex nature of the post-communist transition has also had an influence on the development of the media throughout the past decade. The positive developments of recent times have created the conditions for positive developments for the media as well.

REFLECTIONS ON THE CONCLUSION OF A DECADE

According to media experts, on the conclusion of the first decade of the post-communist transition, in the media systems of the Southeast European countries ones saw:

• in political terms, decentralization of the mass media system accompanied by the emergence of pluralistic press, radio and TV systems;
• in legal terms, liberalization and deregulation of the mass media system, corresponding to the European patterns;
• in economic terms, demassification and fragmentation of the public media, accompanied by higher selectivity standards and social feedback;
• in professional terms, departure from former corporate media standards and introduction of new formats, styles and liberal journalistic ethics;
• in technological terms, the revolutionary advent of new media incorporating national media to the global superhighways (*The Global Network\Le Reseau Global* 2000).

Indeed, even pessimists should be able to see the undeniable changes that have taken place in the region, ranging from 'the Live TV Bloody Revolution' of December 1989 in Bucharest to 'the Live TV Velvet Revolution' of October 2000 in Belgrade.

In general, in all of the countries of the region one finds today a pluralistic spectrum of all orientations and hues of the print and electronic media, which constitutes an important achievement, especially if we consider it as a point of departure. The vertical propaganda (party-nation) imposed by 'the ultimate voice', the Communist Party, exists no more.

Opinions, whatever they happen to be, are being freely expressed. Southeast Europe is no longer the region of closed mouths. The democratic changes in Croatia and Serbia have brought down Tudjman and Milosevic's last media strongholds.

Timothy Garton Ash's characterization of Milosevic's regime as 'TV dictatorship' was a clear expression of the fact that that the Serbian dictator (but the Croatian one was not lagging behind, either) had turned the media into the main instrument for the manipulation of public opinion. Actually, the Serbian and Croatian TV were more of private videos of the rulers than state TV stations.

The decade of transition in the media was characterized by political pressure, economic problems and chaotic media law regulations, on the one hand, and rapid increase of the media outlets, on the other.

'No comparison, whatsoever, is possible between the poor landscape of communist media, which was politically biased and used a wooden language, and the present media, characterized by diversity, dynamism and rapid change', wrote Marian Chiriac and Daniel Cain (2000: 29).

A realistic judgement should be, on the one hand, that the free press constitutes perhaps the clearest achievement of the new Balkan democracies, and on the other, that the role of the press in the past decade had been a contradictory one. The media was a driving force in the democratization of Balkan societies, and also an instrument in the hands of the nationalist forces, which brought about the bloody dramas in the end of this century. In our region the media have left behind the old days of communism, but the contours of their future are still unclear.

A CHAOTIC LEGAL FRAMEWORK

In all the countries of the region the constitutions adopted in the post-communist period guarantee the freedom of expression. Regardless of this, however, the road to the creation of a comprehensive and modern legislation for the media has not been an easy one. Perhaps one of the biggest problems of the regulatory reform affecting the media has been the fact that such a reform was not carried out *en bloc* in any Balkan country. It was done only gradually.

Indeed, in some cases developments have even been paradoxical. Despite the positive amendments to its legislation on the media, Romania still keeps the Law on the Press of 1974 in force. In October

1993 the Assembly of Albania adopted the Law on the Press, a law which, because of its restrictive spirit, came up against criticism from the journalists' community and human rights' groups both within and outside the country. One of the first acts of the new Albanian legislature was the total abrogation of this law in September 1997. Both those countries now are involved in a discussion of whether a Law on the Press is necessary, or otherwise.

In general it can be said that, despite much debate, after almost a decade a status quo has been agreed upon, according to which press laws are not necessary. An interest group, made up of journalists for the most part, thinks that any regulation of print media would, in fact, restrict press freedom.

However, all countries, or almost all of them, have passed broadcast acts, which regulate the private and public electronic media (Albania, Macedonia, Bosnia, Bulgaria, Romania and so on). One should add here that in all these countries the licensing of the radio and TV stations has been the subject of a heated debate. 'The war of frequencies' has not been absent in the countries of the region, either.

In June 2000 the SEE countries signed the Stability Pact Media Charter in Salonica and pledged to adjust their legislation on the media to the spirit of the Media Charter within a short time. The Media Charter affirmed the engagement of the governments of the region to respect the freedom of expression according to international standards and to support the development of the free media in the region (see: *Stability Pact Media Charter*, http://www.stabilitypact.org)

In the penal codes, especially, there are still strong reminiscences of an old spirit that reflects the first stage of the post-communist transition, when all the countries of the region figured on the 'laggards' list or had semi-authoritarian regimes that tolerated only 'a press, which is partly free' (*Media Studies Journal* 1999: 58).

In Articles 205, 206 and 238 of Romania's Penal Code there are 'penalties for insult, calumny and offense brought to the authorities'. The same holds for Albania's Penal Code, with the difference that the expression 'authorities' is replaced by that of the 'the President of the Republic' and 'the foreign representatives visiting the country'. Similarly, Bulgaria's Penal Code, in the case of calumny brought to 'public officials', envisages heavier penalties than in cases of slander against private persons (*Education and Media in SEE* 1999: 28). Regardless of the extent to which these articles have been applied, it can safely be said that their existence in the penal code, although it is simply a relict of the near past, still constitutes an element of self-censorship.

In some countries of the region, such as Bosnia, Albania and others, information laws or acts have also been adopted (the Freedom of Access to Information Act in Bosnia-Herzegovina, October 2000; the Law on the Freedom of Information on Official Documents in Albania, June 1999) which guarantee free access to information. Adoption of these acts marks, at least in the legal sense, an opening of the governments to the public and the media and is intended to turn information from state 'ownership' to public 'ownership'. However, a law of this kind is still missing in some countries of the region, such as in Macedonia, Yugoslavia and Romania.

Croatia and Yugoslavia, which acceded to the democratic mainstream later than the other Balkan countries, have a longer road ahead toward working out a legislation on the media. After President Kostunica's advent to power, the repressive Law on Public Information adopted in October 1998 was no longer enforced.

As for Kosovo, at present legislation on the media consists only of what is called the Kouchner Law, which prohibits the use of 'hate speech'. This law has been coldly received by the journalists' community and, especially, by the international journalists' organizations. This is due mainly to the fact that the first legislative act on the media in Kosovo was not of a positive, or affirmative, nature, as for example, would be an act on the freedom of the media, which has never existed in Kosovo, but a law intended to show the Kosovar journalists the 'red lines' of what was forbidden to them. The well-known Kosovar publicist, Shkelzen Maliqi, compared the Kouchner Law to a 'paper bugbear' intended to scare the journalists (Maliqi 2000)

In general we may conclude that, although positive steps have been taken, the laws regulating the media are not yet satisfying. There exist many contradictions among the laws on the media, constitutions and international obligations. It cannot be said that a just balance has been struck between necessary regulations and the freedom of the media. The Media Charter offers a good opportunity to bring the legislation on the media of the whole region into line.

It is not a rare occurrence in the Balkans for laws to be written according to European standards and then to be applied according to Balkan standards. Working out a modern legislation on the media is one thing, and its implementation is quite another thing. A number a factors bearing on the economy, infrastructure, politics, tradition and so on, influence the way in which the legislation is applied.

AN EXTENSION OF POLITICS?

The relationship between the media and politics in the period of post-communist transition has been a very complex one and has been characterized by many contradictions. Politics has had an influence on the development of the media more than anything else.

Obviously, the state's direct control over the press has been dramatically reduced, especially in more recent years. Censorship has disappeared, but its effects have remained. In most Southeast European countries the media have been exposed to political pressure, though there are important differences in the intensity of political attempts to silence independent media that are critical to the government.

Milosevic's Serbia and Tudjman's Croatia have throughout the past decade been champions of the violation of the freedom of expression. However, in other countries, too, the free word has come up against obstacles. A report of the International Press Institute, which was submitted to the OSCE meeting in Vienna in November 2000, had all the Balkan states on the list of countries in which infractions of the press freedom by the government have been observed. Although they cannot be compared to the authoritarian leaders of the outset of the decade or the first phase of transition, today's Balkan leaders are not prepared to accept a high degree of criticism. More often than not they react violently to criticism, and even more frequently are keener on controlling than being controlled.

There is also another tendency, which may seem as the opposite of the former, but which in fact boils down to the same thing. In some cases you can write what you like, can criticize how much you like, but then nobody reacts. This state of things has been observed in Albania, where the nervous reaction to criticism of the period of the Democratic Party has been replaced with total indifference to criticism in the period of the rule of the Socialist Party.

Indifference to criticism leads to the devaluation of the free word, and actually is an expression of hidden arrogance. It is intended to lull public opinion into sleep, making no distinction between constructive criticism and sensationalism, truth and lie. In other words, you have the right to speak, and we have the right not to listen to you. But, journalists should have the right not only to speak out, but also to be listened to.

Today's Balkan press is rather an extension of politics than a representative of public opinion. A good part of the media continues to be controlled by powerful political groups. In a certain sense, the claim that a number of authors have used to characterize the media situation in other post-communist societies applies to our region, too: 'The press became pluralistic, but not independent' or 'the press became free, but not independent' (Comman 1999, Sparks 2000 and Goban-Klas 1997).

Regardless of the fact that state control over the media has been perceptibly reduced and nobody wields the former monopoly on information, directly or more frequently indirectly, through parliamentary majorities, governments influence the composition of administrative boards of public TVs, or bodies that issue licenses for private audiovisual broadcasts.

Although they cannot be compared to the propaganda strongholds of the period of the New Authoritarianism, in most cases (Albania, Bulgaria, Romania, Macedonia) the so-called public TVs remain 'red carpet TVs', that is, full of government protocol and information. Not without a reason, public stations are considered 'sleeping giants' for their slowness in implementing reform and their dreary style of work. In Romania, the most popular TV station is not the public one, but the private PRO TV. The same occurs in Albania, where KLAN TV is the most popular station, whereas public TV is being watched less and less.

The old state TV stations of the Communist epoch have survived as institutions, and most of their staff has remained what it was. However, their legal position has changed. Today they are officially 'public TV stations. Actually they are subject to the current government, and this is reflected in their programs, especially in the news and current matters', writes Colin Sparks (Sparks 2000: 270).

At the present stage it can be recommended that the process of transformation of state TVs into public TVs be encouraged further, taking into account also the political cost it comports. If this process is dragged out, as has been done until now, the idea of a public TV risks being discredited.

The shift from 'Soviet media model' to 'social responsibility model' seems to have been more difficult than was predicted, not only in the Balkan countries, but also in all former Communist countries. Conservative Victor Urban's government in Hungary has come under criticism for its (illegal) control over public TV. On the other hand, the appointment of the new information director to Czech TV, Jerzij Hodak, who was considered closely associated with former Prime Minister Klaus, led to the biggest protests since the Velvet Revolution of 1989 in that country.

Habits inherited from the time of communism make politicians and political parties constantly try to influence, indeed, control the media, because of the conviction that who controls information holds power still remains strong. Political elites, as a rule obsessed with holding power, 'consider the media to be not a major, but the main, instrument for politics'. 'This vision of the media is one-dimensional, over-politicized and simplified, believing in a missionary role for the journalists and an ideologized press' (Goban-Klas 1997: 37).

It would perhaps be more appropriate to say that now, rather than state interference, a new partisanship is what damages the media more. The Balkan press appears today to be rather 'shooting journalism' or 'revolver journalism'. This is above all a reflection of the nature of politics, which is conceived rather as a conflict than as a dialogue. This is also a reflection of the fact that Balkan societies are more political societies than information societies or civil societies. A conflict-ridden and highly politicized society unavoidably infects its media and involves it in its conflicts and wars, that is, society uses it as a major means for waging those conflicts and in the process destroys its independence, impartiality and professionalism.

If we follow the dialectics of the relationship between the media and politics, we can affirm without hesitation that throughout the decade of the post-communist transition the media have much less modelled and influenced politics than politics has modelled and influenced the media. Part of the media has been unable to resist the pressure and allurements of politics (and not only politics); another part has simply been unable to imagine its role outside partisanship. Actually the conception of the media as a vital element of democracy should not lead to partisanship. The difficult economic situation, on one hand, and the relatively high level of corruption, on the other, could not fail to have an impact on the development of the media, which, just as the other segments of society, is not immune to monetary temptation.

The fact that the media has found itself in a polarized political environment could not fail to leave its traces either. In Albania, the free press initially emerged as a party press. Subsequently some steps were taken toward an independent press, but the threads that link the journals with the headquarters of the political parties generally still exist.

In Serbia, the media that until yesterday were under former President Milosevic's control today have switched to the side of the winners, President Kostunica and his DOS allies. The day after Milosevic's political demise the journal *Politika* and the Serbian Radio and Television started criticizing the old regime and extolling the merits of the new one. Actually one had the impression that no essential change had occurred in these media; they had changed only their boss.

Still the Balkan media are more and more playing a watchdog role in regard to the governments of the region. The proliferation of private channels is an important factor for the democratization and opening up of the audiovisual landscape. Little by little the media are becoming free from gross political manipulations. In Macedonia there are 159 broadcasting channels, in Albania 100, in Romania 144, in Yugoslavia 700 and so on (*Education and Media in SEE* 1999; *Balkan Media* 2000) Peter Gross, however, expresses an interesting idea when he says, 'We in the West were wrong in assuming the media will help to establish democracy. Independent, impartial, professional media are expressions of well-entrenched societies and function in their support. They cannot be spontaneously created in a society in transition to help that transition' (Gross: 9–10).

BETWEEN DILEMMAS

In the course of the past decade we have seen how the politics of war created the media war. 'If you ask me how we should stop this war, I would say only three words: "Media, media, media"'. This already famous sentence belongs to Cardinal Pulic of Sarajevo.

In his report on the role of the media in the origin of the wars in the former Yugoslavia (1995), UN emissary Tadeusz Mazowiecki comes to the conclusion that the media are to blame for stirring up racist ethnic hatred thereby directly contributing to the outbreak of these wars.

Mark Thomson, in his famous book *Forging War*, paraphrased the well-known expression of Clausewitz like this: 'War is continuation of television news by other means' (Thompson 1996: 1)

The slaughter happened in Bosnia not only because the Butcher of the Balkans willed it, but also because he and others found ready mercenaries to serve their ambitions. The 'campaigns' of the media were the forerunners of military campaigns; the mercenaries of the microphone and pen led the mercenaries of the Kalashnikovs and mines. As Adam Michnik puts it: 'The Balkan war first started in the newspapers, radio and television stations' (Michnik 1995: 74). The journalists found themselves facing the dilemma: either to be 'patriots' or professionals. A great part of them chose the first alternative, the other part rejected it. The former, 'the patriots', turned into mere instruments of the official nationalist propaganda of Milosevic and others. The latter refused to become such instruments, although this was very hard to do. *Oslobodjenie* in Sarajevo, *Radio B92* in Belgrade, *Federal Tribune* in Zagreb, *Koha Ditore* in Pristina, and so on, can be considered the resistance front of the free media in the Balkans against nationalism and authoritarianism.

The fact that some media segments have served the policies of genocide and stirred up national hatred raises the dilemma: how can these voices that incite people towards hatred be silenced without impeding the voice of freedom? In other words, should press freedom be limited in order to defend democracy? Or, to put it differently, what should be done when the journalists and the media trespass 'the red line', as for example, when they stir up hatred and violence?

Umberto Eco argues that 'we must define the limits of tolerance, and for this to be done we must first know what is not to be tolerated' (quoted from *Prime Time for Tolerance: Media and Challenge of Racism*, International Federation of Journalists 1997: 3).

NATO's air campaign on Yugoslavia and the Milosevic regime's ethnic cleansing against the Albanians in spring 1999 constituted an important moment of reflection, and in a sense, a test for the media of the region. The media in Albania and Kosovo backed *en bloc* NATO's air campaign. The media in Serbia opposed it, while the media in the other countries of the region were divided, for and against the bombardments, just as public opinion was divided.

During NATO's bombing campaign the independent media in Serbia were subjected to persecution, censorship, and part of them was shut down or taken over by the government. According to *Reporters sans frontieres* 50 independent media were closed after 24 March 1999. Independent journalists were considered 'Fifth Column', 'Quislings', 'foreign mercenaries' and so on. A good part of them were forced to take refuge in Montenegro. In Kosovo the existence of any kind of media was made impossible. The Kosovar journalists were among the refugees that streamed toward Albania and Macedonia.

On the other hand, Serbian Radio and Television which supported the regime became a target for NATO's air strikes. Twelve workers of the Serbian Radio and Television, journalists, operators and technicians, were killed. A great number of journalists' international associations reacted to this act, although the Serbian Radio and Television had been the mouthpiece of the Milosevic regime. (A comprehensive review of how the media covered the War of Kosovo is given in the publication of the International Press Institute *Kosovo – News and Propaganda War*, 1999).

The war of Kosovo and, subsequently, Milosevic's overthrow have raised new dilemmas and posed new questions. A rather hypothetical question is being asked ever more frequently: what would have happened if the billions of dollars gobbled up by the war had been invested in free and progressive media projects in Serbia? (Brunnbauer 1999: 74). History, however, cannot be turned back like a recorder tape. The first lesson to be drawn from the war of Kosovo is that of the Polish journalist Tadeusz Konwicki: 'I will never direct my pen against other nations' (quoted in Michnik 1995: 74)

Unfortunately the freedom of expression has sometimes been interpreted as 'license for hunting'. Huntington has spoken about the danger threatening democracy from itself. The media may become part of this game, if they are misused, and turn from a mechanism of democracy into a mechanism working 'to reduce or destroy democracy' (quoted in Sartori 1999: 173).

Ironically we are living in a time when, while demand for media products is steeply rising, the image of the media among the public is declining. According to a survey carried out by the Albanian Media Institute about the impact of the media on current Albanian society, 60 per cent of those questioned answered that the media cause trouble, and only 23 per cent said that the media contribute positively. Only 12.5 per cent of those questioned were happy with the newspapers, while the rest expressed unhappiness or indifference (research poll carried out by the Albanian Media Institute in cooperation with Press Now, Amsterdam, in March 1998 on the subject *The Media and Public Opinion in Post-Communist Albania*. One thousand people from all parts of Albania were interviewed. For more detail see: Press Now 1998).

It seems paradoxical: while the free press is one of the most important achievements of the emerging democracies, its public image is generally negative. In our opinion, this does not mean that the public is tired of free speech; rather it is a clear signal that people demand a more responsible press. This will take a long time. The unbalanced relationship between freedom and responsibility in the media is a direct reflection of the balance (better said, unbalance) of this binomial in Balkan societies. We live in a society in which democracy is understood more in terms of freedom and rights than in terms of duties and responsibilities.

Two trends make themselves visible: one considers journalists 'necessary devils' and demonizes them, while the other sees them as representatives of the fourth estate, which at times sets them in the role of a headmaster who knows everything and has the last word on everything. Not without a reason, there is widespread scepticism about journalist ethics and the growing power of the media.

In most countries codes of ethics have been drafted and approved, but in general such codes remain only on paper. While codes exist, in almost all countries mechanisms or the bodies that would implement them, like press councils, press complaints commissions, press ombudsmen and others are missing. While agreeing on the ethical principles of their profession, journalists and their associations have not yet been able to agree on the bodies which would supervise the implementation of these principles, mainly because of the polarization of the media scene. A Hippocratic oath for journalists is still lacking. Creation of such mechanisms remains a priority for the future.

ECONOMIC INDEPENDENCE

The independence of the media first of all presupposes their economic independence. It is still too early to speak about economic independence, because the survival agenda has priority for most media. A number of factors related to the ruined system of press distribution, increased prices for raw materials, the limited advertisement market, etc., have forced the media to link up with various business groups, local or foreign.

In a certain sense, it can be said that not infrequently political pressures have been transformed into economic ones. Journalists sometimes face both political and economic pressures.

Can it be said that former political gatekeepers have been replaced by new economic conductors? To some extent they have. Concentration of ownership and penetration of the big international trusts into national media landscapes certainly set the journalists against the dilemmas described above. In Bulgaria the WAZ group (the German *Westdeutsche Allgemeine Zeitung*) controls the main journals or more than two-thirds of the daily circulation (Petev 2000: 30).

It can safely be concluded that, on one hand, the financial weakness of the media makes them vulnerable to economic pressure exerted by governments or private companies. On the other hand, the Southeast European media are in too weak a position to defend their independence against foreign buy-outs. A policy aimed at reducing the high taxation applied to the printed press in most countries would be recommendable.

NEW INITIATIVES

The year 2000 represents without doubt a turning point in regard to communication among journalists in Southeast Europe. Many walls have fallen and are being replaced by bridges.

A number of regional initiatives are being implemented. Seventeen institutes/centres have set up a network, SEENPM (Southeast European Network for the Professionalization of the Media) and are jointly working for raising professional standards among the journals of the region. SEEMO (South East European Media Organization), an organization uniting the journalists of the region, has been set up, upon the International Press Institute's (IPI) initiative. The Balkan Media Academy, which also publishes the review *Balkan Media*, is operating in Sofia. In the meantime regional initiatives, such as the creation of a Balkan TV, are in their first stages.

Negative stereotypes with decade-long deep roots, and the negative description of one another that has predominated in the media of the region are replaced by a more realistic vision which comes about as a result of direct knowledge and contact. In this process foreign aid and assistance, for many a reason, continues to have decisive importance. We have already entered the stage at which communication and coordination among donors should respond better to regional communication and coordination. Unfortunately some donors continue to go by what they call 'their agenda'. Not always, however, 'their agenda' is also 'our agenda'. The time has come for projects to emerge from reality, and not from the abstract schemes of some donors. The Balkan people need a functioning democracy for themselves, not an exhibition democracy for others.

SOME RECOMMENDATIONS AND CONCLUSIONS

If we attempted to make some recommendations on priorities for the media in Southeast Europe, these would be:

- support for existing initiatives conducive to communication among the journalists of the region, as well as other regional or sub-regional initiatives;
- improvement of legislation on the media in all the countries on the basis of the Stability Pact Media Charter;
- strengthening of journalists' unions, which in almost all countries (with the exception of Croatia) are still weak and ill-organized;
- support for reform of public service broadcasting in all countries, especially Serbia, Kosovo, Montenegro, etc.;
- support for reform of departments of journalism at the universities of the region, which, ill-equipped and deprived of financial means for a normal activity, are still labouring under conservative concepts and under bureaucracy;

- support for projects of media monitoring and research; it is clear that, after a decade, trends, tendencies, achievements and failures in the media development are little known and studied. A Southeast European landscape project would be particularly welcome;
- support for a project of audience research, which stands at a primitive phase in all countries of the region;
- support of a project to assess the existing code of ethics in the region and define more effective ways for setting up mechanisms to implement the codes of ethics;
- support for journalists' training centers in the region, with a view to their foundation where they do not exist (Kosovo), and their modernization where they are at their first steps (Macedonia, Montenegro).

After more than a decade of post-Communist transition and violent conflicts the media should undergo a self-examination and assess its role and responsibilities, as well as the policies followed by the governments of the region and the international organizations.

REFERENCES

Balkan Media (2000); Vol. IX.

Brunnbauer, Ulf (1999): *Education and Media in SEE*, Graz: CSBSC.

Brzezinski, Z. (1995): 'Fifty Years After Yalta: Europe and Balkans' New Chance', *Balkan Forum*, Vol. 3, No. 2.

Center for the Study of Balkan Societies and Cultures (1999): *Education and Media in SEE*, Graz: CSBSC.

Chiriac, Marian and Daniel Cain (2000): 'Romanian Media in the Post-Communist Period', *Balkan Media*, Vol. IX, Spring.

Comman, Mihai (1999): 'Media in Post-Communist Countries, 1990-1999', manuscript.

Goban-Klas (1997): *The Orchestration of the Media*, Boulder CO.

Gross, Peter (1998): 'The First Nine Years', *The Global Network*, No. 9-10.

International Federation of Journalists (1997): *Prime Time for Tolerance: Media and Challenge of Racism*, Bilbao: World Congress of Journalists, 2–4 May.

International Press Institute (1999): *Kosovo – News and Propaganda War*, Vienna.

Maliqi, Shkelzen (2000): *Gogoli prej letre*, Zeri, Pristina, 20 May.

Media and Democracy, Council of Europe Publishing (1998).

Media Studies Journal (1992): 'Media Wars', Spring.

Media Studies Journal (1995): 'Media and Democracy', Summer.

Media Studies Journal (1999): 'After the Fall'.

Michnik, Adam (1995): 'Samizdat Goes Public', *Media Studies Journal*, Summer.

Petev, Todor (2000): 'Transformations of the Bulgarian Press', *The Global Network*, No. 13.

Press Now (1998) *Media and Public Opinion in Post-Communist Albania*, Research Poll. See *Free Press in Southeastern Europe. Albania: Starting from Scratch*, Amsterdam.

Sartori, Giovani (1999): *What Is Democracy*, Tirane: Dituria (in Albanian).

Sparks, Colin (2000): *Communism, Capitalism, and Mass Media*, Albanian edition, Tirana: AMI.

State, Media and Democracy (1999): Access Association.

The Global Network/Le Reseau Global (2000): No. 13.

'The Media of Eastern Europe Are Coming Up Against New Problems', AFP, 4 January 2001.

Thompson, Mark (1996): *Forging War*, University of Luton Press.

Thompson, Mark (2000): *Slovenia, Croatia, Bosnia and Herzegovina, Macedonia and Kosovo*, International Assistance to Media, OSCE Representative on Freedom of the Media, Vienna.

Rewriting School Textbooks as a Tool of Understanding and Stability

MIRELA-LUMINIȚA MURGESCU

DIAGNOSIS

Recent conflicts in ex-Yugoslavia have strengthened the image of the Balkans as a major risk area for Europe and/or for world peace. Although other Southeast European countries avoided being driven into major ethnic conflicts during the 1990s, the overall picture is that of a region where economic backwardness and ethnic prejudices combine in making it vulnerable to nationalist manipulation and instrumentalization. And, as in Western Europe after the two world wars, scholars and political analysts could easily notice that the potential for conflict has been enhanced by the ethno-centric education received by people in school. From the whole educational framework, the blame is often placed mainly on the textbooks used in teaching history and geography. Or, as Wolfgang Höpken has put it, 'textbooks often are held responsible for everything which goes wrong in a society ... Nationalism, xenophobia, antisemitism, violence – all this time and again is declared among others to be the result of "bad" textbooks'(Höpken 1997: 67). Of course, textbooks are not alone responsible for the way people think, but they certainly share at least a significant part of this responsibility. Therefore, improving textbooks would be a significant step in setting up a more stable and peaceful Southeastern Europe.

Before trying to outline what has to be done in this respect, some general comments are unavoidable. First of all, in spite of some common patterns, education systems and the problems of identity formation in Southeastern Europe are far from being homogeneous. In fact, we have to distinguish between at least three different situations.

First, we have a group of states, which, although young when compared with Western Europe, have existed at least for several generations, and some of them for more than a century. In these states – Greece, Romania, Bulgaria, Turkey and Albania – national formation occurred either during the nineteenth century or in the first decades of the twentieth century. Although in these states there are some groups that are not satisfied with the present boundaries and foster dreams of achieving national goals at the cost of various neighbours, most of the population of these states does not consider external conflicts as being a political priority. This does not mean that the image of the self and of the other is not biased. In fact, these people share an ethno-centric vision of the world, which insists that their own state is the creation of their own ethnic group, which has struggled throughout history against malicious 'foreigners' and expansionist 'great powers'.

Economic frustration and social crisis also contributed to this nationalist mindset of the public, especially in Romania and Bulgaria. Besides, during the 1970s and 1980s in both countries the communist regimes have used the ethnic divides in order to consolidate their rule, and have accentuated the ethno-centric education and the suspicion against the most important minorities (Hungarians in Romania, Turks in Bulgaria). Although both in Romania and Bulgaria major ethnic conflicts were avoided, and although the relationship with these minorities has in fact improved during the 1990s, the economic and social crisis of the 'transition' fostered new conflicts (especially the hostility towards the Gypsies) and encouraged various political forces to capitalize on social discontent by putting the blame on 'foreigners' and by presenting themselves as the true defenders of the nation-state against major threats fostered by these internal and external enemies. Besides, political and cultural freedom has led to the retrieval of the most outright nationalist creations and values of the nineteenth century and/or of the interwar period, which had been banned during at least a part of the communist rule. Thus, post-communist nationalism is able to link symbolically with the heroic age of nation-building, and to obscure its connection with the late phases of the communist era. This explains the strong reaction against the attempts to change the history teaching. In Bulgaria the attempt to abandon the term 'Ottoman Yoke' caused a violent press campaign against the responsible education minister. Wolfgang Höpken noticed several years ago that 'the Ottoman Yoke' is one of the stereotypes with a long history in the textbooks, 'probably the most famous one, which did not lose its relevance even in those textbooks claimed to be Marxist' (Höpken 1997: 72); thus we can better understand how difficult it is to defy historical stereotypes developed in the collective memory for such a long time.

In Romania, a textbook that presented in a more balanced way the Romanian–Hungarian relationship and that didn't pay the expected tribute to the 'heroic' medieval princes triggered a fierce public debate in autumn 1999, which culminated with a motion in Parliament to forbid the use of the incriminated textbook; although the motion failed, the intimidating effect upon schoolbook authors and publishers is already visible, and the change of government is expected to bring also a setback in the curriculum (Murgescu n.d.). But even before the change of government, one of the first consequences of the debate was the triumphant comeback in the narrative of the textbooks of the pages devoted to the heroic battles of the medieval princes against the 'grim invaders'. Most schoolbook authors seem to welcome the comeback of a more traditional way of presenting Romanian history. The most eloquent example is the textbook for History of Romanians, coordinated by Ioan Scurtu, one of the leading nationalist historians of the older generation. In the revised edition of their textbook, the authors insert the lesson 'The Romanians in Europe' (demanded in fact by the curriculum, but lacking in the first edition of their textbook). The authors claim pride and underline with bold characters that 'by their ancestors, the Geto-Dacians, the Romanians are one of the most ancient peoples in Europe', 'the Romanians "are born Christians"', and they have defended 'the Christianity against the invasion of the Islamised "pagans"' (Scurtu *et al.* 2000: 5). In the pages devoted to the so-called chronological benchmarks *Romanian civilization in European context* (fourteenth to seventeenth centuries), among 31 selected items there is just one without a direct connection to Romanian history (the fall of Constantinople in 1453), while the remainder are only military and political events (battles and peace treaties) with Romanian participation (Scurtu *et al.* 2000: 62); in this 'European' context there is no place for economy, culture and so on.

Certainly, in none of these countries the biased vision of the past is going to degenerate immediately into major military conflicts. Yet, as proven by the good results of the extreme nationalist Greater Romania Party in the Romanian general elections of November 2000, such an image of the world provides, in conjunction with economic dissatisfaction, a fertile soil for authoritarian, anti-democratic and anti-Western political forces. And, taking into consideration that the share of the vote for the extreme nationalists is bigger among the youngsters nationalistically educated in the 1980s and 1990s, it is obvious that the political risk of maintaining a nationalist bias in school education is high in the medium and longer run, especially if the economic situation does not improve significantly in these countries. A special case is Albania, where the nationalist education is favoured also by the ongoing political problem of Kosovo, and by the fact that the 'greater Albania' project is shared by significant groups within the Albanian society.

A second group consists of new states, which emerged in the early 1990s following the demise of the former Yugoslavia and which defined themselves as nation-states. Some of these states could link to a more recent state tradition, as for example Serbia, while others had to resort to very distant and questionable historical forerunners, as for example FYROM, which tried to present itself as the legitimate heir of the ancient kingdom of Macedonia.

In spite of all the differences, these states share some common patterns. Their very existence was disputed recently by some of their neighbours. What's more, most of them contain significant minorities, and the political elites of these states feel insecure about the loyalty of these ethnic groups. Therefore, nationalism was seen as a means to strengthen the national cohesion of these new states. In spite of warnings that the insistence on ethnicity creates divides inside the new nation-states, and thus weakens them, the attraction of the rediscovered ethnicity, which had been prohibited in Tito's Yugoslavia, prevailed. Therefore, the new textbooks of the new states show a major turn to a nationalist, ethno-centric vision of the world, and insist on the struggle against neighbouring enemies.

And, as an informed analyst points out on scrutinizing the textbooks published at the beginning of the 1990s in several states from former Yugoslavia 'what becomes obvious in comparing Serbian and Croatian textbooks is, that both countries are following a very similar didactical concept in presenting their own history, despite their totally antagonistic contents. Their own history is presented as a history of suffering, of deprivation and endangering, caused always by other nation' (Höpken 1996: 117).

But, in fact, schoolbooks are just a part of the picture. Most of the new states – with the notable exception of FYROM – were drawn into the wars of the 1990s, and war experience added to the bitterness of interethnic and international relations; therefore, in these countries the media and the public discourse are even more biased than the schoolbooks. Certainly, recent political trends in these countries, especially in Croatia and Serbia, allow hope that nationalism will no longer be the core of official education policy. Nevertheless, except Slovenia, which has already improved its curriculum and schoolbooks, not one of these states seems prepared to turn to a more balanced way of teaching history and of presenting its relationship with its neighbours.

A third group consists of territories under the virtual control of Western administrations and military troops, as Bosnia-Herzegovina and Kosovo. These territories have experienced severe warfare, whose consequences are still visible also at the level of school education. Physical destruction has combined with the bitter memory of interethnic conflict. In Bosnia-Herzegovina statehood is extremely fragile, while in Kosovo, Albanians and Serbs have antagonistic visions of the political future of the province, while the West tries to postpone the decision until the conflicting parties will come nearer. Even worse, most of the schoolbooks used in these territories come from the neighbouring nation-states, and reflect their vision and interests.

The Bosnian example shows how difficult it is to shift to a more balanced and neutral way of presenting history. Since the civil war of 1992–95 each of the three ethnic communities has developed a separate education system, with specific curricula and their own textbooks (those of the Croat part being published in Croatia, while those used in Republica Srpska come mainly from Serbia), and with diverging visions of the past. 'For instance, the war in the 1990s on Bosnian and Herzegovinan territory has different names in textbooks – the Bosnian Serbs see it as a civil war against being dominated, whereas the Bosnian Croats refer to it as a homeland war in the defence of the home territory, and the Bosnians feel it was a war of aggression' (Karge 2000: 45). Under these circumstances, it is not surprising that the political and social values taught to the young generation were completely at odds with the very ideas of reconciliation and of building a viable Bosnian state, which are central in the peace process initiated with the Dayton political agreement.

While most political leaders from Bosnia-Herzegovina, and even the Federal Ministry of Education tried to segregate the teaching relevant for identity construction according to the ethnical divides, the Office of the High Representative decided to block such an evolution and to reform the education system in order to increase openness and interethnic tolerance. Under international pressure, in spring 1998 an Education Working Group was appointed and reviewed all textbooks currently used, making several improvement suggestions. Yet, in autumn 1998 the recommendations were leaked to the press and the newspapers started a hostile campaign, accusing the experts and the international community of trying to deny the people access to their own history and identity. Because of this climate, the Education Working Group disintegrated, and the cantonal governments rejected all recommendations for textbook reforms.

Yet, when in 1999 Bosnia-Herzegovina applied to become a member of the Council of Europe, the withdrawal of potentially offensive material from textbooks was made a requirement for accession, and the education ministers of all parts of Bosnia-Herzegovina had to agree. The procedure designed by the Office of the High Representative stipulated that international experts should identify the objectionable material in the existing textbooks, which should be either deleted (blackened), or annotated with a stamp in the local language 'The following passage contains material of which the truth has not been established, or that may be offensive or misleading, the material is currently under review'. Of course, such a measure, which was carried out in autumn 1999, is easily depicted as brutal censorship; its efficiency is also subject to debate, especially because the pupils would naturally ask their teachers about the blackened or stamped passages, and teachers might be tempted to provide a biased answer. Therefore, the international authorities considered these measures just an interim solution, and decided to push the reform farther by deciding that in the future all textbooks should be produced in Bosnia-Herzegovina, and that they should include the history and the literature of all communities living in the country. Yet, owing to the impossibility of finding an acceptable version for the history of the 1990s, and in order to avoid generating new tensions, teaching about the recent war was suspended for four years.

In spite of all particularities of the different countries, there are obviously some common problems of history teaching in all Southeast European countries. We have already outlined the tendency to present an ethnocentric vision of history, which presents 'the nation' as the main historical actor even for periods when it was not relevant, or for processes that happened at a local or regional level. This tendency is stressed in many countries by the didactic division between national history and world history, which are taught in different grades, as distinct disciplines. Equally significant is the tendency to present the whole history as a continuous heroic struggle of the home nation, which had to resist against the hostility of the rest of the world; such a sharp division between 'we' and 'they' allows to explain the present dissatisfactions as the outcome of the malicious action of external factors.

In this respect, the 'eternal' fight with the other is considered to be the main feature of history. An analysis of high-school history textbooks in Bulgaria shows that 'all history textbooks still unambiguously claim that the reason for the foundation of the Bulgarian state has been the need to "close the ranks" against the danger of external harm' (Kazakov 1998: 28). Similar arguments are used to explain the unification of Dacian tribes under Burebista in the first century BC, and such examples can be easily encountered in most of the history textbooks or readers from the area. In this framework, national history is very often mainly the history of struggle against numerous, shrewd and powerful enemies, who try to do injustice to the brave home nation. For example, a Croatian textbook depicts the anti-Ottoman resistance as follows: 'Croatia entered the most difficult era of its history, in the age of the 100 years war against the Turks, who gradually conquered territories after territories, plundered Croatian towns and burned them down, and took the population as slaves. They penetrated even into Styria and Carinthia, but all the inconveniences were beard mainly on the Croatian people' (Karge 1999: 318).

Another sensitive point in textbooks, especially in history textbooks, is the incapacity to surpass the one-sided vision of history. In this perspective, each textbook presents exclusively the version of history of its own political, national or ethnic community. 'It is usually only the experience of one's own ethnic group with the others that is presented, but not the experiences the 'others' have with 'us'. The experiences of Croats during interwar Yugoslavia are not in Serbian textbooks; the experience of Serbian families during the Ustasha regime are at best presented at a superficial level in Croat textbooks' (Höpken 1997: 79).

In this framework, Europe and the West are seen both as models, and as a rich world, which egoistically uses double standards in order to further its own interests and to keep the poorer Southeastern Europe at distance; often, Western states, or the West as an entity, are presented as favouring some of the rivals or enemies of the author's nation-state. Obviously, such an image of the world is linked with the sentiments of economic, social, and political insecurity which are widespread in the whole region. Another common feature of history teaching in the whole region is the authoritarian pattern of the teaching process, the pupils being asked just to learn what the teacher teaches them, while the teaching of analysis patterns and of critical discussion are almost completely lacking. It is obvious that such an outdated way of teaching history is less and less effective; yet, the most simplistic historical information still influences the younger generation, and the lack of analytical abilities determines the youngsters to accept uncritically also the simplistic historical narratives of the media, enforcing thus a very distorted vision of the world.

RECOMMENDATIONS

I. Targets

A first task should be the removal of erroneous, false, exaggerated and/or offending statements about other nations, peoples, social and ethnic groups. In this respect there exists a significant experience in Western Europe, and the Southeast European countries have also made some progress in the late 1980s and in the 1990s (Kofos 1999: 23–7).

Removing the offending elements is just one part of the job. In fact, an expurgated history is less attractive, and the pupils will learn from their parents what they no longer learn from school. Therefore, there is a crucial need to put something instead of the hatred removed. A first step in this direction would be to create a database of sources and narratives revealing the cooperation between the neighbouring peoples, the benefits of mutual understanding, and the disadvantages of being hostile. Then, each part would be encouraged to include in the curricula and in the textbooks episodes or sources from this database.

In fact, such concretely targeted improvements would be just a preliminary step towards a more general change in historical perspective. This should include a shift from an ethnocentric vision of the world, where the school education tries just to legitimate the home nation's claims against the rest of the world, to a vision accepting diversity and supporting change. As stated in the Recommendations of the Sofia Conference in 1999:

> the concept of diversity should extend beyond ethnicity to include all its aspects (for example, age, gender, religion, ethnicity, citizen status), it should be based on the respect for human rights, democracy and pluralism and evolve in response to the complex challenges of countries in transition ... Education for the acceptance, respect and responsibility for diversity includes acquiring competencies such as openness to and interest in others; cross-cultural communication and understanding; critical approach to social reality, including to ethnocentrism; democratic citizenship knowledge, values and attitudes (http://www.see-educoop.net).

Such an evolution towards the teaching of diversity and tolerance might be served by a shift in the contents of the history taught in school. Such a shift would include diminishing the share of political and military history to the benefit of economic, social and cultural history. As put by Christina Koulouri, 'history of everyday life instead of epic heroic accounts might also be more interesting to children' (Koulouri 2001: 22). Introducing local history into a teaching process that up to now has focused almost exclusively on the state level would be also a way to increase sensitivity to the concrete life of common people, to the ways different people lived together, and to multi-perspectivity.

II. Means

Improvement of Curricula and Textbooks. This should include mainly history, but also other identity-forming disciplines such as civics, geography, literature, and religion, which often disseminate hatred even more than history. For this purpose, the crucial level of action is that of the national school authorities (usually ministries and various national agencies).

In the past, and in other parts of Europe, there have been organized bilateral textbook conferences backed by the education ministries of the respective countries, where each part's experts identified the objectionable passages and statements in the other part's schoolbooks, and negotiated their removal. Experience shows that bilateral conferences can help a lot in reducing the 'hostile elements' in the schoolbooks, but that often the two parts remain embedded in their prejudices and limit themselves at taking notice of the other part's objections. Therefore, Falk Pingel from the Georg Eckert Institute has suggested 'to act from the very beginning on a multilateral level, even on a European scale, with participation of experts from within and outside the region. This approach often makes it easier to discuss core problems of national interests, as you have a better chance to find neutral observers in the group when more countries are represented' (Pingel 1999: 49). In fact, Pingel argues that in the framework of multilateral conferences there should be discussion of the general issues and identification of the problems restricted to two or few neighbouring countries, which could be then discussed in subgroups, which should then report about their progress to the larger group.

I fully agree with the need to link the bilateral discussions with a multilateral approach, which would ease finding balanced and mutually satisfying solutions. Certainly, there are several practical problems in organizing this kind of conference, and especially in keeping a good balance between the invested time/means and the outgoing results. A critical issue is deciding if it is better to organize a general conference, which should prepare a 'big spurt' in cleansing the schoolbooks, or if it is more appropriate to organize a series of workshops dedicated to very concrete issues. A general conference would be costly and difficult to organize, but would provide an essential impetus and would help the various national governments understand that the European Union and other international organizations are strongly committed to enforce a change towards a more democratic and peace-supporting education in Southeastern Europe. Nevertheless, such a general conference, even if it is a success, needs to be continued by a clear follow-up programme, which should monitor progress, and make possible corrections if needed.

Such a general conference should be prepared at official (political) level, but also by two think tanks. One should focus on curriculum and textbook analysis, and identify the offending and/or dangerous elements in the existing schoolbooks and curricula (in previous bilateral conferences each part was expected to make its own list of objections to the other's curricula and textbooks, but now it is difficult to expect that each participating country will do all this kind of homework; nevertheless, lists of objections from the participating countries might be also handed to this think tank, and included in the agenda of the general conference). The second think tank should include distinguished scholars with a wide knowledge of Southeast European history and culture, and also of European and world history, who should be asked to design and discuss a list of 'positive' elements that should be included in the curricula and textbooks; the final list should include short presentations for each entry, in order to allow non-specialists to realize the educational significance of such an approach. I want to mention that the Center for Democracy and Reconciliation in Southeastern Europe based in Thessaloniki has already established two committees, which might provide the core of the think tanks asked to prepare the general conference for curricula and textbook improvement in Southeastern Europe.

The concrete organization of such a conference, the level of representation and the balance between general sessions and bilateral or multilateral working groups is to be decided at a political level, and exceeds the scope of this analysis. Yet, what is crucial is that at the end each country should receive a very concrete list of tasks, together with a set of general guidelines. Equally important is also to organize a continuous process of monitoring the progress realized after the conference, and eventually to decide on a renewed conference after about two years.

Relying only on national education ministries and/or agencies would be naïve. Therefore, action at government level should be combined with the activities of the Members of Parliament Network, which is the parliamentary track of the Stability Pact, and whose members might help the government in enforcing the improvements decided by the general conference.

Also useful would be workshops for (actual or potential) textbook authors, which should draw their attention to sensitive topics and to the improvements expected from them. The agencies and individuals involved in the assessment and authorization of textbooks deserve special attention. In fact, these agencies proved often to be vulnerable to pressures from the education ministries, from publishing houses and/or from influential textbook authors. Their authority needs to be strengthened both by improving their composition – at this moment the concrete assessment is made mostly by secondary school teachers, while the established scholars are rarely involved – and by providing them with clear and detailed guidelines. Because of the fact that the curricula are rather sketchy, the guidelines for textbook assessment should include detailed references to delicate problems. Training workshops for textbook assessors would also be helpful.

It will be essential to monitor the evolutions after the general conference. For this purpose, a standing network will be needed. It would be wise to rely on more than one individual and/or institution for each country, and to encourage reporting from NGOs and members of the civil society. The monitoring activity should include first the removal of offending elements, and the insertion of the recommended 'positive' elements, but take into consideration also more general aspects, as for example the balance between political history (which is usually focused on conflicts), and economic, social and cultural history, or the balance between local, regional, national, European and world history (but also geography, literature, etc.). In this last respect, it is obvious that the separate teaching of national history and world history in most Southeast European countries is a way to enforce the radical separation between 'we' and 'others' (Ecker and Pühringer 1999). Changing the curricula by merging these two disciplines would be an important success, but resistance might be considerable and, if so, it might be wiser to wait for a later stage in improving the curricula and textbooks.

GENERAL SUPPORT SCHEMES

It is widely recognized that curricula and textbooks have a limited impact if the teachers disagree with them. Therefore, teacher training is essential for the improvement of history and civic education in Southeastern Europe. This would include both initial training in universities and/or pedagogical colleges, and in-service training schemes. Especially the latter pose a severe logistical and financial problem. Throughout the region (but not including Turkey, which would more than double all figures) we have more than 30,000 history teachers, and if we are to include also teachers of civics, geography, literature and religion, the numbers exceed 100,000. It is obvious that such numbers of teachers cannot be trained solely in programmes designed by NGOs and international organizations. Therefore, it is absolutely necessary to appropriate for this purpose the national schemes for in-service teacher training, and to ensure that these schemes will effectively help the teachers to cope with the new requirements placed on education.

The material difficulties experienced by most of the people teaching in Southeastern Europe are a formidable obstacle for any attempt to improve history teaching. 'Teachers are generally paid badly and especially in rural areas and in isolated parts of a country we notice a severe lack of teaching staff ... Also the enthusiasm for joining in-service-training programs is certainly undermined as long as teachers have to take a second and a third job to ensure their minimum subsistence' (Ecker *et al.* 1999). Because of the fact that in many countries the average wages of the teachers fall below the national average wages, and taking into account that underpaid and severely frustrated teachers are a risk for the democratic and peaceful evolution of the region, there is urgent need for international pressure and help to improve the material status of the teaching staff. As pointed out by Alois Ecker, 'financial and other material support [...] are therefore a precondition for any broad reform of the educational system' (Ecker *et al.* 1999). Such a support would also allow enforcing control mechanisms, in order to ensure that actual class activities really shape the young generation in a more peaceful and democratic way than before.

It would be wise also to diversify the approaches towards an updated teaching of history and civic values. A great number of NGOs have developed various projects in this respect. Targeted help to the most promising initiatives would certainly help in reaching the goal of a democratic and peace-oriented education. One of the initiatives that has proved effective in this respect is the EUSTORY network of history competitions for young people, coordinated by the Körber Foundation (EUSTORY 2000). 'Learning through research' is the concept underlying the EUSTORY competitions; the participants – generally school pupils, but the criteria might vary from country to country – are given a general topic as a frame or reference (for example 'Modernization, Innovation, Changes: Bulgaria in Europe' in Bulgaria, or 'Childhood and Youth Through History' in Romania). Participants are asked to choose a particular subject for their research, to collect historical evidence either from public archives, libraries, museums or from eyewitnesses and personal collections, to analyse it and to present a coherent entry about the chosen subject. Young people, mainly of school age, are thus encouraged to take a critical view of the past and to deal with contradictory perceptions and opinions about the past. In Southeastern Europe, EUSTORY competitions have already been organized in Slovenia, Turkey, Bulgaria and Romania; it would be certainly beneficial to help both extending the model to other Southeast European countries, and reaching an increased number of participants in the countries where such competitions already exist. As shown by the existing experience, such competitions develop local identities, help participants to enlarge their perspective on history, and strengthen thus tolerance and intercultural understanding among young Europeans.

Of course, EUSTORY is just one example of such grass-roots initiatives, although one of the most successful and cost-effective. But combining the international pressure on governments to improve curricula and textbooks with such initiatives is probably the most effective way in providing an education system that encourages civic and democratic values, a sense of social responsibility and solidarity, open-mindedness and respect for diversity.

CONCLUSIONS

It is a well-accepted fact that 'images of the past commonly legitimate a present social order. It is an implicit rule that participants in any social order must presuppose a shared memory' (Connerton 1989: 3). In this respect, Deborah S. Hutton and Howard D. Mehlinger are right stressing that

> school textbooks are the modern equivalents of the village story-tellers. Like fairy tales-tellers in non-literate societies, textbooks in history, geography and civics [...] are responsible for conveying to youth what adults believe they should know about their own culture as well as that of other societies. There are, of course, many sources of socialization in modern society, but none compares to textbooks in their capacity to convey uniform, approved, even official version of what youth should believe. (Hutton and Mehlinger 1987: 141)

Rewriting textbooks does not imply only composing new textbooks according to new values and educational aims. This is just one step in a long and harsh process. The political, economic, cultural and mental changes Southeastern Europe is experimenting with for almost ten years, have and will have a strong influence on the collective attitudes of the people living in this area. In this context, education should not only change the images and the beliefs already existing by mechanically switching them with others, but should be able to create a new historical consciousness. Southeast European societies have to handle not only a tweaking of historical memory, but to bring the individuals to understand and support the necessity of such changes. Education must open 'the ability to develop a historical consciousness' and not to distribute only, as today, 'ready historical images' (Höpken 1996: 120).

On the other hand, we have to bear in mind the fact that setting out programmes and schemes for the betterment of education is in fact a question of time challenge. To want to change mentalities and attitudes means to prepare for a long-term process. Results might be perceived only after a long time. In the same framework, a strong political will, which is able to impose changes in curricula and textbooks is not enough without the ability of managing this policy according to the specific reality. We agree that if 'political support is a necessary precondition for textbooks revision, it is equally important that politics are kept out of textbook writing. To turn textbook writing into a kind of "textbook diplomacy" in order to support foreign policy aims would certainly undermine reconciliation by textbook improvement from the outset'

(Höpken 1997: 70). And, we can add, it could damage not only reconciliation, but also even the idea of changing history teaching and of rewriting the textbooks.

Education programmes should not concentrate only on history textbooks. For several years history textbooks were in prime time, but almost the same importance should be paid to civics, geography, literature, music and drawing classes. For instance, the literary texts selected for primary education textbooks are one of the most efficient tools for instilling not only knowledge, but for creating attitudes and a social and historical consciousness. As Vesna Pesic stresses in her analysis on primary readers from Serbia 'the heroism of Kraljevic Marko in the battle with the Turks is transformed into a norm that should remain intact today, as in the past, determining our modern values, ambitions and relations with the other people' (Pesic 1994: 80).

To conclude, an efficient educational policy regarding the rewriting of textbooks in Southeastern Europe as a tool of understanding and stability should take into account some specific prerequisites:

- the political will of Southeast European governments and political elites to adjust their education policies according to European standards, and thus to base them on democratic values and civic attitudes;
- a strong and continuous commitment of the international organizations to support, to promote, if necessary to impose, and to monitor changes in the education systems of Southeast European countries in order to secure a democratic and non-conflictual education;
- the willingness and ability of a significant group of professional historians to prepare academically and to implement a major change in the teaching of history. This should include both an extensive study of the collective and national memory in Southeastern Europe, linked with analyses on educational policies and textbooks in the last two centuries, and the preparation of a set of concrete changes to be enforced.

REFERENCES

Connerton, Paul (1989): *How Societies Remember*, Cambridge: Cambridge University Press.

Dimitras, Panayote Elias (1994/1995): 'Abus de mémoire dans les Balkans'. *Transeuropéennes*, 5, pp.59–64.

Dimitrova, Snezana and Naum Kaytchev (1998): 'Bulgarian Nationalism, Articulated by the Textbooks in Modern Bulgarian History 1878–1996', *Internationale Schulbuchforschung*, 20, pp.51–70.

Ecker, Alois and CSBSC in collaboration with Andrea Pühringer (1999): *Analyses. Education in Southeast Europe, in How to Construct Civil Societies? Education, Human Rights and Media in Southeast Europe: A Critical Guide*: http://www. medienhilfe.ch

Ecker, Alois and Andrea Pühringer (1999): *First Comments on the National Reports as Regards the Didactic Potential of the Projects Described*: http://www-gewi.kfunigraz. ac.at

EUSTORY (2000): *Looking Back – Looking Forward: Understanding History in Europe*, Paper no.2, Hamburg: Körber-Stiftung.

Höpken, Wolfgang, ed. (1996): *Öl ins Feuer? Schulbücher, ethnische Stereotypen und Gewalt in Südosteuropa*. Hannover: Verlag Hahnsche Buchhandlung.

Höpken, Wolfgang (1997): 'Textbooks and Reconciliation in Southeastern Europe', in *Culture and Reconciliation in Southeastern Europe*, International Conference Thessaloniki, Greece, 26–9 June 1997, Thessaloniki: Paratiritis.

Hutton, Deborah S. and Howard D. Mehlinger (1987): 'International Textbooks Revision. Examples from the United States', in Volker R. Berghahn and Hanna Schissler, eds, *Perceptions of History. International Textbooks Research on Britain, Germany and the United States*, Oxford: Berg.

The Image of the Other. Analysis of the High-School Textbooks in History from the Balkan Countries (1998): Sofia: Balkan College Foundation.

Karge, Heike (1999): Geschichtsbilder in postjugoslawishen Raum: Konzeptionen in Geschichtlehrbüchern am Beispiel von Selbst- und Nachbarschaftswahrnehmung', *Internationale Schulbuchforschung*, 21, 4, pp.315–37.

Karge, Heike (2000): 'History after the War: Examples of How Controversial Issues are Dealt With in History Textbooks in Bosnia-Herzegovina', *UNESCO Newsletter. International Textbook Research Network*, 9, pp.40–45.

Kazakov, Georgi (1998): 'The Image of the Other in the Bulgarian History Textbooks (based on materials from the XI grade history textbooks)' in *The Image of the Other. Analysis of the High-School Textbooks in History from the Balkan Countries*, Sofia: Balkan College Foundation, pp.20–28.

Kofos, Evangelos (1999): 'Textbooks: The Pendulum of 'Loading' and 'Disarming' History: The Southeastern European Test Case', in *Disarming History. International Conference on Combating Stereotypes and Prejudice in History Textbooks of Southeast Europe*, Stockholm: Nykopia Tryck AB, pp.22–9.

Koulouri, Christina (2001a): 'Introduction: The Tyranny of History', in Christina Koulouri, ed., *Teaching History of Southeastern Europe*, Thessaloniki: Center for Democracy and Reconciliation in Southeastern Europe, pp.15–25.

Koulouri, Christina (2001b): *Teaching History of Southeastern Europe*, Thessaloniki: Center for Democracy and Reconciliation in Southeastern Europe.

Murgescu, Mirela-Luminiţa (n.d.): *Between Nationalism and Europeanism, or How to Adjust Two Concepts for One Shoe? Remarks about the Debate on National History and Textbooks in Romania*.

Pesic, Vesna (1994): 'Bellicose Virtues in Elementary School Readers', in Ruzica Rocsandic and Vesna Pesic, eds.,*Warfare, Patriotism and Patriarchy. The Analysis of Elementary School Textbooks*, Belgrade: Centre for Anti-War Action.

Pingel, Falk (1999): 'Easing Tensions Through Textbooks Research and Textbook Comparison: What Measures Can Be Taken in the Balkan Region', in *Disarming History. International Conference on Combating Stereotypes and Prejudice in History Textbooks of Southeast Europe*, Stockholm: Nykopia Tryck AB, pp.38–50.

Ruzica Rocsandic and Vesna Pesic, eds (1994): *Warfare, Patriotism and Patriarchy. The Analysis of Elementary School Textbooks*, Belgrade: Centre for Anti-War Action.

Scurtu *et al.* (2000). *Istoria românilor din cele mai vechi timpuri până astăzi. Manual pentru clasa a II-a*. 2nd edition, Bucuresti: Editura Petrion.

Smith, Anthony D. (2000): *The Nation in History. Historiographical Debates about Ethnicity and Nationalism*, Cambridge: Polity Press.

Corruption and Organized Crime in Southeastern Europe: A Paradigm of Social Change Revisited

OGNYAN MINCHEV

ORGANIZED CRIME AND CORRUPTION: RE-ASSESSING THE PARADIGM OF TRANSITION

'Organized crime' and 'corruption' are two concepts encompassing a variety of substantively diverse realities in the global world. Throughout the developed West both concepts reflect phenomena of deviant behaviour of – primarily – marginal social groups (in the case of organized crime) and politicians, civil servants and businessmen (involved in practices of corruption).[1] Defining 'deviant behaviour' in the context of the established Western institutional systems is based on an explicit normative and procedural framework, distinguishing between legitimate and illegitimate social and institutional acts and activities.

In traditional – tribalist or clan-based societies – social relations are normatively based on particular ('natural') codes of behaviour, which might entirely be defined as 'corrupt' from the perspective of a modern society. In societies in transition – socio-economic, institutional and political – the status of 'legitimate' versus 'illegitimate' (or deviant) behaviour is much less explicit, which makes it possible for a particular vacuum in classifying the diversity of social events to occur. There are at least four different aspects of transition taking place in the post-communist societies of Southeastern Europe (SEE), affecting the process of defining (for the purpose of restricting) organized crime[2] and corruption[3] in all their particular forms of expression.

First, the post-communist societies of SEE change their social system. Political totalitarianism and the centrally planned economies are being transformed into democratic political systems and market-oriented economies. The orthodoxy of post-communist transition, developed in the early 1990s has adopted the neo-liberal belief that once given the chance to develop, a free market takes care of all additional problems, especially if combined with representative democracy and human rights respect. From the perspective of the past ten years in transition, we already know that this vision is not sufficient to guarantee successful post-communist transition.

Second, all societies in SEE and the post-communist ones in particular, are facing the necessity to complete the process of their modernization and adaptation to the institutional infrastructure and the normative standards of modern Europe. The process of modernization of the Balkans has developed for almost two centuries now, but the results of this modern development have been quite controversial. Nationalism has expressed itself in a more radical and Ethan-centred manner in SEE, the economic development has been uneven, and traditional society has been preserved in many important fields of social life. The countries in the region have often changed the models of modernization they have pursued, which has additionally complicated the tasks of modern development.

The former communist regimes in SEE, in particular, had pressed their societies to shift entirely the pattern of modern development from a Western European type of economic and social modernization (with free market economy, representative government and urban-bourgeois individualism) to Soviet type Eastern collectivism and totalitarianism. The Soviet system had stimulated technological modernization (through a forced industrialization process) and partial urbanization, but failed to develop entrepreneurial modern individualist values and institutions, based on them. In effect, modern individualism had always been the 'grand foe' of communism. As a result, the communist system had additionally strengthened the backgrounds of traditional society, incorporating the paternalist values into the hard core of the totalitarian political and societal hierarchy. So, the post-communist societies in SEE are facing today the ultimate need to return to the mainstream European model of modern development after decades of employing a false alternative.

The third aspect of transition, affecting post-communist SEE is the ultimate need to adjust to the system and the process of European integration, adapting European models to local conditions and institutional and legal culture. Europe of today is not simply a modern reality. It is a reality of intense integration and multiple levels of cooperation among the member states.

The last aspect of transition, which incorporates elements of all three above, is the importance of catching up with the post-industrial, post-modern and also post-nationalist process of globalization and multi-cultural diversification. The culture wave of modernity has exhausted its dynamics in the last quarter of the twentieth century and has been preserved into the institutional – 'crystallized' – form of the present

Western civilization. It is an unbearable task to adapt to this civilization without being capable of addressing its present – 'post-modern' – cultural development process. The most challenging aspect of this adaptation reflects the fact that it is impossible to simply 'copy' the Western – or the European – experience. The ultimate task is to catch up with this experience while preserving and enhancing the power of your own identity.

All difficulties which the SEE post-communist societies face addressing those four important aspects of transition, are focused in one major problem: the capability of these societies to develop adequate forms and methods of transforming and adapting their institutional systems to the realities of Europe at the beginning of the twenty-first century.

The ideological background of the alternative anticommunist elites leadership in the late 1980s and in the early 1990s has been designed after a simplified version of the neo-liberal/neo-conservative trends in the West. According to this simplified version, it would be enough to disintegrate the system of totalitarian control, to free market forces and to establish the new democratic political institutions. The 'invisible hand' of the market and the 'civil society' (a concept of growing controversy since 1990) would take care of the rest. The transformative efforts in the early 1990s have tried to observe this very simple model of social change. Unfortunately, quite strange results have followed.

PRIVATIZATION AND CRIMINALIZATION OF LOCAL ECONOMIES

Instead of the invisible hand creating the wealth of nations, the post-communist countries of SEE have received the visible fist of the mafia dealer, of the corrupt statesman or the street racketeer. Instead of the creation and maintenance of legality and constitutionalism, the population in these countries met with interweaving of private-sector crime with public sector corruption.[4] Instead of growing wealth, the SEE societies have faced deepening poverty and inadequate economic policies, aimed at transforming nations' wealth into a background of future market development. What went wrong? First of all – the privatization. The accumulated bulk of publicly owned national product had to go into private hands in societies, where all citizens until 1989 could possess at most an apartment, a Russian-made car and – for those higher in the hierarchy – a country house. In an environment of scarce foreign investment, no legal mechanism could provide a legitimate instrument for decent privatization. This is how the important question about privatization has shifted from the reasonable 'how the privatization is being performed' to the politically dominated concern 'who makes the privatization'.[5] The clientelist approach towards privatization has split the newly formed political class into hostile camps, involved in a zero sum game. This is how the very process of privatization has been postponed for years, and when started – it turned out to be heavily corrupt and non-transparent.

As an illustration to the outlined thesis, some comprehensive examples of regional development could be pointed out. The Freedom House country report on Albania, which is part of the organization's annual comparative study 'Nations in Transit 1999–2000', points out that the privatization process in this country has been marked by a number of allegations of insider dealing involving high-level political figures. At the same time, such charges remain difficult to confirm owing in part to the lack of transparency and of a coherent public-awareness campaign.[6] The country report on Macedonia, on the other hand, says that insiders dominated the privatization process in the country. Many of the most viable Macedonian companies were bought by managers with close connections to politicians and to leading political parties.[7]

In its 2000 Regular Report on Romania's progress towards accession, the European Commission states that the excessive number of economic regulations as well as the often non-transparent influence of the public administration in the interpretation of these regulations are the main ways through which the state continues to play a dominant role in the economy.[8] In Croatia, there is a general believe that the manner in which privatization had been carried out is the main cause of destruction of Croatian economy.[9]

Without a strong system of corporate law and a judicial system that can effectively administer and guarantee its application, the privatization process will further support the withdrawal of resources from the legal sector to the grey sector of transactions. That process leads not only to complete criminalization of the states' economies but also of the region as a whole. Starting with the most 'innocent' forms of mass-scale unauthorized trade, and ending up with drugs smuggling, arms sales and money laundering, the domination of 'grey' and 'black' economic transactions surely prevents any successful transition to decent economic and political institutionalization.

The Freedom House country report on Albania quotes the findings of a survey conducted by the Albanian Center for Economic Research. According to these findings the informal economy makes up about 32 per cent of the private sector in Albania. The involvement in intensive trafficking of drugs, arms and people provides the population new means for survival.[10] The survey also found that 'the informal enterprises have operated in the gray economy for a relatively long period of time, despite accumulating sufficient capital to enable them to join the formal sector'.[11] According to Western financial officials the grey economy in Macedonia is equivalent to at least 20–30 per cent of GDP.[12]

A 1998 survey organized by the National Statistic Institute in Bulgaria shows that the grey economy constitutes 22 per cent of the Bulgarian GDP. About 40 per cent of the employed population is involved in this illegal sector of economy. In 2000, in the opinion of the Prime Minister Ivan Kostov, the grey economy share accounted for 25–30 per cent of GDP.[13]

While the privatization has been politically delayed and jeopardized, the only well organized stratum in the post-communist society – the former communist nomenclature, and in particular the political police servicemen – have seized the opportunities provided by their control over the money, the networks and the data bases of the old system. Secretly created commercial companies suddenly appeared from the underground and claimed the legitimacy of a 'national business' community. Their basic aim has been to take advantage of the reduced capacities of the weakened state institutions and to extract the value of the still-public industry and agriculture. The instrument of this illegitimate redistribution of wealth has been the newly created banking system, operating under almost no control.

In 1996, the collapse of an enormous pyramid investment scheme in Albania led to the breakdown in law and order and provoked a general crisis of statehood.[14] The state faced anarchy, the Albanian economy suffered seriously, unemployment soared over 25 per cent and inflation rose 28 per cent.[15] During 1996, Bulgaria was also on the verge of collapse because of a general weakness in the banking sector. The Bulgarian National Bank, facing imminent foreign payments, had insufficient reserves to defend the currency. In order to decrease the budget deficit, the government raised the value-added tax from 18 per cent to 22 per cent. Inflation rose rapidly. Significant public protests put in jeopardy social peace and political stability in Bulgaria.

This is how a powerful system of corruption has been created in order to allow the control of vested interests over the newly created democratic institutions of power. In the 1999 Corruption Perceptions Index, which is a joint initiative of Transparency International and Goettingen University, the post-communist countries from the Balkan region were ranked as follows: Bulgaria, Macedonia and Romania were ranked 63rd out of 99 surveyed countries and received a score of 3.3 (where 10 represents the least corrupt and 0 the most corrupt); Croatia was rated 74th and its score was 2.7; Albania was 84th with a 2.3 score;

Yugoslavia was ranked 90th and received a score of 2.0. In comparison to those scores, the performance of the Central European countries is better: Hungary was ranked 31st and received a score of 5.2; Czech Republic was 39th and its score was 4.6; Poland was rated 44th and its score was 4.2.[16]

In this context, the individuals of the SEE post-communist countries have witnessed a dramatic reduction of their civilian-citizens' status. As it was well pointed out in the 1999 UNDP Special Report on 'Human Security in South-East Europe', 'the whole process of transition in Eastern Europe in the last decade can be seen as a dramatic security trade-off: the old regimes provided basic social security, while the new regimes offer political freedom and new social and economic opportunities. For most ordinary citizens of Eastern Europe, however, the period of transition has been notable primarily for the rise in insecurity'.[17] The analysis in this report shows that from the post-communist countries in the region, only Slovenia has managed to return to its 1989 GDP level. Generally, the governments in the SEE countries have failed to develop comprehensive strategies for reforming their economies and societies and to provide for human security and development.

RESURGENCE OF 'TRADITIONAL' PATTERNS OF SOCIAL COHESION?

Instead of creating social solidarity, law and order under equal and just conditions for all, the newly established political systems proved to be weak and vulnerable, serving the system of organized crime and institutionalized corruption in an environment of disintegrating public morality. Most citizens have felt to be the losers in this new game, where the few winners have benefited through enforcing the 'jungle law' into a disintegrating post-communist society. The failure of governments to deliver the rule of law and to implement consistent policies undermines the confidence in institutions as well as in democratic process, in general. In this context, Goldstock (1993) also emphasizes that the pervasive effect of widespread interaction between corruption and organized crime and the vast spread of governmental and administrative inefficiency, encouraged by political corruption, seriously affect the public's belief in the integrity and legitimacy of government.[18]

This is how the modern principles and institutions of bureaucracy and civility have failed to serve the individuals in the SEE post-communist societies. Such a degradation of the citizen's status has caused an imminent sliding back to the solidarity of the 'organic' society, to the traditional forms of community – the extended family, the clan or tribal identity.[19] Such a societal move back to previous forms of social integration could not, of course, restore the old traditional societies on the Balkans – history never repeats itself. The people of Balkan post-communism, however, tried to imitate traditional communities, and such an imitation proved dangerous in many of the cases causing a significant de-modernizing effect upon the Balkan societies. This process directly affected the development of the political system of Balkan societies, turning corruption from an event of normative deviation into a basic rule of operating private interests into the national institutions.

The Albanian communities are a typical example of those restored forms of traditional solidarity. The integrity of the clan organization of Albanian communities is based upon a specific set of values and expanding networks of family members and relatives. The traditional cultural inability to separate rational from emotional choices, combined with a number of inbred beliefs, have made it impossible for a large number of Albanians to make the distinction between crime and patriotism.[20] That kind of solidarity, typical not only of Albanian society, has proved a fertile soil for local gangsters, powerful mafia leaders and organized criminals to base their activities on particular territorial, traditional, clan-based or ethnic-based localities. The preconditions for such a post-communist feudal structure have flourished under the growing poverty and collapsed civil security: the Boss mistreats you, but the Boss guards you from another Boss.

Exploring the widespread and endemic corruption within the Bosnian political system, the European Stability Initiative has found out that the international community could not effectively support the key local institutions which are being established there. These new institutions are vulnerable to being abolished or rendered powerless by alternative power structures interested in the preservation of conflict on which their power depends. Political parties, bureaucratic fiefdoms, local war-lords and organized crime manipulate the weak democratic institutions in order to maximize their own influence and access to resources, and prevent them from operating in the public benefit.[21]

The process of civic disintegration of society has proved most dangerous in the multi-ethnic environment. Most of the war actions in former Yugoslavia (even if we count out the initial idealistic-nationalist impetus) and the consequent atrocities have resulted from this new feudal mentality, developing on the shambles of disintegrated civility. In the Yugoslav province of Kosovo, which is inhabited by a predominantly Albanian population, Albanian private power structures and mafia organizations relying on clan loyalties are the most powerful and active factor in the province. Real power in the province is not held by democratic institutions but by these structures, which are interested in the preservation of chaos and conflict environment. They are involved in a broad range of corrupt and illegal activities that brings them enormous profit. The so-called 'Balkan route' – a smuggling channel from Afghanistan to Western Europe – that supplies 80 per cent of Europe's heroin is now dominated exactly by the Kosovo Albanians.[22]

Therefore, we need to provide the answer to a basic question: was it a mistake to abolish the communist system and to give a chance to the enslaved nations of Eastern Europe (the Balkans in particular) to be free and take their chances of freedom? The answer is no, it was not a mistake, it was the right thing to do and history justified it. What was the mistake, then? The mistake has been to count on abstract entities such as 'free market' or 'civil society' to do the job that people had to organize and perform by themselves. While dismantling the totalitarian communist state and its repressive institutions, reformist democrats have forgotten to create a new functioning institutional system, therefore opening the space for organized crime and institutionalized corruption to prevail.

The social cohesion of a modern society is provided through the system of 'formal rationality'(Weber) or 'bureaucracy', establishing the norms and procedures of a functioning civil equality, civic responsibility and civil rights. The post-communist reformers have established the representative institutions of democracy, but failed to develop the public administrative component of governance to execute the political decisions made. Kregar speaks about the 'ritualization' and 're-interpretations' of the modern democratic practices in these countries of transition. In his view, the imitation of those practices is highly developed, but 'cultural patterns are based on friendship and family ties, not on rational choice and legal provisions'. The collapse of real governance (it was left to the 'invisible hand') has dramatically emptied the very representative institutions from their substance and mission. In an environment of growing poverty and disintegrating civility, the clan leader, the 'head of the family', has proven to be more adequately 'representing' his own folks rather than the parliament or the municipal council.

SUGGESTED POLICIES: INSTITUTION BUILDING, ENFORCING RULE OF LAW AND ORDER

All the above narrative scenario is aimed at one particular conclusion. The misunderstanding by SEE reformist post-communist elites of the primary importance of creative institutional work for the purpose of good governance has laid the East European (with few Central European exceptions) post-communist societies into the nest of a consecutive ideological illusion – this time a 'liberal' one. This formative, structural mistake has caused an outburst of organized crime and overwhelming corruption, based on traditional communal revival out of the shambles of communist society. Neither market, nor civil society could function out of the general law and order and normative structure of modern society. As pointed out by Rose Ackerman (1978), 'a country that democratizes without also creating and enforcing laws governing conflict of interest, financial enrichment, and bribery, risks undermining its fragile institutions through private wealth-seeking'.

If we come back to the initial typology of social transformation in Eastern – in particular Southeastern – Europe, suggested above, we will face the conflict between the results of the post-communist transition and the purpose of modernization. It is explicitly important to define the particular strategy of fighting organized crime and corruption in the region. We do not deal with expanded crime activities and corrupt inter-relations within a settled institutional system. We witness crime and corruption as integral parts of a restored traditional type of communities, based on clan solidarity and serving as a general model of economic organization and political governance. What we call crime and corruption is very often only the dominant style of social relations, provided the unsuccessful social adaptation to the Western institutional standards. According to a comparative survey on corruption in Albania, Bulgaria and Macedonia, for the bigger part of the citizens corrupt behaviour constitutes a successful social practice. This attitude coexists with the conviction, which finds further confirmation on a daily basis, that corruption is a highly effective tool for resolving personal problems.[23]

In order to integrate post-communism and modernization into one general strategy of regional transformation, we need to shift the dominant paradigm of perception towards the Balkans and, more generally, towards Eastern Europe. We need to change the 'democratization' paradigm with the paradigm of development. There were only few success stories of the post-communist transition in Europe – Hungary, Poland, the Czech Republic. They have made it not because they have listened to the 'invisible hand' promises or to the advice to replace government with 'civil society' – we all have listened to that. Central Europeans have been successful (including the fight against organized crime and systemic corruption), because they have preserved and strengthened their administrative institutional system, while transforming the communist state into a state of democratic representation. The Habsburg tradition of governance has prevented post-communist Central Europe from collapse of civility and outburst of clan-based solidarity. The 'invisible hand' has been carefully kept under law and order control there, before transforming itself into a 'mafia fist'.

There is no reality in post-communist SEE of today that you can explain with the theories of democratization and free market self-sufficiency. Democratic institutions persist, but they lack representative character: simply, the interests of the voters have never been met by any majority in the Parliament or by any executive team. What we need is to face the problems of the region – and in particular crime and corruption – through the perspective of the development paradigm. The basic strategy of social transformation in the region of today should focus on the purpose of institution building. Public administration comes first, as a legislative background, as a normative system, and as a framework of adequate procedures, able to tell legitimate from illegitimate social behaviour. In order to restrict crime and corruption one needs to transform them from dominant mainstream patterns of life in a post-traditional society, into facts of social deviation, into a modern normative system. As a consequence comes democratic representation, free market, civil society – independent and free, but abiding by the rules, effectively imposed.

The development of basic representative institutions with nominal checks and balances among them and the establishment of a responsible and functional administrative system, capable of guaranteeing effective representation of citizens' interests and to execute the decisions resulting from the democratic process is the departing point of enhancing human rights and civil liberties and resisting organized crime and clan economics.

The strategy of modern development of SEE as a – predominantly – post-communist region should be adapted to the dominant context around the region – that is the process of European integration and EU potential enlargement. The First and the Third Tables of the European Union-run Stability Pact have explicitly included within their priorities the fight against corruption and organized crime in Southeastern Europe. Within the Stability Pact framework, international organizations have already developed special initiatives in these areas – Stability Pact Anti-Corruption Initiative and Stability Pact Initiative to Fight Organized Crime. In general, these initiatives have compact Action Plans and provide a good chance to start an open dialogue between Balkan countries and also to unite efforts to curb negative trends and developments. But the Stability Pact could focus a major effort on behalf of the EU to serve as institutional, legislative and economic background to the entire transformation of the SEE region. To cut it short – fighting corruption in SEE would be successful not if corruption is 'exterminated' (which in some cases would mean to exterminate real life), but when corruption in a Balkan country looks more and more like a corruption case in Brussels – irrespectively whether we like it or not.

Last, but not least, modern development as a strategy to transform the Balkans should bear in mind the fact that we all live in a post-modern global world. We are not in a position to imitate (as some of our grandfathers did in the late nineteenth century) the process of modern development of Europe. This process has come to an end and today we face a Europe of a post-modern culture dynamics, based on the crystallized institutional forms of modern society. That shows once again the importance of an institutional approach – the strategy of modern institutions' adaptation to the cultural environment in the region. Today, though, the process of adaptation would be more complex and diversified. The strategies of modernization should carefully count the impacts of post-modern realities: in particular, these are the globalizing economy and the multicultural environment as inescapable prerequisites of our future lives.

Fighting organized crime and corruption as a part of a strategy of development for SEE should be focused on the mainstream prerequisite of regional development – the regional cooperation in the context of integrated Europe. All efforts to ease the process of cooperation in SEE are being blocked by a list of diverse phenomena, including ethnic conflict, international sanctions zones, political instability and so on. Among the major factors of support for the region's crime and corruption rates are the border crossing formalities and the customs regulations. On the one hand, intense border and customs controls follow the logic of a growing and arrogant organized crime of regional and international origin. On the other, customs and border controls are concentrated grey zones of corrupt deals and criminal activities, which are beyond any control, because of the institutional weakness of the SEE post-communist states.

A comparative survey on corruption conducted in Albania, Bulgaria and Macedonia in January 2000, showed that according to public opinion in those countries the pressure exerted on citizens by public officials was perceived as a widespread phenomenon.[24] At the same time, the authors of the Freedom House book called *Nations in Transit* (2000) explicitly pointed out that customs, the tax administration, judicial system, business licensing and the police are areas where corruption is perceived as most common. Very often, customs revenues are used not only as a source of financing for organized crime groups, but also as a means of fuelling money into political parties and elites. A more concrete example is given for Yugoslavia, where during the Milosevic regime a president loyalist was in charge of the federal customs agency, which allowed Milosevic and his party to control the flow of goods into and out of the country, and to impose arbitrary financial penalties and fees on individuals crossing the border.[25]

The concerted efforts of all countries in the region, and the assistance of the EU and the international community may well assist the transformation of those weak administrations into adequate systems of promoting economic cooperation and human contacts and resisting criminal and corrupt cross-border activities.

The strategy of completing the process of modern development of the Balkans would not easily bring intense positive results, unless the countries and the communities of the region understand the changing nature of the present and future world identities. We will all remain citizens of our own nation-states and live within our national communities. The major strategies of our future, though, lie within the perception of SEE as an integrated identity – part of the European process of integration. In this context, fighting organized crime and corruption – for developmental, or any other purpose – will be a reasonable task only within the SEE regional context of cooperation.

NOTES

1. For details on the relationship between organized crime and corruption, see also Van Duyne (1997)
2. See also Maltz (1985).
3. On a theoretical level , there are different explanations of corruption as a deviation from norms. Explanations address different analytical levels. The first approach, sociological in nature, looks at differences in cultural traditions and values. Here, the central focus is on the so-called moral cost considered as a kind of fixed cost that derives from breaking the law (Rose Ackerman 1978). Johnson (1975) and Alam (1990) employ the similar concept of 'aversion to corruption'. The economic approach in explaining corruption is well presented by Becker (1968): 'A person commits an offense if the expected utility to him exceeds the utility he could get by using his time and other resources at other activities'. Goel and Rich (1989) also demonstrated the importance of different economic variables to explain changes in the observed levels of corruption. The third approach is based on rational choice, but in a game theoretical framework. From this perspective, the choice between corruption and non-corruption depends not only on individual preferences and the institutional context, but also on the strategic interaction with the choices of other individuals (Myrdal 1968; Andvig 1996). Murphy et al. (1991) single out a model of multiple equilibria in levels of corruption and income.
4. See also Holmes (1997).
5. See also Kaufmann and Siegelbaum (1997).
6. Freedom House, Nations in Transit 1999–2000, p.60, available from http://www.freedomhouse.org/pdf_docs/research/nitransit/albania.PDF
7. Freedom House, Nations in Transit 1999–2000, p.438, available from http://www. freedomhouse.org/pdf_docs/research/nitransit/macedonia.PDF

8. European Commission, *Regular Report 2000 from the Commission on Romania's Progress Towards Accession*, 8 November 2000, p.31, available from http://www.europa.eu.int/comm/enlargement/romania/index.htm
9. AIM Press correspondent in Zagreb Milan Gavrovic explained, in his article of 17 December 2000, Tudjman's aim to use the privatization to create 200 rich families which had be the eternal foundation of his power and the power of his party. Milan Gavrovic, 'Partial Revision of Privatization', *AIM Zagreb* 17 December 2000; available from http://www.aimpress.org/dyn/trae/archive/data/200012/01221-002-trae-zag.htm
10. AIM Press correspondent in Tirana Ramzi Lani noted in an article of 16 December 1999 that the Albanian currency 'lek' is almost stable and the inflation in levels close to zero, not so much due to the applied economic policy, but due to the fact that the country gets US$1m per day from the immigrants remittances of nearly 500,000 immigrants who work in Greece and Italy and also a considerable amount of hard currency that circulates in the country owing to the illegal traffic in drugs, prostitutes, stolen cars, etc. Ramzi Lani, 'Albania: Nine Years Later', *AIM Tirana* 16 December 1999; available from http://www.aimpress.org/dyn/trae/archive/data/199912/91216-007-trae-tir.htm
11. Freedom House, *Nations in Transit 1999–2000*, p.59, available from http://www.freedomhouse.org/pdf_docs/research/nitransit/albania.PDF
12. Freedom House, *Nations in Transit 1999–2000*, p.438, available from http://www.freedomhouse.org/pdf_docs/research/nitransit/macedonia.PDF
13. Iliev (2000).
14. The team which worked out the UNDP special report on 'Human Security in South-East Europe' points out that it became clear that the pyramid phenomenon was needed to cover a number of other illegal activities. It also added to the level of criminality and social tension. UNDP (1999), p.22.
15. Louis Zonga, *Year in Review 1997*, *Encyclopedia Britannica* available from http://www.britannica.com/bcom/eb/article/0/0,5716,124532,00.html
16. Transparency International, *The 1999 Transparency International Corruption Perception Index*, 26 October 1999; available from http://gwdg.de/~uwvw/
17. UNDP (1999), p.7.
18. Goldstock (1993).
19. Pinheiro (1994) names 'soft state' a state that fails to supersede personal, family, ethnic and tribal loyalties. In his view, this 'soft state' is perpetuated in new democracies because political institutions are usually very weak.
20. Tsekov (2000), p.70.
21. European Stability Initiative, 'Lessons of Institution Building in Bosnia and Herzegovina', September 1999; available from http://www.esiweb.org/hauptseite.html
22. Stratfor, *The Global Intelligence Update*, 'Kosovo: One Year later', 17 March 2000; available from http://www.stratfor.com/CIS/specialreport/special26.htm
23. Vitosha Research, Comparative Survey in Albania, Bulgaria, and Macedonia, February 2000; available from http://www.online.bg/vr/surveyeng/ci_feb2000/Cor_balkan_mon3_e.htm
24. Vitosha Research, Comparative Survey in Albania, Bulgaria, and Macedonia, February 2000; available from http://www.online.bg/vr/surveyeng/ci_feb2000/Cor_balkan_mon3_e.htm
25. Freedom House, *Nations in Transit 1999–2000*, pp.184, 734, available from http://www.freedomhouse.org/pdf_docs/research/nitransit/yugoslavia.PDF

REFERENCES

Alam, M.S. (1990): 'Some Economic Costs of Corruption in LDCs', *The Journal of Development Studies*, 27, pp.85–97.

Andvig, J.C. (1996): 'Corruption and Softening of Government: The International Dimension', a paper delivered at the International Conference on Corruption in Contemporary Politics, University of Salford, November.

Becker, G.S. (1968): 'Crime and Punishment. An Economic Approach', *Journal of Political Economy*, 76, pp.169–217.

European Commission (2000): 'Regular Report on Bulgaria's Progress Towards Accession', Available from http://www.europa.eu.int/comm/enlargement

European Stability Initiative (1999): 'Lessons of Institution Building in Bosnia and Herzegovina', available from http://www.esiweb.org.

Freedom House (2000): *Nations in Transit 1999–2000*, available from http://www.freedomhouse.org

Goel, R.K. and D.P. Rich (1989): 'On the Economic Incentives for Taking Bribes', *Public Choice*, 61, pp.269–75.

Goldstock, R. (1993): 'Organized Crime and Corruption', *Corruption and Reform*, 7, pp.137–45.

Holmes, S. (1997): 'Crime and Corruption after Communism', *East European Constitutional Review*, 6, No. 4 (Fall).

Iliev, P. (2000): 'The Ruling Close Their Eyes to Shadow Economy', *Standard Daily*, 11 December.

Johnson, O.E.G. (1975): 'An Economic Analysis of Corrupt Government with Special Application to LDC's', *Kyklos*, 28, pp.47–61.

Kaufmann, D. and P. Siegelbaum (1997): 'Privatization and Corruption in Transition Economies', *Journal of International Affairs*, 50, pp.419–59.

Maltz, M.D. (1985): 'Toward Defining Organized Crime', in H.E. Alexander and G.E. Caiden, eds, *The Politics and Economics of Organized Crime*, Lexington: Lexington Books, pp.21–35.

Murphy, K.M., Shleifer, A., and Vishny, R.W. (1991): 'The Allocation of Talent: Implications for Growth', *Quarterly Journal of Economics*, 105, pp.503–30.

Myrdal, G. (1968): *Asian Drama: An Enquiry into the Poverty of Nations*, New York: Twentieth Century.

Pinheiro, P.S. (1994): 'Corruption in Brazil', in D. V. Trang, ed., *Corruption and Democracy*, Institute for Constitutional and Legislative Policy, pp.37–40.

Rose Ackerman, S. (1978): *Corruption. A Study in Political Economy*, New York: Academic Press.

Transparency International (1999): 'TI Corruption Perception Index', available from http://www.transparency.de

Tsekov, G. (2000): 'Criminalization of Albanian Communities and Regional Development in Southeastern Europe', in, *IRIS Quarterly Policy Report*, Sofia: Institute for Regional and International Studies, pp.67–79.

UN Development Program (1999): *Human Security in South-East Europe*.

Van Duyne, P.C. (1997): 'Organized Crime, Corruption and Power', *Crime, Law and Social Changes*, 26, pp.201–38.

How to Control Corruption in Southeastern Europe: The Case of Bulgaria

IVAN KRASTEV

From 1982 to 1987 the word 'corruption' was used by *The Economist* and *The Financial Times* an average of 229 times a year: a notable but modest figure in comparison with words such as 'inflation', 'unemployment' and 'budget deficit'. Between 1989 and 1992, the frequency with which the word 'corruption' appeared more than doubled, reaching an annual average of 502 times. This period witnessed a series of political fundraising scandals in Spain and France and saw the start of 'Operation Clean Hands' in Italy. In the following three years, from 1993 to 1995, Europe's top two financial periodicals used the word 'corruption' 1,076, 1,099 and 1,246 times, respectively.

The map of corruption scandals has likewise broadened. In the late 1980s corruption was associated foremost with Latin America, Southern Europe and Africa, while in the past few years Russia and the other countries in transition have become the main source of corruption scandals.

Transparency International ranks Southeast European countries among the most corrupt in the world. The weak states and the illiberal democracies that mark the political landscape in the region render corruption inevitable in the Balkans. Four Yugoslav wars and several economic sanctions have created a favourable environment for the spread of corruption.

The fight against corruption is a major priority for most of the region's governments and the effectiveness of anti-corruption policies is viewed as a primary indicator for the successful transformation of Southeastern Europe. But, could anti-corruption policies and rhetoric be problems in themselves, and is it realistic to expect that Western models will work in the Balkan environment?

This chapter focuses on the potential risks of the anti-corruption crusade initiated by the World Bank and the IMF and tries to outline the philosophy of successful anti-corruption politics in the region. Bulgaria is an interesting case for exploring the risks of both corruption and anti-corruption rhetoric. At present, Bulgaria is the most stable post-communist country in Southeastern Europe with the most efficient government in the region. Nevertheless the country suffers from both corruption and badly designed anti-corruption policies.

The issue of corruption has transcended the borders of nation-states and largely determines decision making at levels of global financial crisis management. The OECD Convention on Combating Bribery of Foreign Public Officials in International Business Transactions and the IMF and World Bank decision against lending to proven corrupt governments are indicative of a dramatic change in the international finance community's attitude towards corruption and crooked governance. The media and interest groups such as Transparency International have turned up the heat on governments to launch a crusade against corruption. If until yesterday many people saw corruption as an inevitable evil, today corruption has become an intolerable evil.

Identifying corruption as a crucial issue in Bulgaria's development should not make the nation blind to the risks of anti-corruption policies and rhetoric. Under the present circumstances, the price of the anti-corruption policy advocated by 'new moralists' threatens to be as high as the economic and political price of corruption itself. In the course of transition the only feasible anti-corruption strategy is reform of the state. Substituting this goal with any special anti-corruption measures is strategically unjustified. The consensus that corruption must be contained should not render the public oblivious to the fact that there are different strategies for doing this.

Corruption is not a disease – it is a symptom. The fact that most Bulgarians see transition as a period of 'shadow rule' is indicative of an overall crisis in the interaction between state and society, and between state and market. This crisis is encoded in the development of Bulgaria's economy.

The current perception of pervasive corruption may also be traced to recent developments. The last ten years have brought radical changes that have intensified the sense of rampant corruption. Privatization and shock social transformation have created an environment in which corruption has become a main source of wealth and new social status. Such rapid reallocation of so much national wealth is arguably unprecedented in Bulgaria's history. Moreover, the impotence of the post-communist state has created conditions in which organized crime has 'privatized' the policing role of the state, with various shady conglomerates forcing private business to pay 'protection money'. Private economic interests have usurped the right of legitimate public institutions to manage national resources.

The perception of public administration incompetence and a general sense of insecurity have consolidated an atmosphere of permissiveness of corruption within the existing system. When the future seems doubtful or even outright dangerous, corruption has become an option for many public officials. In this sense, the greatest government victory in the fight against corruption is the creation of a renewed sense of prospects and stability.

Monetarization of classical, pre-transition corruption is another major factor breeding a sense of moral disintegration. Under communist rule dominated by an economy of shortages, corruption manifested itself in the form of bartering. In most cases, it took the form of exchange of influence and services – straightforward bribery was the exception rather than the rule. The monetarization of corruption as a business transaction between buyers and sellers has made it more visible and disruptive for the majority of the population.

All these factors help explain why an overwhelming majority believes that corruption in Bulgaria is greater today than in the 1970s or 1980s. Yet none of these factors provide a sound argument for a special policy against corruption. The fact that people see the present situation as chaotic does not mean that combating corruption should replace reforms on the public agenda. The real question confronting Bulgarian society is whether the government will be guided by the logic of the fight against corruption or by the logic of reform.

In this sense, the drive against corruption is very much like the drive against unemployment. Unless the economy is stabilized and there is real growth, any superficial attempt to create jobs will not only fail to improve, but will actually worsen the general economic situation. Special anti-corruption laws and policies other than state and economic liberalization would actually do more harm than good for the reasons given in the following sections.

1. CORRUPTION CANNOT BE MEASURED

Corruption cannot be measured and, thus, the success of anti-corruption measures cannot be judged objectively. The fight against corruption inevitably becomes a public relations exercise. Unlike crime, corruption cannot be measured. We can never check empirically whether corruption under the right-wing Stefan Stambolov government (1887–94) was greater than that under Socialist Zhan Videnov (1994–7). There are several reasons why corruption is impossible to measure, and they are of crucial relevance to the selection of anti-corruption strategies.

The definition of corruption itself is very dynamic, and the domain of corruption has grown steadily after each big scandal. That is why we cannot measure corruption in terms of history, for what constitutes corruption today was not necessarily seen as such yesterday.

The second reason why corruption cannot be measured is that unlike other crimes, there are no 'victims' of corruption and there is no one to report the crime. Both the bribe giver and the bribe taker are interested in keeping their deal secret. What usually leaks to the public are foiled deals.

The only available measure would depend on confirmed cases of corruption, placing us in the absurd situation of claiming only 20 to 30 cases in Bulgaria a year, making the whole anti-corruption campaign ridiculous. Since it is impossible to have objective data on the decline or rise of corruption, it is impossible to judge the efficiency of anti-corruption measures. What is possible to measure and *is* measured by organizations such as Transparency International and Political Risk Consultancy, is the general public's perception of the level of corruption in their country. Yet corruption and perception of corruption are not one and the same. People are inclined to see various forms of administrative incompetence that are not associated with personal benefit as cases of corruption, or to use 'corruption' to define a social environment in which there are no clear rules of the game or where those rules are ignored. In politics, perception is reality, just as in perception, reality is politics.

2. MEASURES THAT COULD BE TAKEN

All measures that could have a short-term psychological effect, reassuring people that the government is determined to fight corruption, will, in the long term, make public administration even less effective, keeping the environment highly corruptible. Measures that the public expects the government to take against corruption, which could change public perceptions, are measures that do not really curb the problem.

In a representative national poll conducted in Bulgaria by the Center for the Study of Democracy and Vitosha Research in June 1998, 34.4 per cent of the respondents said that tightening institutional controls was the most effective remedy for corruption, 20.7 per cent recommended raising the wages of civil servants, and just 5 per cent saw the solution in greater openness and transparency of government.

Tightening institutional controls and wage rises cannot be effective instruments in containing corruption in Bulgaria. Passing anti-corruption laws and imposing greater punishment on corrupt officials cannot work in the present environment for, as Gary Becker (1968) points out in his revolutionary study *Crime and Punishment*, the degree of the punishment and the probability of it being imposed determine the deterrent power of punishment. In Bulgaria's case, the deterrent power of punishment is non-existent, for no matter how much the prison term for corruption might be, the probability of actually sentencing a corrupt official is nil, given the current state of the administration of justice.

Founding a special anti-corruption agency to 'blow the whistle' on corrupt officials in the administration or particular institutions is similarly ineffective. First, the measure requires more public spending and more administration; and, second, such an agency cannot replace an ineffective judiciary. The establishment of such an agency will not curb corruption, but rather will increase the number of actors along the corruption chain, providing the opportunity for more public assets to be 'pocketed'.

Anti-corruption projects are very cost-intensive, cripple the local administration and do not produce any mentionable improvements. Nor do pay hikes, the Bulgarian public's second favourite anti-corruption measure. Several World Bank surveys have proven that not just any, but only a high enough wage rise of civil servants could be an effective anti-corruption measure. Most surveys cite Singapore as a success story in this respect. Notably, however, Singapore's government ministers are among the best paid in the world. If Bulgaria were to decide to apply that standard, the country would go bankrupt in a single month. Given Bulgaria's current financial situation and the presence of a Currency Board, raising the wages of public officials to levels necessary to contain corruption is simply impossible. A lower pay rise would only increase the size of bribes, since 'kickbacks' are directly proportionate to a public official's pay.

Show trials and the pillorying of a handful of bigwigs – another measure that might have a psychological effect on the public – risk that the fight against corruption is used as an excuse for private and partisan vendettas. Political developments in Malaysia in the late 1990s suggested that when a government starts slipping in the polls, it suddenly recalls that its rivals were corrupt.

3. POLITICAL HISTORY

Bulgaria's political history over the past 100 years provides ample evidence that all attempts to pursue anti-corruption policies have invariably led to more state regulation and were essentially anti-market and anti-liberal. Bulgaria's political history shows that liberal reform and anti-corruption policies are not necessarily allies in the effort to change society. The ideology and practice of the Zveno political circle (a small political organization that established a dictatorial regime in Bulgaria in 1934–35) are a case study of an attempt to pursue an anti-corruption policy in Bulgaria. Against the background of widespread public disgust and disillusionment with the political status quo in an environment described by the press as 'totally corrupt', Zveno implemented a political project that was based on total state interference in public and political life, outlawing all political parties and suspending or abridging constitutional freedoms. The case of Zveno shows that unlike the Anglo-Saxon tradition where public anti-corruption sentiment targets big government and excessive administration, in the Bulgarian tradition, corruption is fought with more state regulation and more administration. The anti-corruption rhetoric in Bulgaria has always been anti-market and, in many cases, anti-liberal. Today, some of Bulgaria's harshest critics of corruption in the course of privatization advocate *less* privatization, not more honest privatization.

The political practices of communist rule in the 1980s provide another example of the administrative essence of anti-corruption projects in Bulgaria. Andropov's attempt to replace the command economy with get-tough policies underscores why the government should *not* give special priority to combating corruption.

4. POLICIES TO COMBAT CORRUPTION

Given the public sense of insecurity and conditions of political polarization, policies of combating corruption and anti-corruption rhetoric will facilitate a turn toward populism, destabilizing democratic institutions. Politics in countries such as Belarus, Slovakia (under Meciar), Yugoslavia and Russia provide an eloquent example of how anti-reformist political parties and leaders tend to adopt the fight against corruption as their main platform. Incapable of providing alternatives to liberalization, those leaders will replace the battle of ideas with accusations of corruption and anti-corruption incantations. Unfortunately, this does not mean that reformers are cleaner than their opponents. As Daniel Kaufman's (1997) empirical study shows, corruption has no ideological hue and appears across the spectrum. The findings of this survey show that public opinion does not regard right-wing governments as less corrupt than their left-wing counterparts. An unfortunate conclusion, considering that only a few years ago the idea that rightists were ousted from power because of unemployment, and leftists because of corruption, was regarded as a textbook truth.

These four arguments substantiate my thesis that if the Bulgarian government really wants to curb corruption, it should not 'fight' it but proceed with reforming the state by deregulation, demonopolization, simpler tax laws and greater competition. These types of reforms will eventually eliminate the legislative and administrative environment in which post-communist corruption thrives. The best customs policy is not investing in sophisticated control systems but investing in new border crossings.

CONCLUSION

By changing the logic of investment decision-making, corruption has an economic effect. A corrupt government will try to channel public investment to white elephants or large projects with a high potential for corruption. This explains why poor, corrupt countries love building state-of-the-art airports.

The new awareness produced by the anti-corruption lobby is also a new instrument of civic control that could be used effectively by the media, political parties and NGOs. The strategy that I propose is one controlling the logic of government decision, not a Utopian strategy constraining the motives of decision-makers. This will allow us to go beyond the limits of the legalese and moralistic views of corruption.

The strategy that I am proposing, which is based on new empirical anti-corruption data, calls for an awareness of corrupt governments, not of corrupt government ministers. This awareness will not be enough for the courts, but will be enough for the electorate. When we need to know if our mayor is corrupt, we do not need a government commission to tell us so. The anti-corruption surveys suggest that when the mayor of a city is spending millions of dollars on the construction of a new stadium while the city's infrastructure is falling apart, then the chance that he or his team are corrupt is high enough to warrant criminal prosecution.

REFERENCES

Becker, Gary S. (1968): 'Crime and Punishment: An Economic Approach', *The Journal of Political Economy*, 76, 2 (March–April), pp.169–217.
Kaufmann, Daniel (1997): 'Corruption: the Facts', *Foreign Policy*, 107 (Summer), pp.114–31.

Southeastern Europe and European Security Architecture

RADOVAN VUKADINOVIC

INTRODUCTION

Ever since their creation, the states of Southeastern Europe were experiencing problems with their security. They were feeling the rivalries existing between great powers, they were exposed to their political manipulation and were used as little pawns in great games. At the same time, these countries were seeking footholds in alliances with great powers, which, in most cases, never worked. The mechanisms and institutions of the international relations that should be leading to security, such as balance of power in international relations, diplomacy or creation of alliances, did not bear positive results. On the other hand, all of these states were too weak to even consider some sorts of their own models of security, built by themselves, that would enable them to counter the external powers.

SECURITY IN SOUTHEASTERN EUROPE (SEE)

Security is a widely debated and contested concept in international relations. As Bull says 'Security in international politics means no more than safety, either objective safety, safety which actually exists or subjective safety, that which is felt or experienced'.[1] Coming from a rather traditional explanation of security, which usually was connected with military threats to states and lead to war, in the case of recent Balkans developments we could start with war being the highest threat but also expand the concept. New elements of security should be included: economic, political, social and enviromental, which represent nowadays new issues in the concept of security.[2]

Starting with the term 'internal security', which has a meaning in the frames of one state, one could go further looking for a wider elaboration: regional security. The concept which started to be used very widely is cooperative security, which combines a process of peaceful reconciliation with a first step towards regional cooperation. As a result of all these combined activities, a basis for a stable security could be created.

Defining the area of Southeastern Europe or the Balkans geographically one could start with the geographic division of the area made by Magocsi,[3] who draws regional borders on the basis of major rivers. Starting from the premise of defining regions and rivers as boundary lines, Magocsi introduces three European zones; northern, alps-carpathian and the Balkans. In his interpretation the Balkan area is bound by the Sava Danube demarcation line in the north, stretching to the south to the Mediterranean and Aegean seas. The Balkans consists of: Croatia/south of the Kupa Sava demarcation line, Bosnia and Herzegovina, Federal Republic of Yugoslavia, Macedonia, Bulgaria, Albania, Greece and the European part of Turkey.[4]

'Southeastern Europe' originated in Germany as a distinctive label for a group of countries located in the area between southeast Germany and Russia. Central Europe and Southeastern Europe were created as labels at a time when there was a great rivalry between the German and Russian empires.

SECI and Stability Pact have a wider conception of SEE, and countries like Slovenia, Romania and Moldova are also included.[5]

The geographic, cultural, religious and political characteristics of Southeastern Europe impose several conclusions, which essentially determine the comprehension of the political denotation of the region. The area of Southeastern Europe can be to a great extent characterized by:

- its direct or indirect instability;
- the fact that most countries in the area fall within the group of transition countries or so-called 'new democracies';
- fragile democratic foundations and a lack of extensive and lengthy democratic traditions;
- traditional orientation towards and linkage with great states;
- a lack of agreement and desire for cooperation within a Southeast European framework;
- an aspiration of all states in the area to join the European Union and NATO and, in that manner, depart from the backward image of the Balkans.

RECENT EXPERIENCES WITH SECURITY

During the Cold War era, the Balkans became a sort of buffer zone in relations between the two blocks. Although present in the Balkans through their allies, the two leading powers – the US and the USSR – held that the most important line of confrontation was the one dividing the two German states. The so-called central front was a priority, while the Balkans was left to a controlled development within the two blocs, with two non-bloc states.

Maintenance of the balance in overall relations in Europe implied stability in the Balkans, where each of the two great powers had a possibility of controlling their own allies. Yugoslavia was left with a leading role in the non-alignment policy, and Albania, after its friendship with China ended, entered a grey zone of minor interest.

The collapse of the bi-polar system of international relations has cast a completely different light on the Balkans. It has become clear that this region was unable to build its own security system and that the dissolution of the balance between the two blocs resulted in a security vacuum. Differing from some other parts of Europe, the Balkans has never created some normal geopolitical configuration that would enable the emergence of some commonly accepted central factor with its geopolitical periphery. In some other regions such a centre is a focal point to which the peripheral states gravitate in their efforts to receive some economic, cultural, scientific and other benefits. Since in this case the states were either gravitating to powers that were out of their own geopolitical space (Germany, France, Russia), or were encumbered with problems that were preventing any intensive mutual communication, the centre of the Balkans never really existed.

Partly this could be explained as a result of the existence of different cultural and civilizational experiences and religious divisions. But lack of an attractive centre in the Balkans was a permanent feature of contemporary Balkan history. Every Balkan state was looking toward the West and in the days of the Cold War bloc division was directing political orientation towards the frames of bipolar structures.[6] Yugoslavia, which was expelled from the Eastern bloc, saw the creation of the Balkan Pact in 1953 with Turkey and Greece not as a chance for establishing some new Balkan centre, but as an important link with the West. Through relations with two other Balkan's states Yugoslavia was getting security guarantees and an indirect link with the Western bloc.

During the Cold War era, Balkan states were integrated in the structures of the respective blocs, and as such were representing the periphery in relation to the leaders of the alliance. Yugoslavia, as a non-aligned state, with considerable international activites, did not succeed in becoming a geopolitical centre of the Balkans.

Disappearance of the Warsaw Treaty and disolution of relations in Eastern Europe resulted immediately in security disintegration in the Balkans. Lack of some central force that could be instrumental for stability and development was further strengthened by the accelerated disintegration of Yugoslavia, which only contributed to the spread of a Balkan security vacuum.

The end of the Cold War clearly showed that this region was filled with crisis, with no mechanism or any pivotal point that could act to resolve the situation. The passing of the Cold War era, with relatively minimal security-political forms of overall cooperation in the Balkans, has left all of the Balkan states standing alone in search of their positions. It was easier for Greece and Turkey, since both countries continued their normal relations with NATO. Bulgaria and Romania were left without security guaranteed by the Warsaw Treaty, or even more so by the USSR. Albania has lost its internal security, while Yugoslavia started to disintegrate under its internal crisis and wars initiated by Milosevic's regime.

The traditional differences: civilizational, religious, political and economic have prevented creation of some institution that could be used as a mediator, or as a crisis management centre. Differing from some other European regions (Central Europe, the Baltic) where the new democracies have relatively quickly found their bearings and succeeded in building starting mechanisms for their gathering and joint actions, the collapse of the Warsaw Treaty and the end of the Cold War found Balkan states unprepared. And when new democracies in the Balkans started to contemplate their security they were primarily interested in breaking out from this region and linking themselves with NATO, which was seen as the guarantor of their new security.

New political forces, elected in democratic elections, have gradually started to emerge on the political scene in Balkan states, particularly in the states of the former Yugoslavia. They were also unable to build any form of mutual cooperation in the field of security. For some of them (Romania, Bulgaria) the issue of internal political relations was essential. The new states in the territory of former Yugoslavia were faced with so many new problems, brought by the war, that some joint consideration of security issues was out of the question, at least until the international community stepped in with the first serious instruments for crisis resolving (Washington Treaty in 1994 and the Dayton-Paris Accord in 1995).

CONSEQUENCES OF THE WARS

The wars in the territory of the former Yugoslavia found the European Community quite disoriented. Unprepared for such action, the EC (later the EU) strayed in its efforts to find a solution, which enabled the internal conflict to turn into a full-scale war in the centre of the European continent. The lack of a stable European policy resulted in various approaches and attempts to restore security in this area, through the EU, OSCE and, finally, the UN.

Instability in the Balkans and the significant security vacuum had their impact on the creation of some new political approaches by several powers that had a longer tradition of relations with this region. In view of this new development Germany, France, Russia and Turkey were seeking new footholds for promotion of their interests, or for restoring or maintaining their positions. On the other hand, American policy, initially leaving the resolution of the conflict in former Yugoslavia to the Europeans, gradually started to take over the initiative and finally became the most significant arbiter and key actor in solving of the security problems in the Balkans.

Unsolved national issues that led to conflicts and later to the war in former Yugoslavia, made Europe realize the complexity of the divisions and the problems arising from it. At the same time, Europe was swept by a huge wave of refugees, transferring parts of the security problems out of the Balkan region itself. Although initially there was a belief that it would not happen, this transfer of the crisis and its development had some impact on European security as well, which led to a more prompt European reaction towards stabilization of the situation.

Religious divisions were also soon incorporated into national policies of the newly independent states in the territory of the former Yugoslavia and, at the same time, gave way to speculative calculations on various new axes that could be formed based on religious similarities. Besides this, the engagement of the Catholic, Orthodox and Muslim support opened the way for a stronger proliferation of both political and religious forces (Islam), as well as for searching for allies outside of the Balkan space.

All these retrograde political and religious developments had their effect on the economy as well. The collapse of the socialist system has made the positions of all new democracies in the Balkans more difficult. For Albania, Romania and Bulgaria this transition from socialist economy to free market economy was too fast and too painful. For new states in the territory of former Yugoslavia the war with its consequences also contributed to economic decline. Of all countries of the region today only Slovenia has the same level of GDP as before the war. The economies of all the other countries of the region have significantly deteriorated. This has, of course, resulted in economic unattractiveness of the whole area for foreign investment, which sees stability as one of the basic preconditions for its engagement. Therefore, it might be said that the overall geo-economic interest in this area has significantly decreased.

SECURITY ISSUES IN SOUTHEASTERN EUROPE

After the energetic engagement of the international community, which resulted in the Dayton Accord, the Royaumont Initiative, the EU's Regional Approach, the SECI, the Stability Pact, and finally the fall of Milosevic, it appears that the possibilities of new threats to security have been eliminated from Southeastern Europe. The number of significant international factors present, as well as the presence of military forces in the Balkans – whether through SFOR, KFOR or NATO – should all lead to a conclusion that eventual break-out of some larger conflicts is impossible, moreover, that even some other forms of insecurity are almost totally under control. Of course, all this is conditioned by acceptance of Mr Westendorp's announcement that the international community will keep its presence in Bosnia-Herzegovina for a generation; such a time frame should certainly be applied in Kosovo as well. Within such long-range coordinates, and given such a quantum of military presence and political commitment to staying in this area, security in Southeastern Europe might have a chance to succeed.

Systematizing Attempt

In an effort to systematize possible challenges, we could begin from the division on military and non-military threats. All situations eventually threatening the outbreak of military conflicts could be included in the category of military threats. These could include: Greek–Turkish relations, further disintegration of Yugoslavia, creation of a Kosovo State, emergence of Greater Albania, and similar. It is apparent that these goals could be hardly achieved without the use of military force, as well as that some of them could lead to further escalation of confrontation on a regional scale.

Neutralizing military threats should, by all means, include the unfinished process of conventional arms control within the CFE. This demonstrates the fact that the connection with the remaining European space regarding conventional arms control has not yet been fully established, as well as that SEE has not yet been fully incorporated into the European security system. Although this fact can be compensated for by the existence of Annex II of the Dayton Accord, it would have been better if a comprehensive system, linked to the OSCE system, was built.

Of course, these military challenges should be viewed, at this moment, conditionally. Given the presence of numerous military forces of the international community, it would be difficult even to imagine an outbreak of some military conflict, regardless of the strength of any participating country. The international community has a sufficient military power deployed on the ground to stop any source of military conflict at its root, and the direct military action against Serbia has clearly shown that NATO will not allow any continuing warfare in the Balkans.

Therefore, it may be said that the non-military challenges are far more numerous and threatening. All the conflicts that have not been resolved so far can be included in this group of challenges, regardless whether these arise from history, ethnicity or religion, and which all have their territorial expressions. Further, the problems connected to the economic development, that are experienced all over the region, relating either to the common transitional difficulties, to specific national solutions, or to the economic devastation of the central state of former Yugoslavia (Serbia). Such non-military threats, either by a political decision or by insistence of the political elites, can easily cross the line and become military ones.

Having in mind the fact that the line separating military from non-military challenges is a very thin one, maybe the existing challenges in the Balkans could be classified by taking into account all of the dangers that might lead to instability, regardless of their military or non-military character, and then list them as challenges that could jeopardize security and stability. Within such a classification, the following division could be drawn:

- traditional Balkan conflicts;
- new conflicts, connected to the newly gained independence;
- potential points of crisis;
- new challenges to security.

Traditional Balkan Conflicts

The richness of different religious, economic, political, military and ethnic factors in the Balkans opens up numerous possible conflicts as well. Some of them have their distant historical background, have become an inseparable part of particular national determinations, and are to large extent influencing the present positions of particular states.

Although nowadays such conflicts, regardless of the length of their tradition and their national background, are largely subdued because of the presence of the international community, the possibility of their revival should not be completely ignored.

Greek–Turkish conflicts regarding the territorial demarcation in the Aegean Sea and conflicts over Cyprus[7] are the result not only of the different concepts of national leaderships, but are also grounded in distant historical events and their evocations in both nations. In spite of their membership in NATO, the two countries have been unable to solve these questions and every new incident results in mobilization of all national forces for protection of one country's interests and positions. The South Wing of NATO has been aware of the problems arising from the Greek–Turkish relations for years now, and in spite of all the efforts to build upon the European and transatlantic common denominators, was not successful in diminishing them. Turkish striving for EU membership was for a long time resolutely blocked by Greece. Furthermore, in their different positions in regards to the wars in the territories of the former Yugoslavia, both countries have demonstrated their national biases inherited from the past.

Turks are aware of the fact that their country is bigger and stronger, but the integration of Greece into Europe has offered a strong 'joker' to Greece, which can repeatedly be used in order to demand for adjustments in Turkish behaviour. Having in mind the depth of the crisis in their relations, as well as un-readiness for changes in their perception of each other, it is apparent that such a situation between Greece and Turkey will last. Some day, when Turkey becomes an EU member as well, all the tensions in their mutual relations may perhaps disappear.

Conflicts between Albania and Yugoslavia regarding Kosovo can be included in this category of traditional tensions as well. During the days of friendship and cooperation, immediately after the Second World War, when both countries were within the group of peoples' democracies, both sides claimed that this issue was un-important. Even more so, in the light of the plan to create a Balkan socialist federation along with Bulgaria, both countries were to set an example for other countries. But after the Cominform Resolution of 1948, the Enver Hoxha regime became eager in its attacks against Yugoslavia, in the context of which the Kosovo issue was used as well. After Stalin's death mutual relations were normalized once again, but have never reached the level of relations with other East European countries. The Kosovo issue was re-emerging on various occasions within their mutual relations. However, isolated Albania lacked the strength, as well as interested allies that would support its claims. Only after the collapse of socialism and Berisha's rise to the presidential office, the question of Kosovo was openly re-positioned in the centre of Albanian political action. In an attempt to divert attention from internal problems, Berisha was advocating the gathering of all Albanians in one country, and started calling for the internationalization of the Kosovo issue. Milosevic's regime, because of its policy of genocide, opened the space for the internationalization of the Kosovo issue at first, as well as for the engagement of various international organizations and mediators later. By abandoning the negotiations in Rambouillet, it provoked the NATO military intervention.

The above situation has led to the deployment of the UN, that is, NATO and Russian forces, in Kosovo, to the return of Albanian refugees, to the exodus of Serbian and other non-Albanian populations from Kosovo, to the creation of KFOR as the principal military, political and police force, and to the final exclusion of Kosovo from the Serbian state systems (monetary, transport, economic, educational and so on). Although both the West and Russia recognize the fact that Kosovo is an integral part of Yugoslavia, not even a trace of this claim can be seen in this situation. On the other hand, the West is resolutely expressing its opposition to any secession of Kosovo and changing of borders. The obsession with dangers that the change of borders can represent is still present, and is especially accentuated in the easily flammable Balkan territories. The basic idea is that a controlled stabilization of the situation would create a possibility for multi-ethnic life. According to President Clinton, the most important thing is 'to preserve the democracy, self-determination, freedom, and that in these countries [meaning Balkan countries] there should be no ethnic, religious or racial persecutions, regardless of the national borders'.[8] This is, of course, a very reasonable approach, but the question is to what extent will this satisfy the Albanian population which views the expulsion of Serbian authorities and Serbs as a precondition for their freedom. Finally, UCK's position regarding this issue will also be significant, since it is the organization that is able to control a large part of the Albanians and appears as their political leadership in fulfilling the desire for a total secession from Yugoslavia.[9]

If secession succeeded, then certainly a new set of questions would arise. Namely, would an independent Kosovo become an independent state, would it become a part of present Albania, or would this development be a beginning of a process of the emergence of a Great Albania in which certain other areas populated by Albanian majorities would also be included (parts of Macedonia and Montenegro)?

In any case, the issue of Kosovo, and through that Albanian–Serbian (Yugoslav) relations as well, will continue to be a problem that surpasses regional significance. The international engagement,[10] as well as all other efforts aimed at the restoration of stability in SEE, makes the issue of Kosovo a problem of wider international character, a problem that will continue to test the willingness and abilities of the international community to act within the context of the new world order.

The collapse of Milosevic's regime and election of new Yugoslav president Kostunica in 2000 opened new possibilities for the resolution of Kosovo's problem with in the context of FR Yugoslavia in the future. However, the great majority of Albanians in Kosovo would reject a federal Yugoslav solution and they would claim that in lieu of their own state, an international protectorship is more acceptable for the time being.

The Turkish–Bulgarian dispute, although greatly subdued in recent times, remains present. In a situation where over 800,000 Turks (Pomaks) live in Bulgaria, who were forcefully 'Bulgarized' during the previous socialist regime, it is difficult to establish normal relations overnight. And as the fundamentalism of Muslim provenance is, in different parts of the Balkans, often being mentioned as one of the most significant threats, in all communities where the Muslims are present there is a distrust regarding their true commitment and inclusion into the frameworks of the state they live in. If some consider Muslims in the Balkans as a destabilizing factor, and others fear the emergence of fundamentalist forces in these areas, then Bulgaria with its considerable Muslim-Pomak population has an important problem. Nevertheless, the results obtained from an attempt to incorporate Pomaks into Bulgarian social, political and economic life are encouraging for the future. Even more so given the fact that Bulgaria has clearly committed itself to the European path, which includes a strong requirement of respect of human and minority rights.[11]

Relations between Romania and Hungary, owing to the position of Hungarians living in Romania, were periodically during the Cold War quite tense. In Ceausescu's times the policy of national homogenization demanded that all Romanian citizens demonstrate their loyalty to the nation, that is, the state. A large Hungarian population in Transylvanian areas had a strong sense of national identity, and the fall of Ceausescu's regime was expected to create better conditions for their lives in Romania. Although there was no chance that Romania would cede Transylvania back to Hungary, in various circles among Romanian Hungarians, as well as in Hungary, attempts were made to obtain a status of full autonomy, which would then lead to demands for self-determination. Romanian authorities were firmly against such a course of events, and in some highly tense phases of Hungarian–Romanian relations the situation was even seen as requiring the deployment of European forces. It is interesting to mention that the Secretary of the WEU at the time, Van Eckelen, was pointing to this concrete situation as a possible test for WEU action.

This did not happen, and both states have demonstrated some restraint. This restraint was primarily a result of EU pressures, which made it clear to both states that there would be no closer relations with the EU for them, unless they resumed normal relations between themselves. Also, both countries were influenced by their desire to become members of the Partnership for Peace. All this led to signing an agreement on bilateral relations, which, in part, regulated the issue of the Hungarian minority in Romania.[12]

On the other hand, Romania has also certain problematic relations with Moldova. According to the first expectations by Romanian political circles, a state that was created of Socialist Republic Moldova after the collapse of the Soviet Union – Moldova – was to unify itself with Romania. As that did not happen, some discontent was noticed in Bucharest, illustrated by statements that Moldova was formerly Romanian territory and that it would be only natural if the two countries would unite. But, since in Moldova, along with the population of Romanian origin, there are also Ukrainians, Russians, Turks, Jews and Bulgarians, it was apparent that eventual unification with Romania would mean the beginning of new dramatic events. As a result of fears and of some inspiration from outside that Moldova would become a part of Romania, the Ukrainian and Russian populations created the Transdnestar Republic in the south of Moldova in 1990.

At present Romania is absorbed in its internal problems, which will obviously be very difficult to solve, unless the country quickly speeds up its pace towards the Europe. At the same time this is the principal reason for putting all demands that could give rise to nationalism far behind, for it is clear to a majority of Romanian political forces that Europe would not tolerate such a development. Romania, finding that its inclusion in the list of future NATO members is in its best interest, and having the Associating Agreement with the EU already in place, holds Europe as its priority. This in practice limits the possibility of action for those nationalistic forces that would decrease the autonomy of Hungarians who live in Romania. Besides, the new Moldovan independence is becoming a commonly accepted fact, and the Moldovan political structures are far from seeking any unification with Romania, which, in economic terms, is not a very attractive option. Moldova is nowadays expecting much more from the SECI and an eventual approach to the EU, since this approach is viewed as the only way for its development and for overcoming the economic difficulties.

New Balkan Traumas and New Independence

The break-up of former Yugoslavia has influenced the emergence of some new disputes, and has fuelled some previous animosities among certain nations in this area. It is certain that numerous disputes will continue to arise from these problems, as well as that the international community will have to continue with careful monitoring of the behaviour of the new states.

Relations between Croatia and Serbia have their roots in their common life in former Yugoslavia, as well as in the war that erupted after the collapse of Yugoslavia. By the Dayton Accord, and especially by the Agreement on Normalization of Relations between the two states (1996), a process of gradual normalization was started. The question of Prevlaka remains an open dispute, where Croatia views it only as a security issue, while Yugoslavia demands change of borders in its favour. There are also questions connected with the return of refugees and numerous property issues. Finally, an issue of restitution of war damages suffered by Croatia could be opened as well.

Although the relations between the two countries have entered a phase of certain 'cold peace', it is apparent that time and the instruments of the international community will influence the development of better relations. It is understandable that between the two countries which lived within the same state for several decades numerous links and connections existed, ranging from personal to economic and cultural, links that will continue to exist and develop. Naturally, some changes, democratization among the first, should occur as a precondition for development of better relations – which should this time be founded on mutual interests, rather than on some pan-Slavic illusions or 'brotherhood and unity'. The very moment when interest becomes a basis for development of good neighbouring relations, these two countries will demonstrate their readiness for establishment of European type relations.

Changes of regime in Zagreb and Belgrade have opened the door for a proper normalization of bilateral relations. The Stability Pact has also given a chance for wider contacts in all areas, but still owing to the recent traumas coming from the war, one should not push too fast for better relations. They have to come gradually as a result of a common interest of both sides parallel with settling of some still open issues: the question of legacy of former state, official Serbian apology for the war in Croatia, strict abeyance of Dayton for both countries and so on.

Disputes between Croatia and Slovenia, although not of considerable volume, are felt in bilateral relations of the two countries. The current demarcation in the Bay of Piran is not satisfactory to Slovenia, and represents an issue generating some other, sharper, political accents occasionally to be heard on both sides. It is to be believed that this question can be solved relatively easily, as well as the problems connected to the Krško nuclear plant and to the restitution to Croatian clients of the Ljubljanska Banka. It is obvious that a creation of a better political climate, as well as the toning-down of the positions of both countries would contribute to overcoming these problems. But even at this point, these issues are not of such a nature that could lead to some significant tensions in the area.

The Macedonian–Greek dispute has emerged as a consequence of the collapse of Yugoslavia and the creation of an independent Macedonian state. The Greek side has immediately rejected Macedonian statements about a large number of Macedonians living in Greece, and has at the same time found – in the Macedonian flag, as well as in some constitutional provisions dealing with the protection of Macedonians abroad – justification for resolute Greek rejections of the new state. Analysing the creation of Macedonia foremostly through a prism of Greek–Turkish relations, one of the more serious reasons for Greek concern was a question of further development of Macedonian–Turkish relations. Any new foothold of Turkey in the Balkans is something that the Greek state would like to prevent at any cost.[13] But, the initial mobilization of national charge on both sides gradually gave way to easing of tensions. Greece has finally lifted the blockade, by which Macedonia was completely cut-off in the south; an agreement on changes to be made on the Macedonian national flag and some provisions of the Constitution was reached, while the question of the official name – the Republic of Macedonia – remains open.

Macedonian–Bulgarian relations are also very complex. Although Bulgaria was the first country to recognize independent Macedonia, it does not recognize the existence of the Macedonian nation, opening a possibility for claiming that Macedonians are actually Bulgarians. This could, in some other circumstances, result in some additional dangers for

Macedonia, particularly in situations where Macedonia would become absorbed in some internal problems (for example, an attempt of separation of western parts of Macedonia populated mostly by Albanian minority). But, as the international community is firmly present in Macedonia, with the goal of establishing an integral peace in the whole area, it is apparent that such Bulgarian aspirations could not succeed. Besides, Bulgaria also sees its future within the Europe, therefore the EU would have sufficient resources to eliminate this dispute with minimal effort.

Potential Points of Crisis

If the above cluster of new disputes contains issues that are not producing any serious destabilization, especially after the NATO action in Yugoslavia, a set of open questions and potential new points of crisis looks quite different.

Among these, the questions related to the survival of Bosnia-Herzegovina are dominant. The formula of one state, two entities and three nations should satisfy all existing interests in the best and most democratic manner. Nevertheless, if one tried to imagine such a development in some other environment, and having in mind the recent war in Bosnia-Herzegovina, as well as other historical experiences, then such an outcome might become very questionable.[14] Optimists, who believe that after the war and all the suffering, a certain critical mass of Bosnians who support the peace, development and stability has been created after all, find that the presence of the international community on the ground for a long time is a crucial component of future stability.

If the forces of the international community, with their political, military and economic engagement remain present in Bosnia-Herzegovina long enough, then it could be expected that the above formula would work. In such a case the return of refugees and displaced persons could be achieved; the same holds for the creation of pre-conditions for a multi-cultural existence and certain mutual prosperity. Of course, the key question is how long? Three or five years would not be long enough, while a decade or two should be optimal.

In another, extremely pessimistic alternative, all forementioned hypotheses would fall apart if this time period is shortened, or if the international community is rapidly withdrawn from Bosnia-Herzegovina. In that case the three-sided formula would dissolve, and conflicts over the rights to return, over the territory, revenge and similar would begin, with all sides seeking allies for their cause.

For the past ten years FR Yugoslavia has been the most serious challenge to the Balkan security, and still remains the biggest open question. FR Yugoslavia, in the period after Milosevic, is having lot of problems on all sides. Montenegro is on the brink of separation, Kosovo can be practically written-of for Serbia, Sandzak is demanding autonomy. The same may be said for the Hungarians who were also supported by some nationalistic political forces from Hungary in their aspirations for a full secession from Yugoslavia. Milosevic's regime, which was only capable of surviving and was feeding itself on crisis and which, at the same time, lost every war it initiated, created risks for the very territorial survival of FR Yugoslavia.

However, the Montenegran proposal of creating an alliance of two independent and internationally recognized states – Montenegro and Serbia – was not endorsed either in Washington, nor in Western Europe, nor in Moscow. Kosovo is also still a part of Yugoslavia, and assurances are given that it will remain so. Sandzak and Vojvodina could be granted some level of autonomy, but it would be difficult to envisage the international community supporting their full secession from FR Yugoslavia. It is expected that within a democratic Yugoslavia problems related to the union with Montenegro, as well as the autonomy of the multi-ethnic Kosovo, Sandzak and Vojvodina could be solved. By this, the question of changing borders would be avoided, since no one is keen on opening it.

The question remains what are the forces that should carry-on these democratic changes and open the doors for democratization? It is also apparent that such a democratization would not be limited to Serbian borders, but rather should spread all over the region in a form of a universal process of building-up of civil society, elimination of war criminals, respect of human and minority rights and acceptance of European codes of behaviour. Even if we are getting closer to such solutions, the process is too slow.

Territorial and minority issues, unless a high level of democratization and Europeanization of the Balkans is achieved, will continue to present a significant problem in these areas, and a constant challenge to security. Not a single territorial or minority question in the Balkans has been completely solved so far, and following the war on Kosovo it is obvious that it will be even more difficult to solve them.

The question of Albanians who live in Albania as well as in Kosovo, Montenegro, Serbia, Macedonia and Greece, remains unsolved. Will it be enough to guarantee the human and minority rights in this case, or should a creation of a unique Albania be enabled?

Milosevic's policy has further complicated the Serbian question. That policy resulted in a large number of Serbian refugees from Croatia, Bosnia and Herzegovina and Kosovo, who were practically forced to live in one country. Their return is slow and in many cases questionable, which leaves the question open. Maybe a universal Europeanization of the Balkans is the only solution to this question as well. The same can be applied to the Macedonian national question, since some Macedonians live in Bulgaria and Greece. For the advocates of small nation-states, the Muslim question should also be put on the agenda, since a large number of Muslims live outside of Bosnia and Herzegovina (Sandzak).

Therefore, when listing all these potential challenges to security, it must be concluded that within the present circumstances it is easier and, at the same time, more difficult to solve these issues. It is easier since SEE has ceased to depend exclusively on the actions of the Balkan actors and their 'ways' of solving problems; and more difficult because in the 1990s there was so much bloodshed and suffering in this area that is difficult to ignore or forget. Therefore, all these challenges may be controlled only by careful acting of the international community, its efforts on understanding both historical and present relations, and its willingness and commitment to keep its presence in the area for a longer time. As long as the forces of the international community are stationed in the Balkans it would be hard to imagine any outbreaks of conflict. This is, certainly, encouraging, but at the same time it is burdening the international community with many obligations regarding the further development of this part of Europe.

New Challenges to Security

Basically, the new challenges to the security in this area arise from the geostrategic position of Southeastern Europe, from a permanent lack of resources needed for the organization of a modern and efficient military force, from the inexistence of stronger bilateral and/or multilateral alliances (apart from the Partnership for Peace) and from attempts to create pre-conditions for NATO membership, as soon as possible.

This projection is also the basis on which almost all SEE countries, with the exception of former Milosevic's Yugoslavia, see their future security – which should also guarantee as fast as possible inclusion of the whole region into the European and transatlantic structures.

Along with these classical issues that represent threats to the security, or traditional challenges that are connected to the deployment and use of military force, there are also new forms of challenges emerging. The transition from the socialist system to a capitalist one, the accelerated opening of the whole area of Eastern Europe, as well as the activities of organized criminal forces, have all led to the situation in which Southeastern Europe is also becoming replete with different kinds of new challenges to security. New immigration patterns, terrorism, arms and drugs trafficking, prostitution and the enormous spread of organized crime, are parts of such non-traditional challenges that are to be felt more and more.

New immigration patterns present a significant issue in these areas which are situated at the cross-roads of several regions (East European, Russian, Balkan, Middle Eastern) and where practically every country experiences problems connected to uncontrolled immigration. Immigration is characterized by a number of social and economic problems. Large profits are being earned on 'smuggling' people from various countries, where organized groups have already been created for conducting such activities. Some immigrants are being used as a cheap labour force or for prostitution. In a situation where all countries of the region lack the financial means for effective border controls, possibilities for new immigration channels are being opened.

Terrorism has its long-existing roots, especially in the Balkans, and may easily find strongholds in national and ethnic conflicts. Minority groups, if unsatisfied with their status, or strengthened nationalistic movements (as was the case with the Serb rebellion in Croatia) may easily become prey for the organizers of terrorist activities.

But along with that situation there is always a question of outside support which makes the fight against terrorism even more difficult. Unsolved national questions may always serve well as the basis for inclusion of outside elements, either connected to some state, or to some groups of organized crime.

Arms and drugs trafficking has been growing rapidly since the Cold War system of relations was dissolved. The geographic location of this area, as well as the wars fought in the territories of former Yugoslavia, have all created an opportunity to draw extra profits from trading with arms. The arms embargo, which has proven itself, for the n-th time, as inefficient, has only increased the price of arms that were supplied to all warring sides. In that way, huge extra profits were made, and regardless of the fact that the wars are over, the whole Southeastern Europe will continue to feel the consequences for some time to come. Simultaneously with the arms trafficking, channels for drugs have been opened. In many cases channels for drug trafficking were in place in this area even before the wars of the 1990s, as part of transit routes across Southeast Europe, but a large part of its increase can be linked directly to these wars. Southeastern Europe has become a region of local producers, international trafficking routes, as well as of increasing number of domestic users – addicts.

A wave of prostitution that has swept the area of Southeastern Europe can also be linked to the collapse of the socialist system in the East, to the new freedom of movement and travel, to transitional crisis and failures, and to the wars in former Yugoslavia. Large numbers of prostitutes from the East, mostly from Ukraine, Russia and Romania, in their efforts to get to the West, stay in these areas for some time. In an environment of unregulated social relations, there is a possibility of blackmail and extortion. Many women become victims of organized crime and merciless exploitation. It is believed that at this moment there are over 1,000 prostitutes in Bosnia-Herzegovina, mostly from the East, who are generating profits for all kinds of criminals, as well as for some corrupted government officials.

The spreading and strengthening of the forces of organized crime is certainly one of the most significant security risks in Southeastern Europe. At the same time, crime represents the principal threat to political stability and economic development. Exploiting the chaos, insecurity, lack of proper organization and non-existence of the rule of law, organized crime groups have established their strongholds in Southeastern Europe, and have created links with highly ranked political officials and parts of the military establishments. Such relations, in the times of very slow transitional processes, result in an emergence of special interest groups, strengthen the polarization of internal forces and lead to a situation which constantly undermines the confidence of citizens in the possibility of establishment of the rule of law principles.

Different national mobs (Russian, Turkish, Italian, Albanian and Serbian) are able to find and agree on mutual interests relatively easily and have sufficient space for their activities. To a large extent the Turkish mob controls the area of Bulgaria and partly Macedonia, the Russian mob was traditionally strong in Bulgaria and today is strongest in Serbia, Italian mobs work in Montenegro and Albania, while Albanian organized crime becomes more and more international with a diversified network stretching from Albania and Kosovo to Western Europe. Arms and drugs trafficking, gambling, money laundering, purchase of real estate, attempts in sale of nuclear technology and materials, have all flourished during the war times, especially in the territories of former Yugoslavia.

The events of 1996–97 in Albania led to an enormous growth in the Albanian mob, which presently appears almost stronger than the state authorities. Prostitution, arms and drugs trafficking, tobacco contraband, transport of immigrants, and oil trade are just some of Albanian mob businesses, which have already spread in the direction of Kosovo. This represents a threat of Kosovo becoming completely included in the territory controlled by Albanian mafia which would make the process of resolving the Kosovo problem even more difficult.

Such activities conducted by the groups of organized crime have already achieved a multi-ethnic character, and with some exceptions, the area of their operation is the whole of Southeastern Europe. By eliminating the mechanisms of state control and protection, the mob is representing one of the largest sources of overall crime and corruption which undermines domestic social relations, impairs the possibility of foreign investment, and of economic growth and institutional development of democratic forms of government throughout the area.

The forms of cooperation among the states of the region in fighting against crime have been bilateral or through Interpol, but that is not sufficient. Romania has, for example, initiated the creation of a centre for research and fight against organized crime, Bulgaria has launched a campaign against crime and corruption, and the international community is advocating for the same to be done in Bosnia-Herzegovina. Separate actions of the same sort can be detected in other countries as well. But all this combined has a very limited effect on eliminating crime. It is obvious that SEE countries are facing a completely new situation, that is, acute non-traditional challenges to security in Southeastern Europe. Although it could be argued that this is a development characteristic of all post-socialist societies, it must be added that in Southeastern Europe, owing to the recent wars in the region, the situation is much more complex. What must be increasingly exercised is a firm standing and action of state agencies against joint activities of political officials and organized crime, creation of pre-conditions for joint activity on a regional level and even joint police forces; fastest possible inclusion of Southeastern Europe into existing European systems that would help the stabilization of the area and, at the same time, add to elimination of all those forms of corruption and crime which have become one of the characteristics of the region.

If security of this region would be compared with the situation in some other parts of Europe, it can be stated with certainty that the challenges to security will continue to have their domestic, as well as international sources. Modernizing forces, if they truly aspire towards Europe, must become much more dynamic and engaged. Only by such systematic efforts will it be possible to overcome the existing situation and create the necessary pre-conditions for integration of SEE into Europe.

SOUTHEASTERN EUROPE AS A PART OF EUROPEAN ARCHITECTURE

Inclusion into European security architecture[15] is seen in Southeast Europe as a great opportunity for creation of a new situation in this area. This especially for the countries that are not NATO members and which are trying to get closer to Euro-Atlantic institutions and to achieve their major goals through the currently developing European security network.

Greece, as both EU and NATO member, acts as a principal generator of new European ideas and initiatives aimed at closer collaboration and further development in the region, while Turkey is seeking to capitalize on the present favourable situation and its NATO membership to achieve full EU membership. Bulgaria and Romania are strictly holding to the Partnership for Peace, are active in Balkans cooperation and are trying to fulfil their obligations for EU accession in full. Besides this, both countries, and especially Romania, wish to create an impression that they belong to the group of countries that may achieve full NATO membership during the next wave of NATO enlagement.

Most problematic relations with the new European architecture may be found in the Western Balkans. The so-called unstable stability is a result of the post-war situation and firm presence of international forces in this region. At the same time, the principal cause, and the generator of instabilities in SEE, that is Federal Republic of Yugoslavia after Milosevic still radiates new threats and challenges, either those linked to its own parts (Montenegro, Sandzak, Vojvodina, Kosovo), or those relating to the unstable and very turbulent internal political situation in Serbia. This creates a situation where a key issue, such as security, is tied to the possibility of controlling events in Serbia and to the particular moves the new regime might make in some other parts: Montenegro and Kosovo. Combined with the unstable situation in Albania, such a development might create additional challenges for this area of the Balkans; there might emerge an effect on the fragile Macedonian stability, which is very sensitive to the developments in the neighbourhood.

If Yugoslavia is defined as the centre of the crisis and instability, then it is understandable that the initiative for development of national security systems that would lean on European security architecture is being launched by the countries surrounding it. Slovenia has participated in the Partnership for Peace for some time now, and is hoping to be among the first countries to join NATO. Croatia's new policy has led the country into the Partnership for Peace and is hoping to maintain such a tempo, seeing NATO membership as its strategic goal as well. Both Macedonia and Albania are participating in the Partnership for Peace. Bosnia-Herzegovina, a country consisting of two entities, is undergoing a phase of strong international efforts aimed at decreasing its military forces, and at the same time, through bringing closer together all three national components (Croatian, Serbian and Bosnian), to build a unique military that could then very soon be included in the Partnership for Peace. Taking the present situation into account, the efforts of all these countries to accelerate the accession to NATO and to tie their security to a wider European security architecture, can be clearly seen in every political document dealing with foreign and security policy.[16]

Association, stability and cooperative security are nowadays the most commonly used terms in SEE. Each of those reflects outside views on the region, but also the striving of these countries to achieve stability through a faster association, that could in turn lead to cooperative security. But after experiencing recent wars, ethnic cleansing, waves of refugees and economic hardship, all these countries realize that they are unable to build a cooperative security through their joint actions alone; rather that it has to be supported by outside factors.

Because of existing difficulties, as well as a constant danger that unpredictable developments might result in new instabilities, the countries of the so-called Western Balkans are committing themselves differently to some institutional structures of the new European security. They are actively participating in the OSCE but without any illusions on the significance of this mechanism, especially since it was seen acting on the ground. Much more importance is being paid to linkages with Euro-Atlantic institutions, signifying accession to EU and NATO, and thus becoming a part of well developed European space. Because of this, relatively little attention is being paid to the issue of relations between NATO and the WEU, or to the development of the EU's CSFP. In a desire to find a mode for leaving the Western Balkans behind, seen as a necessary nuisance, North and East Balkans countries are trying to make their own way to Europe as soon as possible. This makes clear that even attempts on creating some forms of regional security, that would be a cooperative one, at this moment, would have very slim chances of succeeding. Almost all of these countries have seen in Yugoslavia a danger, or threat to their own security, and have been aware of the fact that their forces, even if combined with forces of some other countries from Southeastern Europe, could not guarantee their security in the case of new instabilities. Therefore, accession to Euro-Atlantic institutions is seen as a concrete answer to the question of security.

The forms of regional security that would call for creation of a free trade zone in the territories of the former Yugoslavia, opening channels for communication and exchange of ideas, people and capital, do not receive any support for the time being. This very important part of cooperative security is seen as something that is being forced upon these countries from abroad and that is not sufficient to satisfy the needs of the majority of countries. On top of this, there is also a fear that such collective approach could slow down the progress of some countries on their way towards Euro-Atlantic structures. In addition, in Croatia, for example, the fear that through such linkages, allegedly, some new form of Yugoslavia could be recreated is still present.[17]

Viewed in that perspective, it could be concluded that the international community may advocate regional cooperation as a concrete proof of the ability of SEE countries for closer approach to Europe, while the countries of the region will independently, or maybe through some bilateral efforts, try to break out from such frames and find possibilities for faster accession to Europe.[18] Applying the instruments available, especially its military presence, the international community, foremostly the EU countries, will be the ones dictating the direction and the tempo of accession to Europe. Within this, the approach to the architecture of European security will be conditioned primarily on assessments of behaviour of individual countries of the region and on their contribution to the development of regional relations.[19]

The example of 'new' Croatia may be used as a significant illustration of possible changes, and of the ability of international community to rapidly and swiftly change its views in case of positive democratic developments. This is certainly the most important international value of changes in Croatia, changes that should show to other SEE countries all the possibilities that would open to them as well if they follow this path. Even the developments of 2000 in Serbia were partly influenced by the Croatian example and how easy it was to make a first step in transition of regime.

The unstable stability that has emerged in the areas of Southeastern Europe, controlled by the international military force, is certainly better then wars and ethnic cleansing. But, since this process is unfinished, it is apparent that some time will elapse before SEE countries access European architecture. Without a definite solution of the Yugoslav question, which is connected to the emergence of the new democratic regime in Belgrade, there are no chances for resolving a potential crisis, nor for development of some cooperative regional security that could lead the whole region to Europe.

To conclude, one could expect:

- gradual changes toward democracy in SEE and slow start of regional cooperation leading toward a cooperative security;
- for all countries in SEE, Euro-Atlantic integration is a primary aim; in Belgrade hopefully the new regime will look for a way out also in that direction;
- because of war memories, improvements in the so-called Western Balkans area will be not easy and it will need time;
- the presence of international forces will be for some time very much needed and with its help some regional projects connected with European security could be expanded;
- after the stabilization and normalization of regional relations one could envisage the time when the whole area of SEE will be in the European security architecture, sharing stability with all other European countries.

NOTES

1. H. Bull (1997): *The Anarchical Society*, London, p.18.
2. For an analysis of this concept of security see: B. Buzan (1991): *People, States and Fear, An Agenda for International Security in the Post-Cold War Europe*, 2nd edn, Wheatshead.
3. P.R. Magocsi (1998): *Historical Atlas of East Central Europe*, London, p. 4.
4. Ibid.
5. In its regional approach EU is mentioning the following countries: Albania, Croatia, Bosnia-Herzegovina, Yugoslavia and Macedonia. The same group of countries is also defined as Western Balkans. The Institute for Security Studies of WEU includes in the term Southeastern Europe the following countries: Bulgaria, Romania, Albania and the countries from ex-Yugoslavia (Croatia, Bosnia-Herzegovina, Macedonia, Serbia and Montenegro). G. Lenci and L. Martin (1996), pp.10–11.
6. For a wider explanation see: R. Vukadinovic (1997), pp.18–19.
7. Officially Turkey adds to these the question of the Turkish minority in the Trakia region arguing that the Greeks do not recognize the ethnic identity of over 150,000 Turks.
8. President Clinton during a conversation with journalists in Sarajevo, *Herald Tribune*, 9 August 1999.
9. N. Dobrkovie (2000): 'Political Perspectives of the Federal Republic of Yugoslavia – Disintegration vs. Integration', in *Zur Problematik der Stabilisierung des Westbalkans*, Wien, pp.83–5.
10. For more on that, see: *Kosovo and NATO: Impending Challenges*, Washington, 1999.
11. Ts. Tsvetkov (1999), p.33.

12. A. Agh (1998): *The Politics of Central Europe*, London, p.157.
13. D. Triantaphyllou, 'The Greek Approach in the Balkans', *The Southeast European Yearbook 1997–1998*, Athens, pp.212–14.
14. For example, see: M.O. Hanion, 'Bosnia: Better Left Partitioned', *Washington Post*, 10 April 1997; H.A. Kissinger, 'Limits to What U.S. Can Do in Bosnia', *Washington Post*, 22 September 1977; J.J. Mearsheimer, 'The Only Exit From Bosnia', *New York Times*, 7 October 1997; R.N. Haas (1997): *The Reluctant Sheriff: The United States after the Cold War*, New York, pp.124–5.
15. The concept of security architecture has various meanings. We understand this as a 'set of institutions which fulfil a security function, and the way in which their mutual relations are arranged'. W. Kostecki (1996): *Europe after the Cold War: The Security Complex Theory*, Warsaw, pp.166–7.
16. Even representatives of the Serbian new regime are advocating the possibility for Serbia to enter soon PfP.
17. This was a traditional fear of Tudjman which is deeply rooted not only in the ranks of Croatian Democratic Union but is also shared among other Croatian political parties.
18. R. Vukadinovic (1999): *Sigurnost na jugoistoku Europe*, Varazdin, pp.174–5.
19. *Security and Reconstruction of Southeastern Europe*, Sofia, 2000, pp.24–7.

REFERENCES

Heuberger, V., H. Riegler and H. Vidovic, eds. (1999): *At the Crossroads: Disaster or Normalization?, The Yugoslav Successor States in the 1990s*, Frankfurt am Main.
Bezopasnost Rossii i Cernomorskij Region, Moskva 1997.
Sopta, M. (1997): *Bosnia and Herzegovina Beyond Dayton*, Zagreb.
Brzezinski, Z. (1997): *The Grand Chessboard: American Primacy and Its Geostrategic Imperatives*, New York.
Clement, S. (1997): *Conflict Prevention in the Balkans: Case Studies of Kosovo and FRY Macedonia*, Paris.
Frolov, A.A. (1994): *Vzglijady i koncepcii regionalnoj bezopasnosti v SSSR i Rossii*, Moskva.
Gnessotto, N. (1994): *Lessons of Yugoslavia*, Paris.
Guskova, J. (1996): *Jugoslavenska kriza i Rusija*.
Kosovo, mezdunarodnye aspekty krizisa (1999): Moskva.
Larrabee, F.S. (1993): *East European Security After the Cold War*, Santa Monica: RAND.
Larrabee, F.S. (1996): *The Balkans*, Santa Monica: RAND.
Larrabee, F.S. and Th.W. Karasik (1997): *Foreign and Security Policy Decision Making Under Yeltsin*, Washington.
Lenci, G. and L. Martin (1996): *The European Security Space*, Paris.
Petkovic, R. (1998): *XX vek na Balkanu: Versaj-Jalta-Dejton*, Beograd.
Prins, G. (1999): *European Horizons of Diplomatic Military Operations*, London.
Shoup, P. and G.W. Hoffman, eds (1990): *Problems of Balkan Security: Southeastern Europe in the 1990s*, Washington.
Security and Reconstruction of Southeastern Europe, (2000), Sofia
Cotey, A., ed. (1999): *Subregional Cooperation in the New Europe: Building Security, Preosperity and Solidarity from the Barents to the Black Sea*, New York.
Larrabee, F.S., ed. (1994): *The Volatile Powder Keg. Balkan Security After The Cold War*, Washington.
Ullman, R., ed. (1996): *The World and Yugoslavia's Wars*, New York.
Tsvetkov, Ts. (1999): *Bulgarian Security Policy: Alternatives and Choice*, Groningen.
Valinakis, Y. (1994): *Greece's Security in the Post Cold War Era*, Ebenhausen.
Vukadinovic, R. (1991): *The Break up of Yugoslavia: Threats and Challenges*, The Hague.

Vukadinovic, R. (1978); *The Mediterraean between War and Peace*, Zagreb-Beograd.
Vukadinovic, R. (1992): *Le fin de la Yugoslavie et Instabilite Balkanique*, Paris.
Vukadinovic, R. (1994): *In Search of Security for the New Balkans*, Vienna.
Vukadinovic, R. (1997): *Postkomunisticki izazovi europskoj sigurnosti od Baltika do Jadrana*, Mostar.
Zamfirescu, E. (1996): *Mapping Central Europe*, The Hague.

The Albanian Question in the Aftermath of the War: A Proposal to Break the Status Deadlock

EVANGELOS KOFOS

WAR AIMS AND ALBANIAN ASPIRATIONS

The conclusion of the military operations, in June 1999, terminated the age-old Albanian–Yugoslav/Serbian conflict for control of Kosovo. Simultaneously, it invigorated Albanian nationalism. In a very short time, it became evident that this new powerful force aspired at a major role in shaping developments in a wider area, traditionally referred to by Albanian nationalists as the 'Albanian space'.[1]

When, early in 1999, the United States and NATO took the decision to intervene militarily in order to break the diplomatic impasse over Kosovo, they did not anticipate that they would unleash an equally uncontrollable force in the region. Although euphemistically they had termed their military engagement a 'humanitarian operation' for the protection of the hard pressed Kosovar Albanians, they had also assigned themselves a dual task: a political one, aiming at the curtailment of Serbian rule over the province, and a punitive one, targeting the downfall of the Milosevic regime and the personal demise of its leader. This is clearly documented in certain clauses of the pre-war Rambouillet draft agreement, the wartime indictment for war crimes of Milosevic, and the contents of the UN Security Council resolution 1244/1999, which acquired the strength of a peace treaty codifying the terms of the victors.

Different was the Albanians' perception of the war. To them, the military engagement appeared as the culminating phase of their century-old contest with the Yugoslavs/Serbs for control of the land of Kosovo, the hearth of the Albanian national movement of the latter part of the nineteenth century. As such, it was their national liberation struggle. By their ten-year old passive resistance under the leadership of Ibrahim Rugova, by their armed insurrection, led by UCK and joined by Albanians from other regions of the 'Albanian space', by their sacrifices and skill, but also by the folly of their adversaries, they had successfully engineered the involvement of the international community to their side to win the war.

In seeking redress for a decade of gross human rights violations, the Kosovar Albanian fighters had also set for themselves a twin objective: to liberate Kosovo from Serbian rule and to establish a national Albanian independent Kosovo republic. Submerged under the publicity focusing on the war goals, was the Albanians' anticipation that success in Kosovo might clear the way for the redemption, in one way or another, of fellow Albanians living in adjacent regions and countries.

What followed in the spring and summer of 1999, was a strange fusion of the objectives of the two war partners, US/NATO and UCK, to force the Serbs out of Kosovo. While the international partner endeavoured to terminate Serbian administration and secure for the Albanians a self-ruled, multi-ethnic international protectorate, the UCK reverted to the time-tested tactics of the victor, so popular in the history of the region, of evicting the defeated 'enemy' from the contested land.[2] With hindsight, it can now be assessed that in the spring/summer of 1999, two wars had been fought over Kosovo, each aiming at its own twin targets. Nevertheless, at the conclusion of the military operations, despite the forced withdrawal of the Serbian military and civilian personnel and the removal of all vestiges of Serbian government institutions, neither of the two war partners had fulfilled its objectives. The US and NATO, now operating under a UN umbrella, were compelled to divide their energy between two important but contradictory goals: on the one hand, to achieve the reconstruction of Kosovo and promote stability throughout the war-ridden Western Balkans and, on the other, to secure the destruction of the Milosevic regime and the punishment of its leader. As for the Albanian nationalists, they soon came to realize that Kosovo's independence, not to speak of 'Greater Albania' visions, would not be offered on a plate.

ILLS OF POST-WAR MANAGEMENT

Understandably, these two variants of war aims, deeply affected the post-war behaviour and the perceptions of peacemaking by the two war partners. The US/NATO actions and subsequent initiatives were legitimized by the United Nations as undertakings of the international community, rendering Kosovo a virtual international protectorate. Thus, one of the partners – now, the 'international community' through KFOR and UNMIK – found itself pursuing peacemaking and stability operations, while continuing 'its war' against Milosevic Serbia. This oxymoron scheme of contradictory war and peace aims, handicapped an equidistant approach toward all the inhabitants of the protectorate. More important, it conveyed the wrong message to the Albanians that the international community was in Kosovo as 'liberator', not as arbiter mediating between the two warring parties. On their part, Albanian Kosovars expected the US and NATO to offer their support to their claim for an independent status and, possibly, to take a benevolent view of Albanian aspirations in the adjacent regions of southeast Serbia and FYROM.

Managing the war-ridden Kosovo proved a task of enormous difficulties for the international community. With the establishment of the interim UN/NATO protectorate, international agencies, foreign governments and NGOs sought to lay down the foundations and the framework of a viable democratic society. During the initial transitional period, there were serious obstacles of control and authority to be overcome, that need not be addressed in this chapter. The rapid and total removal of the Yugoslav administrative edifice had created a critical vacuum. The international military and civilian authorities were not able to fill it for various reasons: they were handicapped by insufficient knowledge of the local terrain, by a dearth of necessary equipment and personnel, by insufficient authority, if not the will to address vital political and security problems. As a consequence, it was no surprise that they showed considerable inertness in enforcing from the beginning a scrupulous observance of law and order for all the inhabitants of the province, irrespective of creed and ethnic background. Thus, the road was left open for unruly, vengeful and, at times, adventurist Albanian elements to enforce their own 'law' in the land. The mass exodus of Serbs, Roma and other ethnic groups was a foregone consequence. Along with it, the ambition to build a multi-ethnic society was placed in jeopardy.[3]

A second obstacle was the lack of communication between the international authorities of Kosovo and the Belgrade government, while Milosevic was in power. During the critical initial stages of the setting up of the protectorate, the exclusion of the Serbian factor from developments in the region, both inside and in the periphery of Kosovo, acted adversely in avoiding further calamities. This malignancy did not augur well, either for the survival of the Serbian minority within a multi-ethnic society, or for the prospects of a negotiated settlement. In a way, it explains the inability, or rather the unwillingness, of leading international actors to lay out a roadmap for the future status of the region. Almost fatalistically, they appeared resigned to operating an interim *de facto* international protectorate which had retained the *de jure* status of a province of the Republic of Serbia within the Federal Republic of Yugoslavia. It is interesting to note that even after the October–November 2000 electoral defeat and removal of Milosevic from the political scene in Belgrade, the future status of Kosovo remained in limbo. Under the circumstances, it was a foregone conclusion that the task of resolving the Kosovo imbroglio would once again attract the attention of militant Albanian nationalists.

Indeed, the other partner, the Kosovar Albanians, after rejoicing at their 'liberation' from Serbian rule, they came to realize that the removal of Serbian administration and military presence from the territory did not automatically signal the commencement of the process toward independence. Thus, they were compelled to pursue to the end the targets they had set for their 'own war'. To nationalist Kosovars, not only the eviction of the Serbian administration but also of the Serbian population as a whole could guarantee their undisputed control in a future independent Kosovo.[4]

Initially, acts of terrorism against the Serbs and other minorities could be explained – but not justified – as a reaction and revenge for ills suffered at the hands of the Serbian civilian authorities, police and paramilitary forces. Top of the list of Albanian grievances were the years of suffering under an oppressive, totalitarian Serbian regime, the forced evictions of hundreds of thousands of Kosovar Albanians during the war, the systematic destruction and looting of their property and a considerable loss of Albanian lives. Nevertheless, the fact that two years after the end of the war such acts continued to target individuals and entire localities which had not been implicated in wrong doings against Kosovar Albanians, can hardly qualify as acts of revenge; more so, since they were directed collectively against the persons, properties and even the religious and national shrines of all the non-Albanian communities in the territory.

This 'reverse ethnic cleansing' certainly resulted in a significant shrinkage of the Serb, Roma and other non-Albanian groups. In the end, however, it proved counterproductive. The remaining Serbs found refuge in self-protected enclaves, thus, sustaining a claim for a future 'cantonization', an anathema to Albanian nationalist aspirations. Furthermore, it taxed considerably the reservoir of pro-Albanian sentiment among international observers and world public opinion. The 'ugly Albanian' was gradually replacing the 'ugly Serb' as the outcast of the Balkan region.

FROM THE KOSOVO PROBLEM TO THE ALBANIAN QUESTION

The two-dimensional Kosovo war effort had also a third, 'hidden' goal which transcended the borders of Kosovo: the vision of 'Greater Albania'. It referred to the yearning of all Albanians, living dispersed and divided into five Balkan lands that, one day, they may be united under the same national state roof. This was an aspiration reminiscent of similar national projects promoted by almost all the Balkan peoples during their drive for national emancipation and unification in the nineteenth and early twentieth centuries. It is true that during Hodxa's communist regime, the Albanians of Albania had been treated to an overdose of nationalism. But that was of a xenophobic rather than the expansionist variety. With the collapse, however, of the communist regime, the disintegration of the SFR of Yugoslavia and the miserable treatment of fellow Albanians in Kosovo, an irredentist nationalism resurfaced. In the early 1990s, the 'Greater Albanian' ideology became popular in the Republic of Albania and found its way even in revised school textbooks.[5]

A quasi codification of Albanian nationalist visions was undertaken by the Academy of Sciences of Albania in its brochure, 'Platform for the Solution of the National Albanian Question', which was published in Tirana, on 20 October 1998. Official Albanians tried to distance themselves from its contents, but failed to disclaim it publicly.[6] The fact that its circulation coincided with the commencement of the guerrilla activity of the then 'phantom' UCK, gave rise to suspicions of interlocking channels of irredentist nationalism between nationalists in the Republic of Albania and the Yugoslav province of Kosovo.

During these years, the first priority for the majority Albanians in Kosovo was to combat Serbian administrative oppressive policies by means of a passive resistance movement and a clandestine parallel system of administration. Gradually, the Kosovars' plight attracted the attention and support of the international community. When the crisis assumed the form of an armed confrontation with the Serbian army, the Kosovars wisely exercised restraint in projecting irredentist aspirations outside the confines of Kosovo.[7]

Irrespective of the variety of tactics promoting the national vision, Albanian nationalists throughout the 'Albanian space', shared a common nationalist triptych: that history had been unjust to the Albanian nation by leaving more than half of the Albanians and the 'Albanian lands' under foreign rule in neighbouring states; that the Albanians had the right to seek their national independence and/or unification, exactly as the other Balkan peoples had achieved their own; that if, under current European realities, 'Greater Albania' was not feasible, then the 'unification' of the Albanians could come about by alternate routes, not necessarily territorial ones. On this third point, more concrete views began to be shaped after the Kosovo war.

THE EVOLUTION OF THE ALBANIAN QUESTION THROUGHOUT THE 'ALBANIAN SPACE'

The Republic of Albania

Since the emergence of an independent Albanian state in the early twentieth century, and until the outbreak of the war in Kosovo, no Albanian would contest that the Republic of Albania, the only independent component of the 'Albanian space', remained the metropolis of the Albanian nation. Nevertheless, beset as it was by insufficiently developed institutions, social upheavals, damaging political and clan cleavages, and elementary economic structures, its leadership position gradually began to erode. The Kosovo war seriously challenged the Republic's ambition to appear as a twenty-first century Albanian 'Piedmont'. The establishment of the interim international protectorate in Kosovo, which was on the road of attaining self-rule, had a negative and a positive impact on Tirana's 'patriarchical' role.

On the positive side, the mass entry of almost half a million Kosovar refugees and the hospitality extended to them not only in Albanian camps but with Albanian families as well, strengthened community ties and gave tangible credence to feelings of common nationhood and brotherhood. Foreign observers at the time noticed the frequent references among refugees of words and phrases such as 'brothers', the 'same blood', 'same family', 'one nation', and so on.[8] Furthermore, the essential truth which emerged from this osmosis among fellow Albanians, long divided by impregnable borders, revealed a newly discovered strength and pride in themselves. Although borders still existed, and conditions differed from region to region, Albanians throughout the 'Albanian space' came to realize that together they constituted an important regional player who could not be ignored. These changes had also a profound effect in shaping a modern version of the Albanian national question.

On the negative side was the realization, particularly among Kosovar refugees, that the social and economic fabric of Albania, particularly in the underdeveloped rural border areas of the north, was below those of Kosovo which had enjoyed much higher standards of living within former Yugoslavia. The fact that the refugees chose to return to their devastated towns and villages, as soon as the fighting stopped, was attributed, to a considerable degree, to these adverse parallelisms. On returning to Kosovo, new and old elites in the Kosovar political establishment were taking in their own hands their future, unchaperoned by Tirana. Moreover, as self-governing institutions began to shape, it was evident that a new Albanian political centre was emerging from the ashes of the former Yugoslav Autonomous Province of Kosovo.

With the euphoria of victory, it was only natural that nationalist visions of grandeur were reintroduced in Albanian debates. Tirana gradually came to realize that the old slogan for a 'Greater Albania', unified around the Albanian Republic, appeared antiquated and had a cost. Already, the international community, conscious of the dangers inherent in the nationalist pronouncements of certain Albanian political leaders, had sought to keep the Republic at a distance from developments in Kosovo. Thus, the term 'Greater Albania', reminiscent of the slogan of 'Greater Serbia' and similar grandiose schemes of nineteenth-century Balkan nationalism, was allowed to fade away from the public eye and ear. With the exception of certain nationalists (most prominently, Sali Berisha, whose provocative statements could be interpreted as advocating change of borders), nationalist rhetoric was clad in more politically correct language. Leading politicians, including Rexhep Meidani, adopted a moderate attitude towards nationalism. Socialist Party leader, Fatos Nano, on various occasions, stated that there was no more need to redraw borders, but to 'render them irrelevant'. Ensuring freedom of movement for the Albanians in the Balkans would deflect the yearning for 'Greater Albania'.[9] And Paskal Milo repeatedly claimed that 'Greater Albanian' could be assessed as a historical vision for Albanians, but could not be seen as a political aspiration of our times.[10]

Kosovo, FYROM and Presevo

Similar were the views of moderate Albanians in Kosovo and FYROM. They, too, had realized the high political and national cost they would have to pay, if they attempted to make radical nationalism their political platform. In Kosovo, Ibrahim Rugova, following his victory in the municipal elections of 2000, aligned himself with the radicals' demand for early independence. He was careful not to antagonize the international protectors by publicly endorsing irredentist views or violent actions in the Presevo valley and Western FYROM.

In 1998, the Prime Minister of FYROM, Ljupco Georgievski, introduced a co-habitation scheme of Slav and Albanian Macedonians in government. In response, the head of the Democratic Party of Albanians (DPA), Arben Xhaferi, succeeded in rallying around a moderate line most of the ethnic Albanian politicians. His platform made no reference to changing of borders or to federation schemes in FYROM. In repeated statements and interviews, he indicated that the basic Albanian grievances referred to the ethnocentric perception of the Slav Macedonians for the state, which undermined the multi-ethnic fabric of the country. The Slav Macedonians, in his view, continued to be seized by a proprietor's mentality – 'from the factories to the state itself' – a remnant of the old socialist-communist indoctrination. Basically, however, the stated priorities of the Albanian Macedonians focused on three premises: stability, acceptance of FYROM in the European process and eradication of inequalities between Albanian and Slav Macedonians.[11] Privately, Albanian leaders would confide that inter-ethnic relations were rapidly deteriorating to a situation of 'animosity'.[12] This was made very clear in military clashes around Tetoro in 2001.

Meanwhile, the deteriorating situation in the mostly Albanian-inhabited Presevo valley of SW Serbia, posed a new threat to the delicate stability achieved in FYROM. Early in 2001, armed activity was recorded in FYROM's border regions. Radicals of a so-called 'Albanian Liberation Army' (UCK), attempted to test the recipe, 'success through violence', so adroitly used by their fellow Albanians in Kosovo and Presevo. They sought not only to challenge the mono-ethnic legal structure of the Slav Macedonian state, but also the authority of their own moderate politicians. To judge by their pronouncements, their goal was to force constitutional changes which could lead either to a condominium or a federal structure for the state. Xhaferi had been probably aware of such tendencies within his community, at least a year earlier. He feared that if the ruling Slav Macedonians failed to make concessions to the demands of moderate Albanians, the latter might be overtaken by radical activists.[13] In March 2001, events proved him right.

In 1999, the first skirmishes had occurred between the newly founded 'Liberation Army of Presevo, Medvedja, Bujanovac'(UCPMB) and Serbian police. They were patterned along the old UCK tactics of 1998. In less than a year, the movement escalated into a full scale insurgency. The guerrillas controlled the five-kilometre demilitarized zone on the border with Kosovo and they infiltrated into the neighbouring towns and villages of the Presevo valley. It is important to remember that the decision to commence the armed activity across the border into Serbian territory was taken while Milosevic was firmly entrenched in power in Belgrade. The UCPMB had the support of the old UCK establishment and access to its hidden caches of arms. In an interview with this writer, the former leader of UCK and head of Kosovo Protection Force, Agim Ceku, had no difficulty to reveal that not all UCK arms were turned in. He added that the Kosovars would reciprocate, if necessary, the support they had received from their brethren in Presevo during the war.[14] Initially the UCPMB's stated objective was to protect the Albanians of the region from Serbian excesses. At the time, this was the right argument to a receptive audience in the West. With the collapse of Milosevic's regime and the reticence of the new democratic leadership in Belgrade to deal with the insurgents, the guerrillas went all the way to provoke a 'collateral' Serbian onslaught on Albanian civilians. It was a trap, which had been tried successfully in Kosovo. When Belgrade failed to accept the challenge, militants abandoned pretences and went public with maximalist demands for outright independence and future union of Southern Serbia – now 'Eastern Kosovo' in the nationalist jargon – with an independent Kosovo republic.[15]

What exactly prompted Albanians in Kosovo and the Presevo valley to open a new theatre of armed conflict is a debated question. Undoubtedly, the provocation scenario is a plausible one. But in the view of a seasoned British analyst, shared by other international observers, the escalation of the guerrilla activity not only in Presevo but also in the border areas of FYROM, should be attributed to the frustration of ethnic Albanians throughout the 'Albanian space', with the nebulous state of the future status of Kosovo. This frustration was compounded by fear that the political change in Belgrade might tip the scale against them and their dearest aspirations for a free and united Albanian state would once again be abandoned.[16] Probably, a more credible explanation might be the assessment of Albanian nationalists that a general conflagration in central Balkans, would compel the international community to concede, as a lesser evil, to the Albanian national demands.

TOWARD A PAN-ALBANIAN MOVEMENT?

Despite centrifugal forces among Albanians throughout the 'Albanian space', significant initiatives were undertaken for coordinating the activities of the various Albanian centres. Meetings between Albanian leaders from Albania, Kosovo, FYROM and other regions became a routine. Their primary aim was to establish a kind of a coordinating forum which would tackle issues of common interest and project common political stands in international bodies. This trend became visible in conferences of international organizations, meetings with NGOs and 'think tanks'.[17] Similar pan-Albanian initiatives for economic cooperation and cultural integration were gaining pace. Top priority was assigned to developing new road, rail and even sea routes. They were aimed to link regions inhabited by ethnic Albanians who had been separated since Ottoman times by the erection of national borders. The communication network would stimulate personal and trade links and would provide needed port facilities to land-locked 'Albanian' regions.

Of particular importance to cultivating a pan-Albanian physiognomy throughout the Albanian communities of the Balkans, were plans for unifying the educational system of Albania and Kosovo, intensifying cooperation between Albanian-language educational institutions, including universities, and writing uniform school textbooks.[18] The reasoning in support of such initiatives was clearly outlined by Luigj Juncaj, President of the Democratic Union of Montenegrin Albanians, in a September 1998 interview: 'We want the same curriculum for all Albanians in the Balkans. The three subjects language, literature and history are to us the most important because with these subjects we can strengthen knowledge about our common Albanian culture, heritage and national consciousness'. Responding to criticism that such initiatives might be the prelude to setting up institutions for a 'Greater Albania', Fatos Nano gave a rather sybilline answer: 'It will be a movement not in support of a Greater Albania but will serve the great European Albanians'.[19]

In short, one could probably detect in these initiatives and pronouncements the seeds of a pan-Albanian movement of independent and/or autonomous Albanian entities, patterned, *mutatis mutandis*, more closely to the pan-Arabian movement of independent Arab states, with features of the nineteenth century pan-Slavist movement. An interesting analogy between Germans and Albanians was outlined to this writer by a prominent Kosovar journalist. (He might have been more accurately speaking of 'Germanophones' and 'Albanophones'.) The Germans, he contended, were dispersed in Central Europe among two independent 'German' states (Germany and Austria), a federal multi-ethnic state (Switzerland) and a self-ruled region (North Tyrol in Italy). The corresponding Albanian entities would also comprise two independent entities (Albania and Kosovo), a federal multi-ethnic state (FYROM) and self-ruled regions (Presevo valley in S. Serbia, and border regions of Montenegro).[20] It is interesting to observe that, a year later, at the time when UCPMB was stepping up its offensive in the Presevo valley, an Albanian Montenegrin politician was making a concrete demand for an Albanian self-governed province adjacent to Albania.[21] What remained to be seen, however, was whether radical Albanian nationalists would be attracted by such long-term processes for political-economic-cultural integration or would resort to violent tactics for changing international borders.

THE VIOLENT OPTION

Apart from Kosovo, ethnic Albanians in other territories of the SFR Yugoslavia had also to contend with political privations of various degrees. In the former 'Socialist Republic of Macedonia' the human and political rights of the Albanians were far from satisfactory, despite the glossy picture portrayed at the time, by Yugoslav propaganda.[22] The destinies of the Albanian communities in the two regions – the Autonomous Province of Kosovo and the Socialist Republic of Macedonia (SRM) – were abruptly severed following the secession from the Yugoslav federation, in September 1991, of what became the independent state of the 'Former Yugoslav Republic of Macedonia' (FYROM). The Yugoslav/Serb and Slav Macedonian authorities adopted different methods in handling the aspirations of their respective Albanian communities. The former, faced from the outset with demands for secession and independence and a mass movement of passive resistance, resorted to oppressive measures. The consequences are well known. The latter chose the road of the incorporation of ethnic Albanians into the political system of FYROM, without, however, conceding to Albanian demands for an equal dual partnership of two constituent nationalities. On their part, the ethnic Albanians, despite their objections and grievances, chose to work through the system without abandoning their aspirations. The experiences and the tactics of both groups offered Albanians, throughout the 'Albanian space', a legacy of two different roads to achieving their common national aspirations.

Understandably, the aura of victory befitted the warriors of UCK. Their popularity among the Albanian populations throughout the 'Albanian space' and among the nationalist diaspora was impressive. At the end of the war, UCK was expected to disarm. Nevertheless, many veterans remained in military uniform and were legitimized in the ranks of the Kosovo Protection Force, while large caches of their weaponry were stacked away, apparently to be ready for a 'second round'. Certain of UCK leaders chose to enter politics. Riding on their popularity, they expected to win in the first elections. Their expectations, however, were not fulfilled, as in the national Kosovar elections of 2001, the electorate, probably encouraged by the international protectors, offered its choice to moderate leaders, headed by the veteran politician, Ibrahim Rugova.

Despite the setback, a brewing discontent was spreading among radicals and the youth because of the slow pace in setting up the institutions of an independent state. This was compounded by their concern at the political changes in Yugoslavia. It was feared that the ascent in Belgrade of democratic forces, despite enjoying the confidence and support of Western powers, might thwart their claims to 'Eastern' and 'Southern Kosovo' (the Presevo valley and the northwest provinces of FYROM). Understandably, supporters for a policy of action by military means would have only contempt for theoretical exercises in futility, such as struggling for a free of borders 'spiritual unity' of the Albanians. On the contrary, the guerrilla tactics, which had successfully lured the international community to intervene on the Albanian side in Kosovo, was a tempting pattern to be copied at the opportune moment. The armed clashes which broke up in the border regions of southwest Serbia and northwest FYROM, in February–March 2001, confirmed this view.

THE PREDICAMENT OF THE INTERNATIONAL COMMUNITY AND THE NEW CHALLENGES

Despite the insurmountable obstacles for the reconstruction of war-ridden Kosovo, almost two years since the establishment of the international protectorate, a marked improvement was becoming evident, mainly in the economic and the institutional field. The holding of municipal elections, followed by national ones, was acclaimed as a turning point. Nevertheless, the core issue of interethnic relations, remained in abeyance. In considerable ways, it had regressed. Repeated acts of terrorism and bombings fed an unending stream of non-Albanian refugees and confined the Serbs in enclaves, protected by the KFOR. The military engagements of UCK offsprings in Presevo and FYROM, early in 2001, gave a clear warning that violence was gaining the upper hand in promoting the Albanian irredenta.

Under the circumstances, the international community is challenged to re-evaluate, from a zero-sum basis, its previous assessments of the Albanian problem. A long list of factors which in the past conditioned its policy options is no longer relevant. Most of these factors were the result of the wars in the northern republics of ex-SFR of Yugoslavia. Later, under strong pressure by NGOs and pro-Albanian or anti-Serb lobbies, the international community was sensitized to come to the aid of the hard-pressed Kosovar Albanians. In the process, Milosevic's unbending attitude led to a nasty diplomatic confrontation and finally to the US/NATO military intervention against Yugoslavia/Serbia.

At no time, until the end of the Kosovo war, did the international community seek to review critically Albanian nationalism at its merits. Lack of a sober assessment of its components naturally handicapped planners in drawing meaningful long-range strategies.

The only exception was the Former Yugoslav Republic of Macedonia. Out of concern for a possible destabilization of the country which had offered a valuable link in the international *cordon sanitaire* stretching around Milosevic's Serbia, foreign powers, with the US in the central role, sought to defuse interethnic tensions there. The strategy was clear. The Slav Macedonians would be enticed to make certain concessions in such areas as education and a greater participation of Albanian Macedonians in government institutions. In return, the international community would not encourage or condone claims, such as condominium or federation[23] or violent actions which would shake the fundamental structures of the state. Once, again, this approach revealed a tendency to view Albanian nationalism isolated in its specific regional dimension.

Following the war, when elements of aggressive Albanian nationalism began to surface in various regions, the international community chose either to downplay their importance or to bypass them in silence. Its representatives in the field (UNMIK, KFOR, OASE, UN, EU and scores of representatives of foreign governments), plus the plethora of NGOs, preferred to work with moderates. These moderates were no less nationalists than the radicals, in the sense that they endorsed the same scriptures of Albanian national aspirations, but they employed accepted and politically correct language in their arguments. They, too, appeared willing to mute the role, the size and even the clandestine activities of radicals. Certain among them, however, would not fail to warn of dire consequences if their 'moderate' claims were not satisfied.[24]

The international community, *nolens volens*, will have to face realities and re-assess its perceptions and priorities. Therefore, it is worth bearing in mind certain bare truths:

- Albanian nationalism and the Albanian Question are not synonymous terms, although they appear to be moving along parallel lines;

- Albanian nationalism is conditioned by certain invariables (redress of historical 'injustices'; demolition of barriers impeding the free intercourse and movement among Albanians; secure of control – one way or another – of the 'Albanian space' regions; acceptance of the Albanian factor as a major regional player);

- the Albanian Question is the problem that stems from the dispersal of ethnic Albanians over the borders of five countries/regions (Albania, FYROM, Serbia, Montenegro, Kosovo). Its deterioration springs from the fact that just ten years ago they were split only between two countries (Albania, Yugoslavia). The process of the reunification of all Albanians, if not the lands they inhabit, is the motivating political force of contemporary Albanian nationalism;

- in the view of the Albanians, the dissolution of SFRY and the eviction of the Serbian administration from Kosovo have created a favourable conjunction of circumstances to achieve the long-term goals of 'liberation', autonomy and eventually unification. The tainted term 'Greater Albania' has been dropped by Albanian moderates, although in substance they concur with radicals on the pursuit of their long-term national aspirations;

• at this time, all Albanian endeavours focus on achieving the independence of Kosovo at the earliest opportunity and, in this context, the management of this issue would affect the entire Albanian Question in the Balkans.

It is a foregone conclusion that the resolution of the status of Kosovo can no more be seen as an isolated problem, or in the context of the Yugoslav wars. It is true that in the past two years, a plethora of scenarios have been worked out and tabled in international conferences.[25] The revolutionary changes of 2000–01 (elections in Kosovo, the overthrow of Milosevic's regime and the emergence of a democratic government in Belgrade, Albanian guerrilla warfare in southwest Serbia and northwest FYROM), have certainly altered the traditional coordinates of the problem. Hitherto, most scenarios could not depart from the classic perception of Serbs and Albanians, as culprits and victims, the 'enemy' and the 'friend'. With the advent of the Serbian democratic 'Opposition' in power, Western peace planners needed to reshape their basic guidelines and even reset their own role in peacemaking. Instead of being the 'liberators' and 'protectors' of the Albanian Kosovars, they would have to recast themselves into the position of 'honest broker'. This might not prove an easy exercise, particularly as NGO activists, personally involved in rehabilitating a destructed region, have difficulty in reorientating themselves. Political leaders and government officials, however, would need to tackle the Kosovo problem in the wider context of building stability for the entire Southern Balkan region. It may be the only way, for those Balkan and international political elites, which among themselves share the blame for the terrible mess they have created in the region, to exonerate themselves of the onus for creating an image of a Balkan region doomed to instability. The outburst of militant irredentism in the adjacent border regions of Kosovo in 2001 rang a warning alarm. It is worth heeding it.

It is precisely in this spirit that this writer decided to experiment, in the subsequent pages, with a novel approach at loosening the Gordian knot of the future status for Kosovo. Its primary aim is to provide a conducive framework for a negotiated settlement that would take into consideration present realities; would respect the basic norms of international law and practice; attend the vital interests of both Albanians and Serbs; and, more important, secure peace and stability for the wider region.

A NOVEL APPROACH: KOSOVO AS A UN TRUST TERRITORY

The critical starting point for resolving the Kosovo question is not to prolong uncertainty over the future status of Kosovo, in anticipation of more favourable conditions. On the contrary, a carefully drawn roadmap, with the consent of the parties concerned, might reveal the light at the end of the tunnel.

Already, it appears that there is a general consensus of opinion among foreign observers that the prolongation of uncertainty over this issue is the cause of destabilization both inside Kosovo and the wider Central South Balkan region. The time has come for a serious exchange of views. The three major developments in 2000–01, cited above, and the kind of equilibrium which has developed in the bargaining position of two sides might prove catalytic in stimulating a constructive dialogue.

The international community, acting this time as 'honest broker', should take the initiative in early negotiations with Prishtina and Belgrade to set the framework and sustain the momentum for a negotiated settlement. It will be a testing exercise, but a worthy one. It will require the consent of Yugoslavia, which, at this point, rejects any idea of relinquishing its (nominal) sovereignty over Kosovo; it will need the cooperation of the Kosovar Albanians who, at this time, agitate for independence within very tight time limits; furthermore, it will have to elicit the cooperation of states in the immediate vicinity and, certainly, it will depend on the active involvement of the major Powers and international organizations, as the UN, EU, OASE and NATO.

A solution can only emerge from a series of mutual compromises and international legal political and military commitments which would safeguard an agreement of a conditional independence for Kosovo and the gradual removal of Serbian sovereignty from the province.

While imminent independence finds no support at this time, apart from the Albanians at large, it is common knowledge that independence looms large, at some undetermined date, as the most likely conclusion of the tragedy. Understandably, it is of primary importance that Yugoslavia should be enticed to consider eventually a *conditional independence* for Kosovo. The timing and the form of an independent Kosovo entity, however, should be subject to binding and enforceable guarantees for a whole range of outstanding issues. Among them one could list, *inter alia*, the self-rule status of minority enclaves, the protection of historical and religious Serb shrines, the return of refugees, guarantees against the spreading of Albanian irredenta in neighbouring countries, and the legally binding exclusion of the Kosovo entity from 'Greater Albanian' schemes.

Negotiations for the political solution and the mechanisms to bring it about, in the foreseeable future, might prove lengthy and probably inconclusive. It is for this reason that this chapter proposes to explore the opportunities and experience accumulated by an old but tested mechanism of the United Nations; the UN Trusteeship system.[26] It is the mechanism, set up by the framers of the United Nations Organization, in 1945, to administer and eventually lead to autonomy and probable independence the pre-Second World War mandates and certain colonies (Chapter XII of the UN Charter). For all practical purposes, the Trusteeship Council has ceased to function since the emancipation and independence of its last trust territory, three decades ago. A few years ago, the Secretary General of the UN requested the General Assembly to terminate it. As no decision has been taken to this day, the Trusteeship system has not been formally abolished. A revisit of its relevant provisions of the UN Charter might furnish some useful ideas, if not the framework, for resolving certain aspects of the Kosovo problem.[27]

Indeed, in many respects, the UN Trusteeship system provides useful checks and balances applicable to the Kosovo case. Of course, Kosovo, by no means, fits the status of the League of Nations mandates, or, for that matter, of the post-Second World War colonies which were placed under the administration of the UN Trusteeship system. Nevertheless, according to article 77 of the UN Charter not only colonies but also '... other territories [may] voluntarily [be] placed under the trusteeship system by States hitherto exercising exclusive sovereignty over them'.[28] Under this provision, Kosovo could be eligible for the status of a trust territory, provided, of course, that the country holding sovereignty over it, that is, FR Yugoslavia, voluntarily consents to place it under the system.

Trust territories are administered by an Administering Authority (AA) and are supervised by the General Assembly of the UN. The Charter provides that the AA is composed of one or more members of the UN (art. 81). In actual practice, by the decision of the UN, functions of the AA were assumed by individual states which had placed under the Trusteeship system territories hitherto under their sovereignty or mandate. There has been, however, a case – Nauru, in the Pacific – where three UN members – Great Britain, Australia and New Zealand – jointly formed its AA. Nothing precludes the UN, taking into consideration existing circumstances in the case of Kosovo, to establish a collective AA from a number of states, including Yugoslavia, which technically and legally is the grantor state. If necessary, organizations of states, such as the European Union and/or NATO might be eligible to be represented in this body.

Determining sovereignty is a pivotal issue for addressing the Kosovo problem. The views of the Kosovar Albanians for independence at the earliest possible date contrast sharply with the Serbs' refusal to divest themselves of their sovereign rights. Resolution 1244/1999 of the UN Security Council affirms Yugoslavia's legal rights over the region, but in practice these rights are exercised by the international community. In short, it could be argued that whereas the residual sovereignty rests with Yugoslavia, the exercise of that sovereignty has passed over to the international organs administering the province in conformity with the above resolution. Despite legal arguments advanced by all sides, it is apparent that the current legal uncertainty over what in fact is an interim status, perpetuates antagonisms and undermines the prospects for stabilizing the region. Under the circumstances, the proposal to have Kosovo placed voluntarily by Yugoslavia under the Trusteeship system would signify, in fact, the transfer of sovereignty to the UN. Yugoslavia, however, through its proposed participation in the AA of the Kosovo trust territory, would, in essence, share in the exercise of sovereign rights entrusted by the UN to the AA.[29]

Once under the Trusteeship system, Kosovo's future course and status would be guided by the basic objectives of the system, as inscribed in the UN Charter. Article 76 of the Charter could be of particular relevance to Kosovo, in the sense that it recognizes, albeit with some elasticity, the progressive development of the trust territories 'towards *self-government or independence* as may be appropriate to the particular circumstances of each territory and its peoples and the freely expressed wishes of the people concerned and as may be provided by the terms of each trusteeship agreement'. Additionally, the Charter stipulates that the Trusteeship system aims to 'further international peace and security'.

This particular clause about the progressive development of the trust territory 'towards self-government or independence' is of cardinal importance for mapping out the future status of Kosovo. It is a fact that most of the initial trust territories were eventually led to full independence. Nevertheless, from the very beginning, while drawing the trust agreements, the UN paid special attention to the peculiarities of each case. It is not a coincidence that, with one exception (Italian Somaliland, which was programmed for independence within a ten-year period),[30] no trust agreement provided for a set time limit for self-government or independence.

Consequently, it can be argued validly, that once Kosovo is admitted to the Trusteeship system, it is assured that at an unspecified time horizon it would proceed to self-government or independence. In this respect, the 'freely expressed wishes of the people concerned' would be of paramount importance. Given official statements and the current sentiments of the Kosovar Albanians, it is a foregone conclusion that the overwhelming majority would opt for independence. Nevertheless, the drafters of the Kosovo trust agreement, while chartering the course toward the final status for the province, will have to bear in mind the supplementary objective of the Trusteeship system, namely to 'further international peace and security'. In composing a balanced document, the drafters of the trust agreement would need to address the conflicting views, interests and concerns not only of the Albanians and the Serbs, but of other directly concerned parties in the region.

The trust agreement might eventually emerge as the successor to the interim status provided by the 1244/1999 Security Council resolution. It has been said that that resolution, however, was the result of a compulsory arrangement imposed by victors on vanquished. Its aim was to terminate a war and to address its immediate and short-term consequences. On the contrary, the UN trust agreement, while taking into account post-war realities and the need to set up mechanisms of peace and stability of long duration for the wider region, would have to be an open and negotiated settlement. Nevertheless, certain of the provisions of resolution 1244/1999 and subsequent practical applications could be incorporated into the new text, providing a fuller framework for the functioning of UNMIK and KFOR, which would continue to operate in the region for some time under a different form and name.

The terms of administering a trust territory are determined by the Charter and individual trusteeship agreements, signed between grantor states and the UN. In effect, this means that the UN retains sovereign rights and appoints one or more states, usually grantor states, to administer the region..

Local government structures, with clear provisions for minorities, should be put into effect immediately. Given the volatility of certain areas such as Mitrovica, these could be designated as protected zones – 'safe havens' – under a special status of self-rule, within the framework of regional administration. Sites and monuments sacred to Serbs could have a special status of religious autonomy, similar, perhaps, to the self-ruled monastic community of the Holy Mountain, in Greece.[31] By joining the Trusteeship system, Kosovo would gradually move toward 'self-government or independence' according to Article 76b of the Charter. However, this process is dependent on certain conditions, namely, 'as may be appropriate to the particular circumstances of each territory and its peoples, the freely expressed wishes of the peoples concerned, and as may be provided by the terms of each trusteeship agreement'. The primary goal of the system, it should be noted, is 'to promote peace and security' (Article 76a).

Under these circumstances, the kind and the length of the process 'toward self-government or independence' would be at the foundation of the drafting of the trust agreement, although it is clear that because of prevailing conditions, the process will of necessity be a long one and will depend on the way in which the terms of the accord are implemented.

If, as is likely, independence is chosen as the concluding phase of the trusteeship, it will have to be in line with provisions for 'promoting peace and stability', not only in Kosovo but in Southeastern Europe in general. A clear commitment will have to be inscribed in the trust agreement that would forbid actions emanating from Kosovo that might incite or aid terrorism or separatism in neighbouring states, or would promote the idea of a Greater Albania.

A 'Cyprus clause',[32] banning union with third countries without the consent of the signatories to the Kosovo Trusteeship agreement, could also be added. It would aim, on the one hand, to curb agitation among extremist elements in neighbouring countries who might envision violent changes of borders and, on the other hand, to dispel the fears and suspicions of neighbouring peoples.

The trusteeship system provides for a sufficiently balanced and flexible framework to regulate the Kosovo problem. Its provisions would allow sufficient latitude to the UN to supervise the administration of the province and to charter its future status. On their part, the Yugoslavs would secure a role in the administration of the trust territory. Thus, they would be assured of sufficient leverage to secure the necessary safeguards for the Kosovar Serbs and the holy and historical shrines of the Serbian nation in the region and, moreover, to negotiate their own economic and geopolitical interests in the region. In turn, the Kosovar Albanians would see their extended autonomy rights recognized and sanctioned by an international treaty in a clearly defined UN-administered entity, in which they would enjoy overwhelming self-rule privileges. The trust status would create at least a degree of permanence which will contribute to stability and allow the Kosovars time to develop some of their own institutions with elements of a viable civil society. By putting some time between the war and a permanent resolution to the crisis and allowing a more permanent structure to replace UNMIK and KFOR, the Kosovars of all ethnic communities would attain a much greater degree of local responsibility and control. This might also leave open the option of some attachment between Kosovo and Yugoslavia in the context of a loose confederation, if that will be the wish of the people at the conclusion of the trust administration. The important feature, however, is the prospect of conditional independence, this time with the concurrence of the international community and Yugoslavia as well.

Third parties in the region, including Serbia, FYROM and Montenegro, would, similarly, be offered ironclad guarantees against attempts, originating in the new entity, which might upset the territorial status quo in their respective territories. Indeed, by the same international treaty, the realization of Kosovar independence would be made conditional to the abstinence from any act or initiative aiming at 'Greater Albania' schemes, or the fostering of irredentist/separatist movements in neighbouring countries. For an extended period of time, the UN would monitor the scrupulous observance of these obligations. Naturally, the advancement to the stage of a plebiscite, by which the people of the entity would record their will for their political status, will be conditional to the findings of a UN monitoring system.

Faits accomplis could inhibit the prospects for a negotiated settlement. Once again, the timing for urgent initiatives by the international community is limited. The alternative would be the prolongation of hostilities and the vicious circle of recurring crisis of revanchism.

In tabling this proposal, the author was motivated by a deep concern over the escalation, since the end of the war, of violence inside Kosovo and uncontrolled armed activity – 'terrorist' or 'freedom fighting' – in the adjacent regions. Unrest has become a continuing feature of life in Kosovo and across its borders. Violence aims at speeding independence for Kosovo and assuring special status for the Albanian populations in neighbouring states. If, however, Kosovo joins the UN Trusteeship system, the Albanians will rather become advocates of the peace process, than perpetrators of acts of violence and promoters of regional instability; otherwise they run the risk to see their vision of independence disappear into a nebulous future.

Initially, this proposal might provoke reservations by both sides, as both will be required to give up something, although this time of their own free will. But they will also be gaining a great deal, by international agreement and with guarantees. The region as a whole will become more stable, as long as the political situation remains clear-cut. And the long road to inclusion in Europe will no longer be wishful thinking.

NOTES

1. In the Albanian nationalist vocabulary, the 'Albanian space' comprises all the regions traditionally inhabited (also) by ethnic Albanians, namely, the Republic of Albania, Kosovo, the northwest provinces of FYROM, the Presevo valley of southwest Serbia, and the southern regions of Montenegro. Historically, they include the province of Thesprotia (Tsamouria) of northwest Epirus in Greece, which, however, is today devoid of any Albanian population.

2. Evangelos Kofos (1998): 'The Two-headed 'Albanian Question'; Reflections on the Kosovo Dispute and the Albanians of FYROM', in, Thanos Veremis and Evangelos Kofos, eds, *Kosovo: Avoiding Another Balkan War*, Athens: ELIAMEP, University of Athens, pp.49–55.

3. A leading Albanian Kosovar, attempting to explain the shrinkage of the number of Serbs, argued in an international conference in Prishtina, that 'wars have created many ethnic states with less then ten percent minorities' and that a similar trend has taken in Serbia with large number of Hungarians from Vojvodina and Moslems from the Sanjak are emigrating to Hungary and Turkey, respectively. Veton Surroi, publisher, *Koha Ditore*, Conference, 'After 10 Years of War and Conflict: Perspectives for the Future', Prishtina, 4–5 February 2000. The inference was that 'counter ethnic cleansing', in the aftermath of war, is a common phenomenon.

4. Ibid.

5. Miranda Vickers (1998): *Between Serb and Albanian. A History of Kosovo*, London: Hurs & Co., pp.269–72. Eleftheria Manta (2000): 'Alvania kai Kossyfopedio: Apo tin Apomonosi sti Dynamiki tis Ensomatosis' [Albania and Kosovo: From Isolation to the Dynamics of Unification], in, V. Kondis and E. Manta, eds, *To Kosovo kai oi Alvanikoi Plithysmoi tis Valkanikis* [Kosovo and the Albanian Peoples of the Balkans], Thessaloniki: Institute for Balkan Studies, pp.278–85.

6. A good analysis of the *Platform* and its impact in: ibid., pp.286–97.

7. Excellent contributions, analysing the basic aspects of the problem at that time, in: *Conflict or Dialogue: Serbian–Albanian Relations and Integration of the Balkans*, Subotica: Open University, 1994.

8. International Crisis Group (ICG) (2000): *Albania: The State of the Nation*, Balkans Report No. 10.2.2000, p.3.

9. Ibid.

10. ICG, ibid, p.6. In two conferences he spoke about 'the integration of all Albanians into Europe, not of unification of Albanian lands'. Prishtina conference, op. cit. and conference of the Project on Ethnic Relations (PER), *Albanians and their Neighbors: Unfinished Business*, Budapest, 7–8 April 2000. Also personal interview of this writer with Paskal Milo, Tirana, 3 March 2000.

11. Arben Xhaferi interview, *To Vima*, Athens newspaper, 9 February 2001.

12. Personal interview with A. Xhaferi, Kavouri, Athens, 1 December 2000.

13. Personal interview with A. Xhaferi, Prishtina, 5 February 2000.

14. Personal interview with General Agim Ceku, head of the Kosovo Protection Force, former UCK leader, Prishtina, 5 February 2000.

15. Xhaferi interview, *To Vima*, 9 February 2001.

16. Jonathan Eyal, 'Analysis: Nato's Kosovo Dilemma', BBC News 8 March 2001. Also, Xhaferi, ibid.

17. Personal impressions of this writer of international conferences, held in Tirana, Prishtina, Budapest and Athens, during 2000.

18. Interviews with Greek diplomats in Athens and Tirana, February and March 2000.

19. *ICG Report*, 2 February 2000, op.cit, p.8.

20. Interview with Blerim Shalla, publisher of *Zeri*, Prishtina, 5 February 2000.

21. Project on Ethnic Relations (PER), Conference: 'Albanians as Majorities and Minorities: A Regional Dialogue', Kavouri, Athens, 30 November–2 December 2000. Also, statement by the Montenegrin politician Ferhat Dinosa, PER conference, Budapest, op.cit (author's notes). A claim to a 'special status' of the Albanian minority of Montenegro was made by the same politician during the Kavouri, Athens conference, op.cit.

22. Hugh Poulton (1995): *Who Are the Macedonians?*, Bloomington: Indiana University Press, pp.126–37.

23. For the discovery of large caches of UCK weapons in Kosovo, in 2000 and the KFOR's refusal to take any measures, see an interesting report by Steven Erlanger, 'West Scrambles to Keep Balkans Stable', *IHT*, 13 March 2001.

24. Interview with a high-ranking US diplomat in Skopje, August 1998.

25. Interview with A. Xhaferi, Prishtina, 5 February 2000, conceding that radicals may bypass the Albanian moderate leaders if the Slav Macedonian political establishment failed to grant concessions to Albanians. At the same time, Veton Surroi, speaking at the Prishtina conference, 5 February 2000, op.cit., 'advised' the Slav Macedonians that that was the right time to come an agreement with the actual 'responsible' Albanian leadership, adding, almost prophetically, that 'this cannot endure for long'.

26. Papers of the policy conference, 'Options for Kosovo's Final Status, Quo Vadis, UMNIK?', organized by the UN Association of the United States and the Istituto Affari Internazionali, Rome, 12–14 December 1999. In most conferences, the arguments would concentrate either on early or immediate independence or on indefinite postponement of a decision for a final status. (For example, Noel Malcolm and Franz Lothar Altmann, respectively, Prishtina conference, op.cit. Van Eckelen , for postponement, in a Tirana conference, 3 March 2000, and more recently US Assistant Secretary for European Affairs, James Dobins, interview, *Kathimerini*,11 March 2001.) A comprehensive study was prepared by the Independent International Commission on Kosovo, which recommended that Kosovo be placed on a path towards 'conditional independence' within the framework of a Balkan Stability Pact. Report, 30 Nov.2000 (Conclusions, p.1).

27. In October 2000, I discussed my ideas about a probable settlement of the Kosovo status in the framework of the UN trusteeship system with Rand Corporation Balkan specialist Steve Larrabee, who, subsequently, made a summary presentation of the idea in an international conference held in Athens on 1 December 2000, kindly acknowledging his indebtedness to this author for the idea.

28. An excellent analysis of the provisions of the UN Trusteeship system appear in L. Oppenheim's (1955): *International Law. A Treatise*, Eighth Edition, edited by H. Lauterpacht, London, New York, Toronto: Longmans, Green and Co., pp.223–42. For the legal aspects and the way the system functioned: Nicolas Veicopoulos (1971): *Traitè des territoires dépendents. L'oevre fonctionnelle des Nations Unies relative au régime de tutelle, tome II*, Bruxelles–Athènes: Maison Ferdinand Larcier, pp.871–88, 1026–78, 1084–2060. Also, UN *Progress of the Non-Self-Governing Territories under the Charter*, Vol. 1 General Review, New York: United Nations, 1961.

29. It is interesting to note that international trusteeship was also suggested, officially or otherwise, for such diverse territories as Eritrea, Trieste, the Ruhr, Antarctica and the then Formasa.

29. Oppenheim, op. cit., pp.235–6.

30. Ibid., p.231.

31. Nikolaos Antonopoulos (1958): 'I Syntagmatiki Prostasia tou Agioreitikou Kathestotos' [Constitutional Safeguards for the status of the Holy Mountain], Ph.D. Tesis, Kovanis-Nomika Vivlia, Athens.

32. Treaty of Guarantee between Cyprus, Greece and Turkey specified in article 1 that the Republic of Cyprus undertakes not to participate, in part or as a whole, in any political or economic union with any state. To this end it will forbid any action which will tend to aim, directly or indirectly, to the union or partition of the island. Text in Pantazis Terlexis (1971): *Diplomatia kai Politiki tou Kypriakou* [Diplomacy and Politics of the Cyprus Question], Athens: Rappas, p.459.

The International Presence in Kosovo and Regional Security: The Deep Winter of UN Security Council Resolution 1244[1]

ALEXANDROS YANNIS

The fall of the Milosevic regime and the peaceful revolution in Belgrade on 5 October 2000 have restored the dignity of the Serb people as well as their place in Europe and the world. They have vindicated and strengthened the forces of democracy and progress in Yugoslavia, in the Balkans and beyond. They have also sparked euphoria for a Balkan spring that would lead to peace and stability in Southeastern Europe. The Final Declaration of the EU–Balkan Summit in Zagreb on 24 November 2000 acknowledged the triumph of democracy in Croatia and Yugoslavia and stated that 'the recent historic changes are opening the way for regional reconciliation and cooperation. They enable all the countries in the region to establish new relations, beneficial to all of them, for the stability of the region and peace and stability on the European continent'.[2]

On 28 October 2000, only three weeks after the changes in Belgrade, the moderate forces of Ibrahim Rugova achieved a sweeping victory with 58 per cent in the first-ever free and fair municipal elections in Kosovo. A less sweeping victory by Rugova followed, in the 2001 general elections. The advent of democratization and self-government in Kosovo restored the hitherto obscured dignity of the Kosovo Albanians, also strengthening democracy in the region. The elections also vindicated the international presence in Kosovo (UNMIK and KFOR) and the forces that support the rigorous implementation of Resolution 1244 as a precondition for stability in Kosovo and the region. Perhaps above all, the peaceful and democratic atmosphere of the elections and the victory of moderate forces reinforced the confidence of Kosovo Albanians in their future.

Yet, the Final Declaration of the Zagreb Summit adopted by the Heads of States of the 15 EU member states and several other states in the Balkans did not even mention Kosovo. The changes in Belgrade have resulted in a shift of the attention of the international community within the region. While it is essential to continue supporting the consolidation of democracy and the re-integration of Serbia into Europe, it is equally important for stability in the region to continue supporting democracy and the forces of moderation in Kosovo.

Amidst the winds of optimism for a Balkan spring the new president of the Federal Republic of Yugoslavia (FRY), Vojislav Kostunica, speaking in front of an impressive array of high-profile Western politicians and diplomats on 27 November 2000 in Vienna, stated that 'there is hardly any need to stress that the Kosovo issue is the most important European issue today. It is not possible to overestimate its importance because of the fact that it could easily set the entire region ablaze'.[3] Three days earlier Bernard Kouchner speaking as the Special Representative of the UN Secretary General in Kosovo in the EU–Balkan Summit in Zagreb also cautioned against the prevailing climate of optimism and euphoria: 'I feel it is my responsibility ... to alert you that we must not lose sight of the dangers that still lie ahead ... Success in Kosovo and stability in the Balkans will depend on the commitment of both Belgrade and Pristina to become genuine partners in the process of implementing Resolution 1244 and agree to move forward ... This is the only way to avoid sliding back to a new open conflict'.[4]

Much has changed since the NATO bombardment of FRY in spring 1999 and the subsequent arrival of the international presence in Kosovo in June 1999. Much has changed since the adoption of the UN Security Council Resolution 1244 of 10 June 1999 that led to the withdrawal from Kosovo of all FRY military, police and paramilitary forces and to the deployment in Kosovo of an international civil and security presence under United Nations auspices, albeit under separate command – respectively, the United Nations Interim Administration Mission in Kosovo (UNMIK) and the NATO-led KFOR. Much has changed since the UN replaced the FRY authorities in the territory of Kosovo and assumed full interim responsibility for its administration.

This article will review the role of the international presence in Kosovo and the prospects for stability in Kosovo and the region in the light of the changing realities in Southeastern Europe. It will argue that in the absence currently of an international or a local consensus over the future status of Kosovo and of conditions in the region for a comprehensive political settlement, only the vigorous implementation of the UN Security Council Resolution 1244 could prevent Kosovo from sliding back into open conflict. The recent democratic changes in Southeastern Europe cannot alone resolve the Kosovo conflict.

However, they have opened up a window of opportunity for building a hitherto missing local consensus to freeze the status of Kosovo and for a constructive engagement of both Kosovo Albanians and Serbs for the implementation of Resolution 1244.

This is the deep winter of Resolution 1244. What is needed is time to build and sustain a local consensus for the implementation of Resolution 1244 that provides a road map to meet the minimum objectives of both Kosovo Albanians and Serbs and the maximum of neither; and a long-term commitment by the international community to create the conditions for a regional settlement of the Kosovo dispute.

THE DEEP WINTER OF RESOLUTION 1244

The fall of the Milosevic regime was received rather differently in Kosovo. There was no euphoria there about the prospects of reconciliation and a resolution of the conflict. Both Serbs and Kosovo Albanians felt that this was merely another twist in the long history of the Kosovo conflict. Kosovo was as much in limbo as it was when Resolution 1244 was adopted and the international presence was deployed in Kosovo in June 1999.[5]

Many Serbs, particularly the still substantial number of supporters of the Milosevic regime in Kosovo, were simply lost. Others were filled with relative optimism that the worst was over for them and that democracy in Belgrade was about to reverse the course towards independence and trigger the process for the re-integration of Kosovo into Serbia (for example, Serb National Council of Mitrovica). Some more moderate voices considered the fall of the Milosevic regime as a step towards the initiation of a constructive political dialogue between Serbs and the Kosovo Albanian leadership, but under the rather unrealistic precondition that Kosovo Albanians would stop insisting on independence (for example, Fr Sava). In Belgrade, Kosovo was not an issue high on the agenda of the new President. The changes in Belgrade were a rather internal Serb affair.

Kosovo Albanians received the news with a great concern for the impact of the changes in Belgrade on their dream for independence. They were sceptical about the prospect of a change in attitude by the new government in Belgrade towards the Kosovo conflict and nervous about the dramatic shift of attention of the international community within the region (for example, Ibrahim Rugova, Hashim Thaci). Kosovo Albanians had not fought only against the Milosevic regime but also against Serb oppression. The changes in Belgrade had no impact at all on their commitment to independence.

The Kosovo conflict is not a dispute over power or form of government. It is a dispute over control of territory. It is about FRY sovereignty and Kosovo's independence. It is about a secessionist movement in Kosovo and the territorial integrity of FRY. The changes in Belgrade, therefore, alone could not have had any direct impact on the Kosovo conflict. Serbs are basically all against the independence of Kosovo, as Kosovo Albanians are all against the return of Kosovo to Serb rule. Just two months later, in early December 2000, the refusal by Ibrahim Rugova even to start a dialogue at that moment with Vojislav Kostunica was just a demonstration of the limited direct impact of the Balkan spring on the Kosovo conflict.

The changes in Belgrade may have no direct impact on the Kosovo conflict, but the competition over democracy between Belgrade and Pristina that started in October 2000 in both places may in the long run have a positive impact on the Kosovo dispute. This competition over democracy has the potential to contribute to the stabilization of the situation in Kosovo if it succeeds to divert the focus of the two adversaries away from the bone of contention of the Kosovo conflict – its international status. This competition over democracy has in the long run the potential to contribute to a peaceful solution in Kosovo if it manages to build upon the pacifying virtues of democracy and transform the Kosovo dispute into a competition over democratization, modernization and economic development and a competition over international support and resources.

The Kosovo conflict may not be over, but the changes in Belgrade and Pristina offer a window of opportunity to build for the first time a consensus between Kosovo Albanians and Serbs for the implementation of Resolution 1244. A genuine partnership among Serbs, Kosovo Albanians and the international community could in the long run contribute to the stability in Kosovo and the region.

Today this looks more possible than before because the international presence in Kosovo enjoys now relative confidence of both rivals. The previous imbalance when in the streets of Kosovo, the international presence was received as liberators by the Kosovo Albanians and as an occupation force by the Serbs, has been considerably redressed. The Serbs both in Kosovo and Belgrade are prepared to cooperate now with the international presence not only as reluctant partners owing to mere pragmatism but also because they increasingly believe that the international community can be an a constructive actor in Kosovo. The good relationship that the new regime in Belgrade established in a rather short period of time with the major international actors involved in the Kosovo crisis has been crucial. The Kosovo

Albanians continue to maintain a high degree of confidence in the international presence. They remain largely convinced that the international community will not allow Kosovo to fall under the former rule again.

The challenge for the international community is now to build upon this window of opportunity and transform this positive momentum into a consensus between Kosovo Albanians and Serbs over the role, the next steps and the objectives of Resolution 1244 and the international presence in Kosovo. To achieve this, there are three key requirements: first and foremost, time. A consensus is needed about the requirement to freeze the status of Kosovo. The territory of Kosovo will enter a deep winter in which Resolution 1244 will be the sole Northern Star. Second, a consensus over the implementation of Resolution 1244 has to be reached that meets the minimum objectives of both Kosovo Albanians and Serbs and the maximum of neither. Kosovo Albanians should be progressively enabled to develop and run democratic institutions of self-government and substantial autonomy in Kosovo and to become full partners in the process of regional integration, while Serbs should be assisted in achieving greater security and freedom of movement as well as greater opportunities for the return of Serbs back to Kosovo through a system of greater self-government in Serb areas. Finally, success will also depend on the commitment of the international community to maintain a long-term political, military and financial contribution for as long as this deep winter will permit other forces, such as democratization, economic development, social and political transformation and, perhaps above all, regional integration in a wider European perspective, to act upon as restraints for using violence to settle the Kosovo dispute.

FREEZING THE STATUS OF KOSOVO

The Kosovo dispute is fundamentally about the international status of Kosovo and this does not seem likely to be an issue to be settled peacefully now or in the near future. The idea of a departure in the foreseeable future of the international presence from Kosovo and the return of Kosovo to Serb rule, including the return of FRY forces, only raises the spectrum for the return of Kosovo to an open conflict. It would be a tragic mistake to underestimate the commitment of the Kosovo Albanians to their cause for independence and the preparedness of both communities to resort to the use of force to fight for their causes. For the time being, the international presence in Kosovo is the only guarantee for preventing Kosovo from sliding back to an open conflict. This is apparently well understood both within the international community and the region.

Another alternative is independence. The moral and political force of the Kosovo Albanian drive for independence remains intact. Albanians are the overwhelming majority of the Kosovo population and their determination has only been enhanced by their conviction that the FRY has lost its moral right to rule Kosovo owing to its recent ethnic cleansing policy. Clarity about the future status of Kosovo is also a key to economic development and political stability as it could play a critical role in mitigating the continued inter-ethnic violence in Kosovo, particularly if an agreement for independence includes solutions that ensure significant degree of self-government for the Serbs in Kosovo (for example, partition, 'cantonization').[6]

However, the prospects for a negotiated agreement between Belgrade and Pristina granting independence to Kosovo or of some form of internationally sponsored agreement for 'conditional independence' of Kosovo are rather limited at the moment.[7] The momentum for independence that was running high even among some international circles during the spring–summer of 1999 appears now to have considerably subsided. In fact, every day that passed after the adoption of Resolution 1244 and the deployment of the international presence in Kosovo, for the international community the idea of independence was becoming an ever more distant prospect, despite widespread belief among Kosovo Albanians and Serbs as well as many international observers for the opposite. The continued violence against Serbs has been constantly adding grist to the mill that opposes the independence of Kosovo. The progressive consolidation of the international civil and security presence in Kosovo and the collapse of the Milosevic regime have only strengthened the forces that oppose further disintegration in the area.

The international community appears now to have largely returned to the basic premises of its involvement in Kosovo before the escalation of the crisis in 1998.[8] The international community generally fears that independence would strengthen the forces of disintegration in the Balkans with unpredictable consequences in FYROM and Bosnia. It also fears that it could set a dangerous precedent of violent change of borders with potential destabilizing impact on the entire Southeastern Europe, particularly from the perspective of fuelling tendencies for the unification under the Albanian state of all the Albanians in the Balkans. The international community at this moment would generally support solutions that fall short of independence (for example, federation, confederation).

The fall of the Milosevic regime also removed another of the arguments in favour of the independence of Kosovo. The resolution of the Kosovo conflict when Milosevic was in power would have served the interests of the democratic developments in Serbia, as it would have removed a major burden for the new democratic forces, while the historical responsibility of that loss would have been placed on Milosevic.[9] Instead, the independence of Kosovo stands now as a Damoclean sword over the new Belgrade regime. Many Serbs share the view that it is in the interests of both Serbs and Kosovo Albanians to find a pragmatic solution in Kosovo. Yet whether a pragmatic solution would include independence and how strong is the influence of such views among the new Serb leadership and the Serb population is unknown. It is only very difficult at this moment to imagine a Serb leader signing the independence of Kosovo.

In any case, since for the Serbs, essentially any such solution includes some kind of partition, such ideas are double edged. They may resolve the problem, but they may again cause more instability and spread the conflict even further in the region. Kosovo Albanians vociferously oppose partition, particularly as it may have to involve giving up Northern Mitrovica and the Trepca Mines in Northern Kosovo.[10] The future of the tens of thousands of scattered Serbs in other parts of Kosovo is not an easy issue either, as neither geography nor demography are very helpful in this respect. The conflict in Presevo Valley in Southern Serbia has been just another demonstration that partition may be a more complex exercise than its supporters think. The very existence of Bosnia and FYROM may also be at stake. Such solutions may need a regional rather than only a Kosovo-wide settlement, and it is highly questionable whether the region or the international community is ready for such a wider regional settlement at this moment.

Finally, developments in Montenegro could turn out to be the barometer for the prospects of independence in Kosovo. Montenegro's independence would inevitably trigger further unrest in Kosovo and somehow weaken the position of Belgrade. Montenegro's independence could even create the critical mass necessary for the independence of Kosovo. However, an agreement between Belgrade and Podgorica that would keep Montenegro within FRY could also have a significant impact on Kosovo, as it could pave the way for a similar future arrangement for Kosovo.

However, any of these propositions for a definitive political settlement of the Kosovo conflict cannot at the moment form the basis of an international policy in Kosovo and the region. There is currently neither local nor international consensus over the future status of Kosovo. Unless developments in Montenegro lead to a rapid independence in Kosovo, for the international community there is now essentially only one option available: to form a solid local consensus over the need to freeze the status of Kosovo and move on with the implementation of Resolution 1244. This is reinforced by the fact that, in any case, even an agreement for a more definitive solution almost certainly would also require a long-term commitment for a substantial international presence to guarantee and ensure the implementation of its arrangements. Such a situation would also inevitably include, at least for a long transitional period, very similar tasks with the ones envisaged in Resolution 1244.

The problems caused by the ambiguity and uncertainty over the final status of Kosovo can only be addressed by seizing the moment to build a consensus for a partnership between the international community and both Belgrade and Pristina which would set common objectives for the implementation of Resolution 1244. What is needed are time and a policy that aims to move Kosovo out of the current stalemate in which both rivals stubbornly seek zero-sum solutions.

The greatest guarantee for stability in Kosovo and the region at the moment is the perpetuation of the international rule in the territory of Kosovo and the implementation of Resolution 1244. The new government in Belgrade has repeatedly stated its commitment to the implementation of the Dayton Accords and Resolution 1244 as the two pillars of its policy in the region; and Serbs in Kosovo are becoming increasingly convinced about the intentions of the international presence to implement impartially Resolution 1244. Serbs in general support Resolution 1244 because it reaffirms the commitment of the international community to the sovereignty and territorial integrity of the FRY.

Kosovo Albanians remain committed to Resolution 1244 mainly because they maintain high confidence in the international community. They generally support Resolution 1244 because it ensures the continued exclusion of the FRY forces from Kosovo and commitment to self-government and substantial autonomy, which they see as the critical factors that guarantee that Kosovo does not fall again under Serb political and/or military rule. Some form of international presence in Kosovo has been contemplated for some time by Kosovo Albanians as an essential element in the transitional period of any definitive political solution, including independence.[11]

The international community also feels generally comfortable with the idea of perpetual international rule until both parties to the Kosovo conflict are ready for a compromise and a political settlement (positive-sum solutions).[12] While domestic politics requirements in Western capitals may necessitate a rather flexible and modest rhetoric about the commitment of the international community in Kosovo, it is rather clear that the international presence is there for the long haul. Resolution 1244 provides UNMIK and KFOR with sufficient legal and political authority to administer the territory under its jurisdiction. The responsibility and the tasks are enormous but well within both the historical and the institutional role of the UN to undertake any measure required with the aim to achieve its key objective of maintaining and building international peace.[13]

Neither another UN Security Council Resolution is needed nor any change of the mandate of Resolution 1244. Such efforts would only complicate the already delicate exercise of building a local consensus over Resolution 1244. What is needed is a strategy for the implementation of the Resolution supported by strong international leadership and the instruments necessary to fulfil its objectives.

IMPLEMENTING RESOLUTION 1244

A strategy to implement Resolution 1244 should be built on a consensus that meets the minimum objectives of both Kosovo Albanians and Serbs and the maximum of neither. For the Kosovo Albanians, the minimum requirements for a continued constructive engagement with the international presence in implementing Resolution 1244 is the continuation of building self-government and substantial autonomy in Kosovo and the increased opportunity for its population to become full partners in the process of regional integration in a European perspective.

Greater self-government and substantial autonomy require the creation of both the political and administrative institutions that are needed to empower the local population and increase the accountability of the Kosovo leadership.[14] The nervousness of Kosovo Albanians over the impact of the fall of the Milosevic regime on their cause for independence and the shift of international attention within the region only accelerated the impatience of Kosovo Albanians to deepen and enlarge self-government in Kosovo.

Kosovo is not Bosnia. As the elections have demonstrated, the moderate forces of Ibrahim Rugova have won a majority. The demographics in Kosovo are not favourable to any serious inter-ethnic political competition that favours radicalization. The political competition in Kosovo is essentially an intra-Albanian affair and thereby the task of moderate political forces is easier.

An increased role by the Kosovo Albanians in the exercise by UNMIK of its legislative, executive and administrative powers will also increase the accountability of the Kosovo Albanian political leaders. This, when combined with the strengthening of the judiciary and the rule of law, and the further development of an efficient macro-economic framework and a strong fiscal management, could further build the confidence of the local population in UNMIK. Such progress is also essential to sustain the support of the Kosovo Albanian population to an international administration.

Finally, Kosovo should be given the opportunity to increasingly open up to its neighbours and Europe. Its uncertain status should not be allowed to become an obstacle to its participation in regional developments and integration. The political, economic and psychological benefits of Kosovo's integration into the current political, economic and security initiatives in the region could be critical in sustaining a constructive engagement of the Kosovo Albanians with the international presence. Kosovo should become a full partner in all key regional initiatives, also because these are the forces that will bring stability and development in the region. It could be very dangerous to mistake the freezing of the future status of Kosovo with an exclusion of Kosovo from regional integration and some degree of direct involvement in the EU-sponsored stabilization and association process in the region.

Democratic self-government and regional integration of Kosovo are not only requirements for sustaining the commitment of Kosovo Albanians to the political process in Kosovo. They are also two of the basic ingredients for any political settlement of the Kosovo conflict in the future.[15] The other basic elements for a future peaceful solution in Kosovo and stability in the region are tolerance and equal opportunities for security and prosperity for the non-Albanian communities in Kosovo. Continued insecurity and discriminatory treatment of the Serbs and other non-Albanian communities can in the long-run totally discredit Kosovo Albanians as well as the international administration and result in the exclusion and dangerous marginalization of Kosovo from the international community and the process for regional integration.[16]

The minimum requirement for the cooperation of Serbs with the international presence in Kosovo is effective international guarantees for their survival and their eventual full inclusion in the political, social and economic developments in Kosovo, FRY and the region. The triptych for improved conditions of life and stability for the Serbs in Kosovo today is greater security and freedom of movement, greater opportunities for the return of Serbs back to Kosovo, and greater self-government in Serb areas.

Improved security and freedom of life as well as improved conditions for the return of Serbs to Kosovo can be achieved only if the international presence is determined to break the cycle of impunity. This requires ever-improving military, police and judicial policies to prevent criminal acts and to identify, apprehend and punish those responsible for inter-ethnic crime. It also requires sustained policies to stop systematic harassment and intimidation that result in sales of property and land, prompting further exodus of Serbs from Kosovo. The lack of preparedness by the international community for the scale of violence against Serbs that followed the departure of FRY forces from Kosovo rendered inadequate the early response of UNMIK and KFOR and undermined the confidence of the Serbs. While the prime responsibility lies with the Kosovo Albanians, as Aleksa Djilas, the Serb historian, put it 'the possibility of revenge increases the desire'.[17]

An improved political environment is also very important. Further efforts by the Kosovo Albanian political leadership to create a culture of tolerance and mobilize Kosovo Albanians behind the tasks of stopping criminality and attacks against Serbs and creating together with UNMIK and KFOR basic conditions for returns of Serbs to Kosovo could be critical.[18] Success, however, in improving the security situation of the Serbs will ultimately be measured by results and not efforts. Thus, both Kosovo Albanians and the international presence must increase their determination to improve the present security situation in Kosovo.

The other highly challenging and complex task for the international presence in Kosovo with respect to Serbs is the requirement to achieve their integration in the political, economic and social life of Kosovo and build their confidence that there is a future for them there. There is on this issue a vast disagreement between Kosovo Albanians and Serbs on how to achieve these objectives. Kosovo Albanians generally argue that Serbs should basically be treated as an ethnic minority entitled to the conventional rights and protection of minorities. In reality, the treatment of Serbs in daily life is far from meeting basic standards of human rights, partly because of the widely discriminatory attitude of Kosovo Albanians and partly because many institutions that could ensure a fair treatment are either not yet fully in place or they are malfunctioning.

The progressive improvement in the capacity of the civil administration to deliver services and the gradual strengthening of the institutions that can play a critical role in redressing discriminatory behaviour is expected in the long-run to improve the overall situation. However, urgent action is also required. For example, the excessively discriminatory provision of electricity to Serb areas in the middle of the winter and with temperatures below zero is indicative of how serious this problem is. The challenge is vast. UNMIK has to develop a hitherto missing capacity to closely supervise and investigate the conduct of the entire administration. It has to take corrective measures and follow-up initiatives on a daily basis and on a great range of issues to adequately address this huge and somehow underestimated problem.

The bone of contention, however, with respect to the prospect of integrating the Serbs in the political, economic and social life in Kosovo is mainly whether Serbs can be better protected through special territorial arrangements that could ensure greater self-government for them within Kosovo. This is an old issue and a highly controversial one. Since the early 1990s, Serb intellectuals have been proposing various forms of partition of Kosovo that included territorial arrangements to ensure that Serbs rule their own affairs in Serb areas in Kosovo.[19] Later, the then Serb representatives in the Kosovo Transitional Council (KTC), Bishop Artemije and Momcilo Trajkovic, put forward for consideration by UNMIK and the Kosovo Albanian representatives a proposal for the 'cantonization' of Kosovo (August 1999).[20] The proposal envisaged the creation of Serb cantons in rural areas and some form of mixed administration in larger urban areas. The objective was that no Serb would ever be under Kosovo Albanian rule. The Serbs argued that such a proposal merely reflected the history and the realities in Kosovo where Serbs and Albanians have lived for centuries next to each other in some form of coexistence but never together in a Western-like integrated and multi-ethnic society.

The proposal was immediately rejected by Kosovo Albanians as a Trojan horse for the eventual partition of Kosovo, and by the international community both owing to the pressure by the Kosovo Albanians and because it did not comply with the ideal of a fully integrated multi-ethnic society. Bernard Kouchner's suggestion to discuss the underlying objective of the proposal – the need to improve the protection of Serbs in the areas where they live – was also rejected categorically by Kosovo Albanians and certain Western countries (for example, US) at that time. This clear rejection by the Kosovo Albanians of the Serb proposal for 'cantonization' paved the way for the eventual withdrawal of the two Serb representatives from the KTC that happened less than a month later when they formally suspended participation in the KTC in protest for the Agreement for the transformation of the KLA to the Kosovo Protection Corps. Retrospectively, and while the concerns of Kosovo Albanians over further divisions and eventual partition of Kosovo are perfectly understood, this was perhaps a missed opportunity by the international community at an early stage to take more effective action to address the underlying issue of the proposal for 'cantonization'

– the need for a political and institutional model for effective protection of the Serbs in Kosovo.

The 'Agenda for Coexistence' that was launched eventually by the SRSG emanated from this initial failure to accommodate Serb ideas about a model of peaceful coexistence.[21] It aimed to improve security, ensure the delivery of public services and minimum self-rule by Serbs in the areas where they live. It did not, however, foresee territorial changes feared by Kosovo Albanians. It rejected the idea of territorial autonomy for Serbs and kept all new arrangements within the existing municipal structures. Instead, it introduced the idea of 'functional autonomy' for Serbs through the elaboration of a mechanism within the UN administration that aimed to ensure *in situ* delivery of public services to Serbs and other non-Albanian communities. These arrangements were eventually integrated in the Regulation on Self-Government of Municipalities against the protests of Kosovo Albanian political leaders.[22]

In practice, these arrangements were undermined by Kosovo Albanians and their implementation was slow and inconsistent by UNMIK mainly owing to the lack of preparedness of the international bureaucracy to implement such urgent and extraordinary measures. This project was also undermined by the Milosevic regime and its supporters in Kosovo, who were following a policy of non-cooperation with the international presence and had built their own rudimentary parallel structures, which in many respects were more effective in providing assistance to the Serbs in Kosovo than the international administration. The major consequence has been the strengthening of the *de facto* divisions on the ground, such as the ones in Mitrovica, and the failure to build the confidence of Serbs over the commitment by the international community to take all necessary measures to improve their situation in Kosovo.

Several ideas have been contemplated since the arrival of the international community in Kosovo on how to address this issue. They all more or less converge to the core idea of the 'Agenda for Coexistence': the vital need to ensure effective 'functional autonomy' for the Serbs in Kosovo in the areas where they live. They do not necessarily require territorial changes along the lines of the 'cantonization' proposal but they do require stronger institutional arrangements ensuring greater self-government in Serb-dominated areas. These arrangements exist as an embryonic concept in the Regulation on Self-Government of Municipalities (that is, Community Offices) but they need further vigorous elaboration and rigorous backing for their implementation by UNMIK. They include the need to develop an additional administrative layer in rural areas where Serbs are scattered minorities at the level of community and village, and they require innovative arrangements for the special cases of Mitrovica and Strepce.

A New Agenda for Coexistence is needed that could effectively ensure functional autonomy for the Serbs inside the substantial autonomy of Kosovo Albanians. Given the continued resistance by Kosovo Albanians to any idea that includes preferential treatment for the Serbs, the success of such efforts rely almost entirely on the commitment of the international presence to implement these arrangements. The final result could, however, be beneficial for the moderate forces of both Serbs and Kosovo Albanians because it carries the potential to lay the foundations for peaceful coexistence in a multi-ethnic society and a political settlement.

MAINTAINING LONG-TERM INTERNATIONAL COMMITMENT

An indispensable requirement for both Kosovo Albanians and Serbs to become genuine partners in implementing Resolution 1244 is the commitment of the international community to maintain its political, military and financial contribution for a long period of time.[23] Building consensus over the need to freeze the status of Kosovo and focus on implementing Resolution 1244 would be predicated on a long-term international commitment to be the driving force. At the moment what keeps the Kosovo Albanians and Serbs from sliding back into an open conflict is essentially the international presence in Kosovo. There is a 'wall of blood' separating them, and their commitment to resort to the use of force for their diametrically opposing causes is equally strong. Reconciliation and a peaceful solution in Kosovo will need at least a generation.

Long-term international commitment does not necessarily imply undiminished financial contribution or military presence. The challenge of the international community is to maintain a sustainable presence and commitment in Kosovo. For example, the stabilization of the security situation, particularly the changes in Belgrade, has removed a major objective of the initial deployment of the international security presence in Kosovo. The decreased need to focus for the time being on the deterrence of new hostilities between FRY forces and Kosovo Albanians is a major example of the improving operational environment in Kosovo. Expansion and consolidation of the multi-ethnic Kosovo Police Service – a major success story of the international presence in Kosovo – could also increasingly facilitate a better and more effective use of UNMIK Police resources. Thus, KFOR and UNMIK Police could be increasingly enabled to shift their focus and resources to the more critical objectives of protecting the Serbs and other non-Albanian communities as well as of tackling more effectively organized crime.

The progressive establishment of democratic institutions of self-government in Kosovo and the further empowerment of local representatives to run its political and administrative institutions will also most likely soon require smaller presence by UNMIK. Thus, UNMIK may be soon presented with the opportunity either to diminish its presence or to use its resources in a more effective way to focus some on the most challenging and critical political objectives: an effective supervision of the administration to ensure the rule of law and non-discriminatory access to public services, and to speed up economic reforms and ensure equal opportunities for economic development. Thus, the objective of the international presence in Kosovo is not to maintain its current presence indefinitely but to sustain for a long period of time a presence capable of achieving its objectives. It will most likely be a balancing act on a tightrope.

Kosovo needs time to allow other forces, such as democratization, economic development, social and political transformation and, perhaps above all, regional integration in a wider European perspective to create the conditions for a comprehensive political settlement in a regional context. The international presence in Kosovo is a critical factor in allowing time to perform its healing work as it is a critical factor in ensuring that Kosovo does not destabilize further the rest of the region. From Bosnia through Southern Serbia to the borders with Greece, stability in the foreseeable future depends on building peace in Kosovo.

In June 2000, Kofi Annan, in his report on the 'Search for Self-sustaining Stability in South-Eastern Europe' stated that 'without stability in Kosovo, it is difficult to envisage stability in the region. The Kosovo issue ... can only be addressed within a regional context and with international support'.[24] Until the conditions are ripe for a resolution of the Kosovo conflict in the context of a comprehensive regional settlement, nobody can claim with confidence that the worst is over either in Kosovo or in the region.

NOTES

1. The author would like to thank Axel Dittmann, Karin von Hippel and Kyla Evans for their comments and contribution in the preparation of this article. Names in this article are used the way they are found in current English-language publications and usage.
2. Final Declaration, EU–Balkan Summit, Zagreb, 24 November 2000, paragraphs 1–2.
3. Statement by Vojislav Kostunica, 8th OSCE Ministerial Council, Vienna, 27 November 2000.
4. Statement by Bernard Kouchner, EU–Balkan Summit, Zabreb, 24 November 2000.
5. See Judah (2000), pp.311–12. For interesting historical analogies in other periods of the history of Kosovo see also his first chapter, particularly pp.26–32 and also Malcolm (1998), particularly chapter 15.
6. Caplan and Allin (2000), Opinions.
7. About the idea of 'conditional independence', see the Independent International Commission on Kosovo (2000), Part II, Chapter 9.
8. For a comprehensive analysis of the views and policies of the key international actors involved in the Kosovo crisis before the NATO bombardment see Caplan (1998).
9. See above note 6.
10. For a more detailed analysis of the question of the partition of Kosovo see Spahiu (1999).
11. Glenny (1992), p.239.
12. On the discourse about zero-sum and positive-sum solutions in Kosovo see Heraclides (1998), pp.389–443.
13. For an extensive analysis of the evolution of the role of the UN in administering territories see Chopra (1999).
14. For a background on this issue see the *Agreement for the Establishment of the Joint Interim Administrative Structure* that ensured the participation of Kosovo Albanians in the administration of Kosovo, UNMIK unofficial document, 15 December 1999 (document available from the author) and the UNMIK Regulation No. 2000/1 of 14 January 2000, *On the Kosovo Joint Interim Administrative Structure* that incorporated the Agreement into the evolving institutional set-up of Kosovo. See also the UNMIK Regulation No 2000/45 of 11 August 2000, *On Self-Government of Municipalities in Kosovo*, which was the first step in establishing a legal framework for substantial autonomy in Kosovo.
15. Kouchner (2000a; document available from the author).
16. A fairly good early account of the dramatic security situation of Serbs and Roma in Kosovo and its consequences is provided by the Human Rights Watch Report (1999).
17. See above note 5, in Tim Judah, p.312.
18. See also the *Agreement for the Establishment of a Joint Committee on Returns for Kosovo Serbs* signed by the Serb National Council of Kosovo and Metohia, UNMIK, KFOR, UNHCR and OSCE, Gracanica Monastery, UNMIK unofficial document, 2 May 2000 (document available from the author).
19. See above note 10, pp.97–126.
20. Cantonization of Kosovo-Metohia: A Proposal, August 1999, (document available from the author). The proposal for 'cantonisation' was submitted to the Kosovo Transitional Council meeting of 25 August 1999 by Bishop Artemije and Momcilo Trajkovic. It was drafted by the Belgrade Professor Dusan Batakovic and it was based in his earlier proposal for the 'cantonization' of Kosovo of September 1998.
21. *Agenda for Coexistence*, UNMIK unofficial document, November 1999, and *Agenda for Coexistence – Kosovo Community Offices*, UNMIK unofficial document, March 2000 (both documents available from the author). See also the *Joint Understanding between UNMIK–SNC (the Serb National Council of Kosovo and Metohia) on the*

participation of the SNC in the JIAS (Joint Interim Administrative Structure), Pristina, UNMIK unofficial document, 29 June 2000 (document available from the author).
22. UNMIK Regulation No 2000/45 of 11 August 2000, Article 23, paragraphs 11–14. Kosovo Albanians generally rejected these arrangements. The Joint Understanding that was signed by the SRSG and Bishop Artemije in 29 June 2000 raised considerable controversy among Kosovo Albanians who vocally rejected some of its provisions, particularly some of the measures to increase the security of Serbs and the provisions that called for the implementation of the Agenda for Coexistence. The signing of the Joint Understanding also led to the decision by Hashim Thaci in early July 2000 to temporarily suspend his participation in the Interim Administrative Council of Kosovo.
23. The critical importance of sustaining international commitment for stability in Kosovo and the region after the changes in Belgrade was one of the key recommendations in the Statement of Bernard Kouchner to the EU Ministers of Foreign Affairs in the EU General Affairs Council, Luxembourg, 9 October 2000 (Kouchner 2000b).
24. Annan (2000), p.9.

REFERENCES

Agenda for Coexistence; UNMIK unofficial document, Pristina, November 1999.
Agenda for Coexistence – Kosovo Community Offices; UNMIK unofficial document, Pristina, March 2000.
Agreement on the Joint Interim Administrative Structure (JIAS), UNMIK unofficial document, Pristina, 15 December 1999.
Agreement for the Establishment of a Joint Committee on Returns for Kosovo Serbs; UNMIK unofficial document, Gracanica Monastery, 2 May 2000.
Annan, Koffi (2000): *The Search for Self-Sustaining Stability in South-Eastern Europe*, Report by the UN Secretary-General, June.
Cantonization of Kosovo-Metohia: A Proposal; Pristina, 25 August 1999.
Caplan, Richard (1998): 'Crisis in Kosovo', *International Affairs*, October, Vol. 74, No. 4.
Caplan, Richard and Dana Allin (2000): 'Kosovo Needs a Clear Road Map for Independence', *International Herald Tribune*, 19 August 2000.
Chopra, Jarat (1999): *Peace-Maintenance: The Evolution of International Political Authority*, London and New York: Routledge.
EU–Balkan Summit; Final Declaration, Zagreb, 24 November 2000.
Glenny, Misha (1992): *The Fall of Yugoslavia: The Third Balkan War*, London: Penguin Books.
Heraclides, Alexis (1998): 'Ethnonational and Separatist Conflict Settlement and the Case of Kosovo', in Thanos Veremis and Evangelos Kofoc, eds, *Kosovo: Avoiding Another Balkan War*, Athens: Hellenic Foundation for European and Foreign Policy.
Human Rights Watch Report, *Federal Republic of Yugoslavia: Abuses Against Serbs and Roma in the New Kosovo*, August 1999, Volume 11, No 10 (D).
Independent International Commission on Kosovo, *The Kosovo Report*, 23 October 2000.
Joint Understanding between UNMIK–SNC (the Serb National Council of Kosovo and Metohia) on the participation of the SNC in the JIAS (Joint Interim Administrative Structure); UNMIK unofficial document, Pristina, 29 June 2000.
Judah, Tim (2000): *Kosovo: War and Revenge*, New Haven and London: Yale University Press.
Kostunica, Vojislav (2000): Statement, 8th OSCE Ministerial Council, Vienna, 27 November.
Kouchner, Bernard (2000a): *A Stable Kosovo: Essential for Regional Stability*, UNMIK unofficial document, June.

Kouchner, Bernard (2000b): Statement, Meeting of the EU Ministers of Foreign Affairs in the EU General Affairs Council, Luxembourg, 9 October.
Kouchner, Bernard (2000c): Statement, EU–Balkan Summit, Zagreb, 24 November.
Malcolm, Noel (1998): *Kosovo: A Short History*, London: Macmillan.
Spahiu, Nexhmedin (1999): *Serbian Tendencies for Partitioning of Kosova*, Budapest: Central European University Press, June.
UNMIK Regulation No. 2000/1 of 14 January 2000; *On the Approval of the Kosovo Joint Interim Administrative Structure.*
UNMIK Regulation No 2000/45 of 11 August 2000; *On Self-Government of Municipalities in Kosovo.*

Ten Concepts That Will Define the Future of Kosovo (A Personal Note)

VETON SURROI

1. THE POSSIBLE

On 14 June 1999 on the hill in front of a house in Prishtina in which I hid for more than a month I saw British paratroopers establishing their pattern of patrol. As they climbed the hill in an orderly fashion, six of them moved their legs left and right as if part of one body.

Just two days before a lonely Ukrainian custom-made UAZ armoured jeep was making its routine patrol. It carried armed Serb paramilitaries who were responsible for looting the neighbourhood and not allowing any inhabitants to return to it. Its dark green mask colours and tinted glass brought immediate discomfort.

Just a day later, white UN non-armoured Toyota four-wheel-drives with the new UN Administrator for Kosova, Sergio Vieira de Mello, would become a customary feature of the hill in front of the house where I did not need to hide any more. The description of that hill, the few days preceding and the few days succeeding the British paratrooper patrol can, I think, identify Kosovo's present. In a matter of days, that territory experienced the greatest historical change. An almost century-long Serb armed presence disappeared, for the first time in the history of Kosova an external armed presence that wasn't hostile to the local population came in and for the first time the UN embarked on a novel state-building exercise in Europe. During the whole preceding decade conventional wisdom would explain why such an event, as experienced in June of 1999, would be impossible. The days of that June, nevertheless, showed that the time we were living through was the *time of the possible*.

2. IRREVERSIBILITY

The three things I was told, in East and West, would never happen were the end of communism in Europe, the disintegration of Yugoslavia and the military intervention in Kosovo (with its liberation). The time of the possible made these events reality, and in fact made them part of the same event. As communism was making its collapse, the complicated structure of multi-ethnic Yugoslavia did not undergo a democratic transformation, making its death imminent. Its violence and capacity to threaten present and future regional stability created the preconditions for the military intervention in Kosovo. Now, can these processes be reversed: can communism, Yugoslavia and Serb rule over Kosova be revived?

Nationalism wanted to replace communism and its totalitarian format; it succeeded in a good part of Yugoslavia, but the different nationalisms do not have the potential of totalitarian rule that communism had. Communism was global, nationalism by definition needs to be particular.

There may be no doubt a future in communications between the peoples of ex-Yugoslavia, but communications are one thing and a state entity that will encompass the peoples and territories of Tito's Yugoslavia is a totally different thing. Tito's Yugoslavia broke up when the right to democratically communicate between its parts was not established.

And yes, a democratic Serbia will want to have a say on the affairs of Kosovo but this will not revive the Serb rule over it. Serb rule can be established only if the Kosovars want it, and that would be a rather astonishing expression in self-determination, a reverse of what the Kosovars aspire to.

The times of possibility have created, or are part of a process of *irreversibility*.

3. THE REVOLUTION

As I walked into my everyday life, after the NATO troops marched in, I realized that I needed to establish some sort of communication with the Authorities. And there were at least two levels of them. On the one side were the Albanian authorities derived from the right of the KLA insurgents to assume power through arms, and on the other side were the international authorities who derived their right to assume power through a far greater military strength supported by international political agreements. In any case, I would not be dealing with any form of political authority known to me in Kosovo before 1999. I would not be dealing with the Titoist Communist authority known until 1990, which was based on the right of the victor after the Second World War. I would not be dealing with the Milosevic regime, which derived its power from the Anschluss of Kosovo in 1989, nor with the Kosovar 'parallel society' which was developed as an Albanian peaceful response to the Milosevic use of brutal force.

In any case, I would be dealing now onwards with a revolutionary power. If *it*, becomes possible, and irreversible, it must be a *revolution*.

4. UN-DETERMINISM

A window of the shop in front of my office was broken while the streets of my city were still not filled with all the people who were forced out of it during the war. While I was expecting the return of refugees, meeting occasionally one or two in front of my office, I was overwhelmed by the clearly identified feeling of liberty.

Liberty, revolution, a day of history … I thought about the notions I could read in the past and in different environments, and suddenly I was feeling them. I thought that the change was so big that it would be part of everybody's mind. As I saw the window of the shop shattered, and five grown-ups looting, I soon realized that the noble notion of Liberty was quite rapidly overcome by the notion of post-revolutionary reality, that of the everyday life.

Along with the windowpane, I think that another valuable thing which was also shattered was the belief that once the Serb oppressor is out and NATO forces in, there ought to be an automatic behaviour of the population that will resemble the behaviour of the population of Western European countries. The end of oppression, the victory of the revolution, however irreversible, will not create, though, a predetermined future. The looters of the shop were not driven by the forces of history, but were rather invited to act by the lack of institutions of law and order.

Kosovo is *un-determinist* as anything else.

5. STATE BUILDING IN TIMES OF DISINTEGRATION

The common denominator of the Albanian political movements throughout the twentieth century was state building. Whether at the end of Ottoman Empire, the Second World War or after it, political movements left and right were explicit in the form of their requests for a state. It sometimes was called autonomy, sometimes Greater Albania, sometimes Republic of Kosovo within Yugoslavia, and lately an independent Kosovo, but in any case it was about the ability to exercise state rights through the rule of the Albanian majority.

The Kosovar state building movement now coincides within a double revolutionary process, unparalleled in Kosovar history and its environment. The first is the process of disintegration of the Former Yugoslavia, something which had momentarily occurred during the Second World War, but in a historic interim. The second, is the process of integration within Western Europe. In both, the common denominator is the end of the Cold War. With the end of the Cold War, the magnetic poles of the ideological conflict that held the old European order disappeared. The new magnetic pole became the Western integration, be it in the form of the EU or the transatlantic alliance. The disintegration of Yugoslavia is in fact part of the process of the Western integrations. Slovenia, a former part of Tito's Yugoslavia will within the next two or three years become a full member of the EU.

The Kosovar natural allies, thus, are both the end of the Cold War and the Western integrations. But the state-building process in times of post-Cold War Europe for Kosovo has an additional characteristic: it has to be done through a democratic process. Differing from the whole Western European experience where the state was built first, while the democracy was built or expanded later, Kosovo of the twenty-first century has simultaneously to build both state and democracy

6. TRANSITIONALITY

Kosovo is living through at least three transitional processes. The first transition is from communism to democracy. The end of the Cold War caught Kosovo being overrun by Milosevic's forces, abolishing all forms of self rule. Under the conditions of Milosevic's control it was impossible to engage in political and economic reforms that former Communist countries went through. Kosovo is today caught with a total lack of experience in democratic institutions and economic structures, in terms of property and production, inherited from socialism.

The second transition is from minority to majority rule. Kosovo was not only ruled, in ideological terms, by an non-elected minority, but in ethnic terms as well. Establishing a system of apartheid, the Serb authorities factually institutionalized the right of the ethnic Serb minority to rule over Kosovo. The 1999 revolution brought conditions for a new rule, of the majority, but this new rule still has to develop a new quality, that of protection of the minorities from majority rule.

And, the third transition is the one from multi-ethnic state formation to nation-state. Kosovo has always been part of a model of either colonial rule (in the Ottoman empire) or softer forms of alien administration, such as the Kingdom of Yugoslavia, and the centralized versions of the Yugoslav federation (the exception being the autonomy 1968–89). The death of both the Ottoman empire and the various forms of Yugoslavia have brought new conditions for the state-building process of the Kosovars, the process of the nation-state in a rather inverse way. Namely, not the state of the ethnic Albanians, since that was already formed in 1912 in Albania, but of political Kosovars, who are ethnic Albanians in their majority.

7. STATEHOOD CONDITIONALITY

There is one point of consensus between Kosovars and the international community as far as the future of Kosovo is concerned: it is going to be a state. Resolution 1244 of the UNSC, the ruling law of Kosovo talks about a process of establishing self rule and then determining the permanent status through talks. This in effect means that Kosovo needs to be a state, without making a decision now about whether it is sovereign or not. Where the Kosovars and the international community differ is the degree of sovereign rights that Kosovo should have, namely whether in the future it is going to be a fully recognized international subject or not.

If such is the case, four basic requirements of its proper functioning will also be the measuring yardstick of the ability of Kosovo to stand on its own. The Kosovar society will have to engage in building democratic institutions, economic restructuring, establishment of tolerance in internal relations and good neighbourly relations.

The extent to which these conditions are fulfilled will determine the extent of the proper functioning of the self-rule in Kosovo, under UNSC 1244. But at the same time, the extent by which these conditions are fulfilled will determine the degree by which the international community will support the Kosovars and their aspirations for an independent state. The UN mission in Kosovo, would, then, through this interpretation measure its own success through the extent by which it has helped the Kosovars build their state.

8. ETHNIC POLYCENTRISM

Ethnicity has been the driving force of the Kosovar state-building process even before the end of the Ottoman empire. It is still a driving force, in and around Kosovo. The Kosovar case, though, has created a specific case within the pattern of national movements in the case of the disintegration of Former Yugoslavia. Differing from the Serb and the Croatian movements that were ethnocentric, with the capitals of the respective nation states becoming capitals of the national movements, the Albanian national movement has not ended up with one centre.

Kosovo has been developing its own policy regardless of the policies developed in Albania. And this has been true in the last years for the Albanians in Macedonia as well. The Albanians' political movements are *polycentric*.

This polycentrism is important for the Kosovars not only in terms of concentrating on the state-building duties within the boundaries, but because it brings at the same time a great degree of rationalization to the national question as a whole, namely to the communication within the Albanian nation. Through a polycentric approach, the question of communication between the Albanians becomes actually a question of communication between the countries of Southeastern Europe where the Albanians traditionally live. The Albanians, therefore, will have a vested interest in the flexibility of the borders, their permeability, rather than rigidity.

The Kosovars, through this approach, see their state-building process as one of integration of the region.

9. FINALITY: INTEGRATION/REGIONALISM/SOVEREIGNTY

For years I have been personally advocating that the question of Kosovo needed to be dealt with on a two-step approach. The first would be to an internationally agreed self rule that would give democratic content to the Kosovar shell. The second would be an inclusive decision making on the permanent status of Kosovo.

In 1999 this approach was adopted by the international community, throughout the negotiating process in Rambouillet and Paris and further with the bombing campaign and the establishment of the UN Administration.

Coincidentally, this is the approach which to a great extent has characterized the EU debate. First, it is important to concentrate on the functionality of EU, and afterwards in the second stage, on its permanent status, namely the finality of the process of integration.

For Kosovo, this is not a cosmetic coincidence. One of the fundamental questions about its future has to do with the new concepts of sovereignty. When the time comes to discuss the permanent status, what kind of sovereignty needs does Kosovo want to project? Does it want full control over monetary policy in the way a non-EU sovereign state has, while at the same time it adopts the Euro as its own currency? What does full sovereignty in matters of defence mean today, in view of the NATO military presence in the foreseeable future? What forms of sovereignty will be applied to the border regime, having in mind both the needs for much better trans-border communication and the abilities of borders to maintain state structures (customs which are almost the only source of budgets in the region)?

These are all questions that define the future, but they define the present as well.

10. THE DAY AFTER

If in reaching this point we used the two-step approach, there is a need to introduce a third step. It is necessary to fill the Kosovar shell with democratic content and economic viability in the first stage; it is important to have a multilateral democratic process to define the future status in the second stage; but then beyond it is of utmost importance to discuss the day after the status is defined.

Namely, the status will be defined both through the degree of transformation of the Kosovar society and the ability of Kosovo and its neighbours to live in an accommodated fashion. But the day after needs to include the third element, the EU. What will the relations of this region be with the EU, when will it be within the EU, through what kind of a procedure? All of this will dictate to a great extent the dynamics with which Kosovo and the region will be transformed.

In 2001, part of the debate about where the EU is going was also linked to the ability or the inability of the Polish farmers to produce less or more potatoes. In a Europe and world of greatest ever interdependencies, any debate about the EU enlargement has an impact on the future of Kosovo, therefore the one on the Polish potatoes as well.

Yugoslavia at the Crossroads: Reforms or Disintegration?

PREDRAG SIMIC

The victory of democratic forces in the elections in Serbia and Croatia and the departure from the political scene of two main protagonists of the Yugoslav drama – Slobodan Milosevic and Franjo Tudjman – indicated during 2000 the end of the drama of former Yugoslavia. Soon after the victory of the Democratic Opposition of Serbia (DOS), FR Yugoslavia was returned to the membership of the United Nations and OSCE, and admitted to the Stability Pact of Southeastern Europe. The new authorities, applying for the admission to the Council of Europe, indicated their intention 'to bring Yugoslavia to Europe', that is, to guide it towards accession to the European Union. Reacting to the government turnabout in Serbia, the international community lifted most of the sanctions imposed on FRY and by the end of 2000 granted financial and humanitarian aid amounting to US$500m. The return of FRY to international organizations and admission to the Stability Pact revived regional initiatives and opened scope for a more active action of the EU in Southeastern Europe, as confirmed by the success of summits in Zagreb and Skopje. In short, the three-month period of 'Yugophoria' has shown a great potential of democratic and integrating processes in Southeastern Europe that progressed very slowly in previous years due to the breakup and war in former Yugoslavia, absence of investments and international isolation of FRY (geographically the central country of the region). However, at the beginning of 2001 optimism retreated before renewed threats to regional security that could no longer be directly attributed to the legacy of Milosevic's regime. Although the focus of the crisis shifted towards Macedonia, FR Yugoslavia found itself among the countries whose security and even survival was threatened by the new escalation of the Kosovo crisis and requests of Montenegrin authorities for confederate constitutional arrangement, that is, secession from the common state.

Almost two years after the international administration (UNMIK) and international peace force (KFOR) came to Kosovo and Metohija, ethnic violence has not been arrested, but only changed its direction, making Serbs and other non-Albanian population its main targets. Despite the presence of UNMIK and KFOR, paramilitary units of formally disbanded 'Kosovo Liberation Army' (KLA) remained the dominant factor in Kosovo as well as among ethnic Albanians in southern Serbia and in Macedonia. The crisis spilled from Kosovo and Metohija first to southern Serbia, where the so-called Liberation Army of Presevo, Bujanovac and Medvedja (UCPBM), composed of KLA members made an incursion into the so-called Ground Safety Zone (GSZ) established in June 1999 as a buffer zone between KFOR and the Yugoslav Army (YA).[1] Despite the October victory of democratic forces over Milosevic's regime in Serbia, the GSZ has not been abolished and in the meantime it has been turned into a testing ground for action of Albanian terrorists, who demand accession of Presevo, Medvedja and Bujanovac to Kosovo and Metohija. Towards the end of February and during March 2001 the crisis also spilled from Kosovo to Macedonia, where KLA members founded the so-called People's Liberation Army (PLA) and started conflicts with Macedonian security forces in northern (Tanusevci, Kumanovo) and northwestern Macedonia (Tetovo). Further escalation of this crisis would jeopardize Montenegro (eastern parts of this republic are predominantly populated by ethnic Albanians[2]), southwestern Serbia (the Raska region, that is, Sanjak), Albania (relations of predominantly Muslim north and predominantly Christian south), as well as overall relations on the south of the Balkans, including Greece and Turkey, that is, the southern NATO wing.

The second threat to the survival of post-Milosevic's Yugoslavia is aggravation of crisis in relations between its two federal units. Contrary to expectations that the fall of Milosevic's regime will open a democratic dialogue between Montenegro and Serbia about the future constitutional arrangement of the Federation, the authorities in Podgorica towards the end of 2000 issued a *Platform for Negotiations with the Government of Serbia about New Relations between the Two States*, demanding separation of Serbia and Montenegro into two sovereign states that would subsequently, according to this proposal, constitute a union of states. Somewhat later, at the proposal of the president of FRY, Vojislav Kostunica, the ruling coalition in Serbia, DOS, adopted a *Proposal for Reconstruction of Yugoslavia* that also advocates constitutional changes while preserving the federal state in the form of 'minimum federation'. Having in mind that the Federal Republic of Yugoslavia currently represents a relatively unstable bond of three different units – Serbia, Montenegro and Kosovo and Metohija – it is not difficult to assume that secession of Montenegro might have direct consequences for the status of Kosovo and Metohija and could trigger a *domino effect* that would produce consequences from Bosnia-Herzegovina to Macedonia, while the number of states in the region could rise from the present ten to as many as twelve to fifteen.

Although different by character and political objectives, these processes have a common dynamic: for example, one of the main arguments of advocates of Montenegro's independence is that pro-reform course in this Yugoslav republic must not depend on the developments in Serbia and Kosovo, that is, that Montenegro 'must not be the hostage of the Kosovo crisis'. On the other hand, Albanian politicians in Kosovo and Metohija support Montenegro's independence, stressing that it would contribute to independence of Kosovo and creation of a single Albanian state in the Balkans in accordance with their thesis that 'Yugoslavia is a country in the process of disintegration that must be brought to its end', that is, to the revision of state borders in the Balkans and creation of ethnically homogenous states. It seems that the international community pursues contradictory goals in the Balkans – while it wants to preserve multi-ethnic, multicultural and multiconfessional community in Bosnia (contrary to the desire of two of its three constitutive peoples), in Kosovo and Metohija it *de facto* tolerates the creation of ethnically homogenous state with extremely revisionist intentions towards the neighbours. Unlike SFOR in Bosnia-Herzegovina, KFOR and UNMIK in Kosovo and Metohija are not ready to actively oppose a 'greater state' movement and prevent spilling of the crisis to neighbouring areas. Thus, they are becoming hostages of an obsolete policy and perhaps even the victims of a possible broader armed conflict in the south of the Balkans.

THE PROBLEM OF MONTENEGRO

Security of FRY and its closest neighbourhood depend, primarily, on the future relations between its two members – Serbia and Montenegro, which are already for a long time in crisis. After the proclamation of independence of Slovenia, Croatia, Bosnia-Herzegovina and Macedonia, the two remaining republics of the Socialist Federal Republic of Yugoslavia – Serbia and Montenegro – proclaimed the 'Third Yugoslavia', that is, FRY, on 28 April 1992. However, while this decision in Montenegro was reached at a referendum, the citizens in Serbia did not have the opportunity to give their opinion about the new state. Slobodan Milosevic's regime decided instead of them. In spite of crises in Croatia (Krajina) and in Bosnia-Herzegovina, the closeness of Milosevic's Socialist Party of Serbia (SPS) and Montenegrin Democratic Party of Socialists (DPS), led at the time by Momir Bulatovic and Milo

Djukanovic, kept the common state together until the latter half of the 1990s. Soon after the Dayton Peace Agreement and victory of opposition parties in local elections in Serbia, a conflict broke out within the ruling party in Montenegro between Milo Djukanovic and Momir Bulatovic, which ultimately led to the split in the party into Democratic Party of Socialists (led by Djukanovic) and Socialist People's Party (SNP) founded by Bulatovic. Although in the summer of 1997 the Montenegrin deputies in the Federal Assembly voted for the election of Slobodan Milosevic for president of FR Yugoslavia, approaching presidential elections in Montenegro widened the cleft within the ruling party in this republic.

At the presidential elections in Montenegro held in October 1997, Milo Djukanovic won over Momir Bulatovic by a close margin. This event marked the beginning of the cold war between Belgrade and Podgorica that in the following years led to the erosion of federal institutions and actual confederalization of the country. Djukanovic's tight and disputable victory[3] was confirmed by Democratic Party of Socialists's landslide in the early parliamentary elections in Montenegro in May 1998. Attempting to mitigate the consequences of Bulatovic's defeat in Montenegro, Slobodan Milosevic removed Radoje Kontic from the office of the Federal Prime Minister, appointing Momir Bulatovic to this post. Thus political cleavages were transferred from Montenegro to the relations between the Montenegrin and Federal Governments. In the meantime, the new authorities in Montenegro changed the law which stipulated that the share of political parties in the Montenegrin delegation in the House of Republics of the Federal Assembly is determined in proportion to their election results, that is, in proportion to their representation in the republican Assembly. Instead, the parliamentary majority decided that Montenegro's delegation in the House of Republics of the Yugoslav Assembly should be composed only of its representatives. This caused a reaction of the Constitutional Court of Yugoslavia which ruled that such a law is in contravention with the 1992 Constitution of Yugoslavia. However, somewhat later the Constitutional Court of Montenegro contested the competence of the Constitutional Court of Yugoslavia, endorsing the decisions of the Assembly of Montenegro and the ruling party. In return, Milosevic's regime decided that the new deputies from Montenegro cannot take their seats in the House of Republics and instead kept the former deputies close to Momir Bulatovic until the elections for the Federal Parliament in September 2000.

Since summer 1998 onwards the relations of the federal and Montenegrin authorities continued to tighten not only due to the exclusion of authorities in Podgorica from the decision-making in internal and foreign-policy of FR Yugoslavia but also due to increasing independence of Montenegro from the federal state, that will ultimately leave the Yugoslav Army as the only federal institution in Montenegro. In the struggle against Djukanovic's authority, the Milosevic regime implemented various forms of pressure, including economic sanctions, refraining from payments into the republican budget[4] and frequent blockades of trade between Serbia and Montenegro. The authorities in Podgorica reacted by taking control of the customs in the territory of Montenegro and refusing to pay the revenues from customs and federal taxes into the federal budget. Consequently, the Constitution of FRY was disavowed in practice, while relations between Serbia and Montenegro became confederate. Aggravation of relations between the Milosevic's regime, on the one hand, and US and EU, on the other, were favourable to the authorities in Montenegro, who got an important place in the policy of international isolation and pressure on Slobodan Milosevic. Podgorica not only received political support and possibility for international promotion, but also considerable technical and financial aid that made Montenegro the second largest recipient of US aid per capita (after Israel). The 'shadow economy' became the second important source of income as it flourished under international trade sanctions against FRY and chaotic situation in Bosnia after Dayton, in Kosovo and Metohija, and in Albania.[5]

Although Montenegrin authorities refrained from open conflict with Belgrade, thus leaving Milosevic with free hands on the national plan, it nevertheless weakened his position in relation to the country's major political problem at that time – the problem of Kosovo and Metohija – that in 1997–98 escalated into an open armed conflict. At the end of 1998 and beginning of 1999 Milosevic's regime entered into the conflict with the US in which the Montenegrin authorities attempted and largely succeeded to stay aside. Moreover, during NATO intervention Montenegro accepted almost 100,000 Albanian refugees from Kosovo and Metohija, thereby clearly articulating its independent position in relation to Milosevic's regime. Contrary to Western expectations, Milosevic survived the war with NATO and loss of Kosovo and Metohija, so that the problem of relations between the two members of the Yugoslav federation reappeared on the agenda. In the first post-war months, Montenegrin authorities watched carefully every move of Serbian opposition and assisted in its contact with the US and EU, seeking the best position both in case Milosevic remained in power and in case of his downfall. Since the decisive conflict between the regime and opposition did not occur at that time, at the beginning of August 1999 the official Podgorica proposed its first platform on reorganization of the Yugoslav federation, which remained without the response of then authorities in Belgrade, while on the opposition side only the Serbian Renewal Movement explicitly supported the platform.

Temporary consolidation and mounting repression of the Belgrade regime worked in favour of the authorities in Podgorica, who came to be regarded by the West as an important stronghold in the conflict with Milosevic's regime. At that time the number of police in Montenegro increased from 10,000 to about 25,000, incidents with members of the Second Army of the Yugoslav army stationed in Montenegro became increasingly frequent, while the media in Montenegro warned of the possibility of a military coup, seeing in the newly founded Seventh Battalion of special army forces the unit entrusted with this task. Owing to the assistance provided by USAID, EU and other international organizations the authorities in Montenegro embarked upon the process of legislative changes with the aim of harmonization with European Union law. In practice, the effects of reforms were much more modest: according to the data of Montenegrin economists, GDP of this republic dropped to only 40 per cent of GDP recorded in 1989, unemployment tripled, and the main economic sectors, such as tourism, did not seriously undertake privatization.[6] Neighbouring Italy frequently launches allegations about a high degree of criminalization and connections with the Mafia in the Italian province of Puglia, which the Montenegrin authorities reject as a rule. In this period, the gap between Serbia and Montenegro continued to widen: the Belgrade authorities were more and more often closing the border between two republics partly as a form of political pressure on Podgorica and partly with the aim of protecting the Serbian market from the influence of the increasingly open Montenegrin market. The single Yugoslav market finally collapsed when Montenegro introduced the German mark as legal tender in addition to the dinar and somewhat later completely eliminated the dinar from its payment system. These factors had a decisive influence on economic and political developments in Montenegro towards the end of the 1990s, leading to the emergence of a new political and intellectual elite that would become the main protagonist of the policy of Montenegro's independence. On its part, the 'shadow economy' contributed to the establishment of a new business class whose interests are closely interconnected with the interests of Montenegrin authorities and who are considered to be the main inspirers of their policy.

The turnabout in relations between Belgrade and Podgorica came about in mid-2000, when Milosevic's regime, under growing pressure from the US and erroneously believing that it has sufficiently weakened the opposition in Serbia, decided to change the federal Constitution and introduce direct elections for the president of Yugoslavia. The intention was to enable Slobodan Milosevic to have another term at the helm of the federal state. Unlawful change of the Constitution on 6 July 2000 sounded an alarm for the Serbian opposition and for the West, as well as for the authorities in Montenegro. Although some opposition parties in Serbia were hesitant whether to participate in the federal elections under these conditions or to boycott them, under the pressure of the US and EU most of the opposition gathered within the Democratic Opposition of Serbia (DOS) and decided to participate in the elections scheduled for late September. However, Milo Djukanovic refused American requests, justifying his position with illegitimacy of constitutional changes. Interests of Montenegrin authorities and Serbian opposition became openly divided on this issue, although the latter badly needed the help of Montenegrin voters in their showdown with Milosevic's regime. The somewhat unexpected but very convincing Democratic Opposition of Serbia victory of 24 September elections and large-scale protest of Serbian citizens in Belgrade on 5 October, when they finally removed Milosevic from power, caused mixed feelings in Podgorica: while support of the Montenegrin authorities to Serbian opposition gave obviously the reason for satisfaction, Milosevic's fall objectively reduced the importance of Djukanovic's regime for the US and EU.

Thus the presidential and parliamentary elections led to a somewhat paradoxical situation: while the authorities in Montenegro boycotted them and refused to recognize their result, Bulatovic's Socialist People's Party participated in them and hence became the only candidate from Montenegro for setting up the new Federal Parliament and Government. Despite political differences between the Socialist People's Party and Democratic Opposition of Serbia an agreement was reached and, since Vojislav Kostunica was elected president of FRY, Socialist People's Party representative Zoran Zizic was given the mandate to form the new Federal Government. The old conflict between the authorities in Podgorica and the Federal Government thus passed on to the new authorities, established in the federation as the result of Democratic Opposition of Serbia victory.

Arguments underlying the political platform of Montenegrin authorities about independence and possible confederate arrangement between Serbia and Montenegro are quite similar to those advocated in the late 1980s and early 1990s by Slovenia, the first republic that separated from then SFRY (thus starting a chain reaction in Croatia and Bosnia-Herzegovina). As already mentioned, they proceed from the statement that Montenegro has the longest uninterrupted state tradition among all Yugoslav republics, that it has negative experience with three Yugoslav states,[7] that it has developed stable democratic institutions and processes, that it has progressed in the transition process and is approaching European integration, that it has established harmonious inter-ethnic relations, that it has stable relations with neighbours, and that it does not want to be the hostage of unsolved problems in Serbia, primarily Kosovo and Metohija. To corroborate this stand, Montenegrins quoted that the so-called Badinter Arbitration Commission back in 1991 classified Montenegro among Yugoslav republics that do not have political obstacles to become independent states. It is interesting to note that constitutional experts close to the authorities in Montenegro think that democracy in Serbia and Montenegro would not enable a stable community because of great disproportion in the size of two republics (population in Serbia is almost 19-fold more numerous than in Montenegro, which rules out the principle 'one man – one vote'). Unlike Slovenia and Croatia, which saw the expression of their independence primarily in international recognition, their own army and economic independence,[8] the authorities in Montenegro insist on economic independence, but not on a separate army, stressing that Montenegro does not need armed forces. Nevertheless, supporters of Montenegro's independence recognize close historical interconnection and similar interests of Serbs and Montenegrins as well as of Serbia and Montenegro, emphasizing that independence of Montenegro would not mean complete severance of links between the two peoples and two republics and that these ties would be preserved through a confederate union.[9]

The platform of FRY President Vojislav Kostunica and Democratic Opposition of Serbia recognizes the shortcomings of the present constitutional arrangement and also advocates a reform of a Serbian–Montenegrin federation towards federal state with minimum joint functions: the Federal Government would have only five departments in its competence, while the option of a unicameral Federal Parliament is not ruled out. According to this proposal, protection of basic rights and freedoms, foreign policy, national defence, elements of economic system and transport and communications would be the sole areas in the competence of the federal state. To ensure equality of two different-sized federal units, this proposal sets forth several principles according to which the federal institutions would operate. The first one is that all relevant decisions – laws and other regulations – would be adopted by both parliament chambers by absolute majority, while both chambers would have general competence. According to this proposal, the federal bodies would have two types of competence. The first one includes issues in the exclusive competence of the Federation, such as foreign policy, national defence, monetary system, customs system, transport, law of obligations and securities. The second one includes issues in the joint competence of the Federation and member-states, such as: basic rights and freedoms (including minority rights), ownership relations, fiscal system, banking system, commercial law, pensions, property and personal insurance. Although similar in many respects, these two proposals differ in the character of the common state: while the Vojislav Kostunica/Democratic Opposition of Serbia proposal envisages a federal state (federation), the Montenegrin proposal advocates an alliance of states, that is, confederation of two internationally recognized states.

During February and March 2001 a series of meetings and discussions on this topic took place between Belgrade and Podgorica both at the government and non-government level, where a three-year moratorium has been proposed, but a compromise has not been reached. Soon afterwards, the Assembly of Montenegro adopted a series of decisions, including the decision to schedule early parliamentary elections and the new Law on Referendum. According to this law, referendum would be considered successful if a simple majority (+50 per cent) of registered voters cast their votes, while a simple majority of this number (one-quarter of registered voters) would be sufficient to decide the outcome. Only nationals of Montenegro with permanent residence in this republic would be eligible to vote in the referendum. Provisions of this law have been criticized, while the US administration and the European Union openly warned against its provisions. The major objections refer to the fact that the fate of Montenegro (and of the Yugoslav Federation) could ultimately be decided by only one-quarter of registered voters in Montenegro. Second, the provision of this law granting voting rights on the referendum only to citizens with permanent residence in Montenegro excludes a large number of Montenegrin nationals who live in Serbia.[10] Third, a unilateral decision of Montenegro would inevitably have consequences for the future of Kosovo and Metohija and, probably, the entire region. In spite of the almost unanimous stand of the Serbian political public that they would accept whatever the decision of Montenegrin voters and the mutual desire to preserve the Serbian–Montenegrin community in the federal or confederate form, the breakup of the Yugoslav federation would probably have serious consequences for Serbia and drift the interests of Serbia and Montenegro apart. While the former would be primarily oriented toward the Central European area, the latter would become a predominantly Mediterranean state. Further political and economic fragmentation of Southeastern Europe would also be one of the consequences of the breakup.[11]

During the election campaign in Montenegro, two options became polarized. The first one, championed by Milo Djukanovic's Democratic Party of Socialists and Social-Democratic Party (SDP) urges Montenego's independence and confederate union with Serbia, while the other one, promoted by Predrag Bulatovic's Socialist People's Party, Dragan Soc's People's Party (NS) and Bozidar Bojovic's Serbian People's Party, strives to preserve the federation with Serbia. It is interesting that the Democratic Party of Socialists declined the offer of the Liberal Alliance for the establishment of a purely separatist bloc in Montenegro before the elections and maintained its position about redefinition of relations between Montenegro and Serbia. In short, the first group maintains that by remaining in the federation Montenegro would over time lose the attributes of statehood and would be reduced to one of the regions in Serbia. The other group claims that independent Montenegro would very soon become the target of territorial aspirations of its neighbours, above all Greater Albanian nationalism of ethnic Albanians in Kosovo according to the same blueprint that was used in Macedonia. These warnings proceed from the fact that a larger part of Montenegro, including Podgorica, is within the borders of 'Greater Albania' as shown on the maps of Albanian extremists in Kosovo and Metohija; that Albanians are the most numerous national minority in Montenegro; and that in case of independence of Kosovo and Metohija Montenegro would border with two Albanian nation-states, which could not leave indifferent the numerous Albanian minority living on the east and northeast of Montenegro.[12] Advocates of Montenegro's independence refute such statements, believing that independent Montenegro would be a civil and economically prosperous state, which would maintain ethnic balance between Montenegrins, who account for two-thirds, and national minorities who make up one-third of its population.

KOSOVO AND METOHIJA: THE FAILURE OF INTERNATIONAL MISSION?

Unlike Bosnia and Herzegovina, where civil war ended with a traditional peace conference and a comprehensive political agreement,[13] the war in Kosovo and Metohija was interrupted by NATO military intervention, while the mandate for international administration (UNMIK) and peace force (KFOR) was established by UN Security Council resolution 1244 and Military Technical Agreement signed in Kumanovo. Although time has shown that the Dayton Peace Agreement was an 'unfinished peace', the two-year experience of international administration in Kosovo and Metohija indicates that in this case it is rather an 'unfinished war'. This is corroborated by the fact that since the signing of the Dayton

Agreement not a single armed conflict occurred in Bosnia-Herzegovina, while in Kosovo and Metohija political violence continued (in reverse direction) after the arrival of UNMIK and KFOR. Under the pressure of political and ethnic terror, about 250,000 non-Albanians, predominantly Serbs, Montenegrins and Roma, left the province after 10 June 1999. Their property was looted, while a large number of Christian religious and cultural monuments were damaged or demolished. Small Serb enclaves were preserved mainly along the border with Serbia proper in the northern part of Kosovo and Metohija, but they are exposed to continuous pressure of militant Albanians, such as the March 2001 unrest in Kosovska Mitrovica or terrorist attack on the bus near Podujevo at the same time.

The local Albanian population that did not accept KLA rule or simply happened to be the target of criminals, many of whom came from northern Albania, suffer as well. At the local elections held towards the end of 2000, the Kosovo Albanians mainly voted for Ibrahim Rugova's Kosovo Democratic League (LDK), but political violence of formally disbanded KLA escalated soon after the elections, when Rugova's political advisor was killed in a terrorist attack.[14] At about that time the crisis began to spill into southern Serbia when members of the so-called Liberation Army of Presevo, Medvedja and Bujanovac (UCPBM – a KLA wing) started to make incursions into the Ground Safety Zone established along the administrative border between Kosovo and Metohija and Serbia proper. The crisis in Presevo valley threatened the trans-European transit corridor No. 10, that is, the highway and railway line Belgrade–Skopje–Thessaloniki–Athens, because the foremost UCPBM positions are only 900m away from these transportation lines. At the beginning of 2001 Albanian extremists from Kosovo and Metohija seized control of the village of Tanusevci in northern Macedonia and started attacking Tetovo, attempting to embroil the ethnic Albanian population in the entire Macedonia into the conflict. The immediate cause of these attacks was the signing of an agreement about the definition of the border line between Yugoslavia and Macedonia at the summit of Balkan states in Skopje (23 February 2001), which the Albanian political leaders both in Kosovo and Metohija and in Macedonia rejected unanimously. Following initial hesitation over the response to the attack of KLA on Tetovo, the international community gave the signal to Skopje to roll back militarily Albanian forces.

In the Serbo-Albanian ethnic and territorial conflict in Kosovo and Metohija, the Albanian leadership has sought for years and has finally got NATO intervention and international administration in the province. Two years after the NATO intervention and introduction of UN interim administration, the interests of Albanian national movement, on the one hand, and UNMIK and KFOR, on the other, are becoming more and more conflicting. Convinced that time works for them, the Kosovo Albanian leaders exert pressure toward final resolution of the status of Kosovo and Metohija, that is, recognition of independence, opening at the same time crisis spots in all neighbouring areas populated by ethnic Albanians, such as southern Serbia,[15] western Macedonia[16] and, in the future, probably also eastern Montenegro. Somewhat paradoxically, UNMIK and NATO missions in Kosovo and Metohija found themselves in a position similar to Milosevic's regime: although with superior military force, they were unable to stop violence and to reinforce the policy of normalization of inter-ethnic relations. In such circumstances, Albanian extremists continued national mobilization and training of paramilitary formations without much problem, with the strong support of Albanian diaspora in Western Europe[17] and the US.[18]

UNMIK and KFOR try to fulfil their mission avoiding confrontation with KLA which has formally been demilitarized and transformed into the Kosovo Protection Corps (KPC), but in practice its political and command structure, troops and armament have been preserved. From them emerged somewhat later UCPBM in southern Serbia and PLA in Macedonia. The US, which has for many years discreetly and since the latter half of 1998 openly supported KLA[19] as an ally in the fight against Milosevic's regime in Serbia, is not yet ready openly to admit that KLA, similar to the Taliban in Afghanistan, has turned from an ally into a regional security threat. The interests of Kosovo Albanians in Washington are still represented by a strong Albanian lobby and by a group of influential congressmen and senators not willing to support a major shift in the US policy in the Balkans despite the downfall of Slobodan Milosevic's regime. In addition, the Pentagon's position regarding the protection of US forces and 'zero losses' in Kosovo and Metohija imply either the retreat of American troops to fortified bases or their limited engagement, leaving a wide scope for action of KLA and its successors. Although the rules of engagement of European soldiers are somewhat more flexible, more or less similar limitations apply to them as well.

The consequences were already obvious in the crisis in the Presevo valley that started in November 2000, where Albanian paramilitary groups, armament and equipment came from Kosovo and Metohija in spite of checkpoints and border controls by KFOR. Something similar happened later in northern Macedonia, particularly during the conflicts in Tetovo, where KLA members crossed the border to Macedonia in the region of the Sar Moutain without much problem. Moreover, KFOR units stationed in Macedonia to prevent the conflict retreated from Tetovo as soon as the first German soldier was wounded in the clashes between Albanian extremists and members of Macedonian security forces.

In short, increasingly open conflict of interests between Albanian extremists and KFOR inevitably raises the issue of revision of the goals of international presence in Kosovo and Metohija and UNMIK mandate. In this regard the international community has two options at hand: either to attempt to carry out its mandate and reach the goals set by UN SC resolution 1244, risking armed conflict with Albanian extremists and casualties in KFOR ranks; or to succumb to Albanian requests and recognize the independence of Kosovo and Metohija, risking further expansion of conflict all the way to the creation of a large Albanian nation state in the Balkans. Both options put NATO in a particularly delicate position not only because of a possible failure of KFOR mission in Kosovo and Metohija, but also because of the fact that one member of Partnership for Peace – Macedonia – is de facto faced with cross-border aggression and that neither NATO nor other PfP members have so far shown readiness to come to its rescue. Moreover, escalation of crisis in the region bears the risk of a new Balkan war that could embroil other PfP as well as NATO members. In such circumstances, NATO and the US have shown readiness to offer certain cooperation to their recent adversary – Yugoslavia – without which it would be very difficult to secure military balance in the region.[20] Contrary to the statements that the US could withdraw from the Balkans, the US and NATO will probably take other political and military steps to stabilize their military presence and reinforce relations with old and new partners in the region.[21]

Contrary to the reactions of the former regime and expectations of Albanian extremists, the new authorities in Belgrade refrained from the use of force against UCPBM in southern Serbia, restricting the role of security forces to containment of the conflict within the Ground Safety Zone (GSZ). The newly founded Coordinating Committee of the Federal and Republic of Serbia Governments under the leadership of Serbian Vice-Premier Nebojsa Covic soon released its plan which implied political negotiations and economic and other measures for development of this region, as well as re-integration of the local Albanian population into government and other institutions of the Republic of Serbia. Positive reaction of the international public to this approach of Serbian and Yugoslav authorities made UCPBM lose initiative, bringing the crisis in the Presevo valley to an impasse, where the only way out was cooperation between former adversaries: the Yugoslav Army and NATO. NATO responded positively to the request of Serbian and Yugoslav authorities for abolition of GSZ by dividing it into three sectors, the first one extending along most of the border between Montenegro and Bujanovac (Sector A), the second one, 93 km long, between Bujanovac and Presevo (Sector B) and the third one between Presevo and Macedonian border (sector C). Special forces of the Yugoslav Army in cooperation with KFOR first entered the tactically most risky Sector C (occupying only 25 square kilometers), but were soon granted an authorization to enter Sector A. This was the first time that NATO and Yugoslav armed forces established operational cooperation in practice.[22]

THE YUGOSLAV DILEMMA

Two years after the end of the war in Kosovo and Metohija, six years after Dayton and ten years after the beginning of the war in SFRY, Yugoslavia and the Balkans are facing another turning point: although hardly any of the main protagonists of the breakup of the former Yugoslav federation are still active on the political scene, the crisis continues, threatening to open another chapter of the Balkan drama. Thereby, the course of the crisis follows the logic that has been known since the very beginning of wars for the Yugoslav legacy: wars in western republics of ex-Yugoslavia more or less ended by the Dayton Peace Agreement, although that does not mean that firm state structures with certain future have been established. Bosnia-Herzegovina, for example, does not stand the risk of a new armed conflict, but the policy of the international community in Bosnia-Herzegovina even six years after the Dayton Peace Agreement has not managed to achieve the main political objectives. This former Yugoslav republic is still a deeply divided society which functions largely owing to international presence and international financial assistance. Instead of having the competencies of the UN special envoy and international administration transferred over time to joint government organs, quite the opposite happened in practice: weakness of joint organs made the international administration gain more and more competencies. Moreover, at the beginning of 2001 the Croatian community in the so-called Herzeg-Bosnia started to work towards the separation from the Muslim (Bosniak) part of the Federation and creation of the third entity, contrary to the Washington Treaty and the Dayton Agreement. In spring 2001 Croat soldiers left the Union Army and Croat civil servants withdrew from the Union state institutions. However, it is highly unlikely that this process could cause regional tensions, let alone that it could escalate into an open armed conflict.

The situation is quite different in the southern Balkans, where the Kosovo crisis remained smoldering in spite of international presence, jeopardizing all neighbouring states and threatening to cause a wider armed conflict. Even if the latter were avoided, Kosovo and Metohija will probably remain the source of long-standing military and non-military threats to regional security, a potential source of international terrorism and an important crossroads in illegal trafficking in narcotics and arms in Southeastern Europe. Although the desire of Montenegrin leadership for independence will not cause armed conflict with Serbia, the breakup of the Yugoslav federation would considerably disturb the present balance of power in the region, providing a fertile ground for further escalation of the Kosovo crisis that may cause a series of wide-reaching armed conflicts in southern Balkans. The post-Milosevic and democratic FR Yugoslavia could be in this regard an important factor of regional balance, as could be seen to some extent in the crisis management in southern Serbia. If Yugoslavia managed to curb the present crisis, it could play a similar role in regional integrating processes being geographically the central country of Southeastern Europe, as well as the country with special national interests for integrating processes in the region because of the consequences of the breakup of SFRY.

NOTES

1. Already in the Milosevic–Holbrooke Agreement (October 1998) a no-fly zone was established along the administrative border between Kosovo and Serbia extending 25km into the territory of Central Serbia. The Military Technical Agreement (MTA) signed in Kumanovo established also a Ground Safety Zone extending 5km into the territory of Central Serbia. More about this in Simic (2000).
2. Even the Albanian leaders who are members of the ruling colaition in Montenegro do not miss an opportunity to stress that 'Albanians in Montenegro are aware that they are living on their own land that was awarded to Montenegro on the Berlin Congress by the will of great powers and that they accept such state of affairs as long as the authorities in Podgorica respect their rights'. Statement of Ferhat Dinosha at the Council of Europe conference, Strasbourg, October 1999, and at the Project for Ethnic Relations conference, Budva, January 2000.
3. Djukanovic's opponents claimed that the elections abounded in irregularities: between the first and second rounds the number of registered voters rose by 13,000, at certain polling stations voting was permitted past the closing time, some even claimed that police drove voters to certain polling stations, etc.
4. For example, for the payment of pensions to retirees of the federal bodies and Second World War veterans.
5. During and after the fall of Sali Berisha's regime.
6. Montenegrin economists see the reason in the fact that Montenegro, as part of the Yugoslav Federation, was under international sanctions and could not get commercial credits for creating new jobs.
7. The 'First Yugoslavia' – Kingdom of Serbs, Croats and Slovenes – was founded in 1918. The 'Second Yugoslavia' – Socialist Federal Republic of Yugoslavia (before that Democratic Federal Republic of Yugoslavia and Federal People's Republic of Yugoslavia) – was founded in 1943, and internationally recongnized in 1945. The 'Third Yugoslavia' – Federal Republic of Yugoslavia – was founded by Serbia and Montenegro in 1992.

8. The main campaign slogan of Franjo Tudjman's Croatian Democratic Union was: 'Croatian rifle on the Croatian shoulder and Croatian billfold in the Croatian pocket'.
9. It is worth noting here that in the initial phases of its emancipation Slovenia did not insist on full independence either, but only demanded constitutional transformation of the former Yugoslavia towards the so-called assymetric federation, in fact a kind of confederation.
10. According to the census taken in 1991, there were 140,000 Montenegrins living in Serbia. However, if one adds to this the part of Montenegrin populaton that consider themselves Serbs or who are the first- or second-generation immigrants from Montenegro, that number would range between 600,000 and 800,000. By comparison, the population of Montenegro numbers about 650,000.
11. Until the breakup of SFRY there were six states in the Balkans. Their number by the late 1990s rose to 10, while the continuation of the crisis could increase it to as much as 12–15.
12. Appearance of KLA slogans in Plav and Gusinje and claims presented on its web-site that KLA has four units in Montenegro alarmed the public in Montenegro and sparked fierce polemics between the supporters of the two political options in Montenegro.
13. In spite of that, five years after the signing of the Dayton Peace Agreement, Bosnia-Herzegovina is not re-integrated and remains a deeply ethnically divided society, tending toward final split. This was confirmed by political conflicts between the leadership of the Croatian Democratic Community with international adminsitration in Bosnia-Herzegovina and the request for secession of the so-called Herzeg-Bosnia, populated by the Croats, from the Muslim part of the Federation.
14. International Crisis Group (2000).
15. In the terminology of the Albanian national movement, the area of Presevo, Bujanovac and Medvedja is called 'eastern Kosovo'. Territorial aspirations of Kosovo Albanians extend to the entire territory of Serbia south of Nis and Raska region (Sanjak).
16. In the early 1990s Albanians in western Macedonia demanded federalization of Macedonia and a high degree of autonomy for this territory that they named 'Illyrida'. Having in mind the experience with the autonomy of Kosovo and Metohija in Serbia, it is hard to imagine that this would be anything else but an interim construction that would lead to final division of Macedonia.
17. The Albanian political organization with the greatest political clout is probably the People's Movement of Kosovo (Levizja Populore e Kosoves – LPK) founded in 1990s in Geneva by the followers of Enver Hoxha and Adem Demaqi and former political prisoners. LPK was the kernel of the former KLA. More about this: Simic (2000), and Judah (2000).
18. The most influential group of Albanian diaspora in the US is the Albanian-American Civic League (AACL) founded in Washington, DC in the late 1980s by the American congressman of Albanian descent Joe Diogardi. See: http://www.aacl.com.
19. The turning point was the spectacular meeting of then American envoy for the Balkans, Richard Holbrooke, with Ljum Haxhiu, member of KLA leadership, in Drenica in June 1998.
20. This dilemma has an internal component in the American policy owing to an obvious difference in positions between the Administration and Congress where a strong Albanian lobby is active. During February and March 2001 that difference was present in relation to demands forwarded by the Congress to the new authorities in Belgrade.
21. An example of this kind is military arrangements with Bulgaria.
22. It is interesting to note that already in mid-March the Federal Ministry of Defence proposed to the Federal Government to apply for addmistion of FRY into the NATO's Partnership for Peace programme.

REFERENCES

Cohen, Lenard J. (2001): *Serpent in the Blossom – The Rise and Fall of Slobodan Milosevic*, Boulder: Westview Press.

Dragoljub Popovic, *et al.* (2000): *Zajednica Srbije i Crne Gore – predlog ustvane rekonstrukcije SR Jugoslavije (Community of Serbia and Montenegro— A Proposition for the Constitutional Reconstruction of Yugoslavia)*, CLDS, Beograd – Smederevska Palanka.

Government of Montenegro (28 December 2000) *Platform for Talks with Government of Serbia on New Relations Between Two States*; http://www.ceps.be.

Hayden, Robert M. (1999): *Blueprints for a House Divided – The Constitutional Logic of the Yugoslav Conflicts*, Ann Arbor: The University of Michigan Press.

Judah, Tim (2000): *Kosovo: War and Vengeance*, , New Haven and London: Yale University Press.

International Crisis Group (2000): *What Happened to KLA?*, 3 March, http://intl-crisis-group.org.

Milosavlevski, Slavko and Mirche Tomovski (1997): *Albanians in the Republic of Macedonia 1945–1995*, Skopje: NIP Studentski zbor.

Prlja, Dragan (2001): *Srbija i Crna Gora – Pogled u budu}nost iz evropskog ugla*, paper presented at the round table 'Serbia and Montenegro – outlook for the Future from the European Viewpoint', Beograd: Friedrich Ebert Foundation, 10–11 March.

'President's Kostunica's Proposal for the Reconstruction of Yugoslavia', *Tanjug*, 10 January 2001; endorsed by the Democratic Opposition of Serbia; http://www.ceps.be.

Simic, Predrag (2000): *Put u Rambuje, kosovska kriza 1995–2000 (A Road to Rambouillet: the Kosovo Crisis 1995–2000)*, Belgrade: Nea.

Sovereignty, Europe and the Future of Serbia and Montenegro – A Proposal for International Mediation, discussion paper, European Stabilisation Initiative, Berlin, 12 February 2001.

Greece and FYROM: A Partnership for Stability in Southeastern Europe?

ARISTOTLE TZIAMPIRIS

INTRODUCTION

In the early 1990s, Greek foreign policy was dominated by the dispute with the former Yugoslav Republic of Macedonia (FYROM)[1] that was centred around the new republic's exact name.[2] Strong popular reactions, enormous mass demonstrations, the imposition of economic sanctions, and the unwillingness of both sides to compromise, created an explosive situation with partisan, political and regional consequences.[3] As Yugoslavia violently disintegrated, FYROM managed to maintain a poor, precarious but peaceful existence, while Greece's international prestige was badly damaged. An Interim Agreement was eventually signed in September 1995 between the two states, although it did not resolve the name issue.[4]

Five years later, bilateral relations have improved to such an extent, that FYROM's Prime Minister Llubco Georgievski has characterized the new situation as a 'small miracle'.[5] Unfortunately, the extent and quality of this development has not been widely reported or sufficiently analysed and appreciated by the international community. Nevertheless, it has the potential of creating an important source for stability in Southeastern Europe (SEE).

This essay will first assess problematic developments in FYROM, and explain why the new republic's very existence has been threatened. An analysis of Greece's rapprochement with FYROM will then be presented, focusing on the country's national interest in maintaining good bilateral relations and securing the young republic's continued territorial integrity. Finally, a series of specific policy-oriented actions will be recommended, which involve Greece and major international organizations. Their implementation would strengthen FYROM's relations with the European Union (EU), reduce any internal threats to domestic stability, and help solidify a partnership with Greece that would contribute towards peace and development in SEE.

FYROM AT THE CROSSROADS

FYROM's coalition government, comprised of both Slav-Macedonian and Albanian political parties, is facing a series of challenges and problems.[6] First of all, the country's economic situation is not particularly good. This is at least partly due to the adverse consequences of the Kosovo Conflict: the (temporary) influx (of more than 400,000) refugees; the disruption to international trade in goods and services; the closing of transportation routes through the Federal Republic of Yugoslavia; the damage to consumer and investor confidence; the reduction in access to international capital markets; and the setbacks to the process of structural reform and development, including weakened government.[7] The Kosovo-related cost to FYROM's economy was eventually estimated at US$1.5bn.[8]

A remarkable effort to address these problems ensued, that had unexpectedly impressive results as regards the republic's inflation rate and balance of payments situation.[9] However, FYROM's government is facing considerable opposition and charges of corruption in its necessary drive to privatize certain sectors of the economy.[10] Furthermore, unemployment was estimated by the International Monetary Fund at 32.4 per cent, while per capita GDP was only US$1,698.[11] These statistics are particularly problematic for a state confronting complicated ethnic relations, since it cannot offer (at least for now), a high level of development and prosperity as a counterweight to nationalistic aspirations.

As regards FYROM's ethnic conundrum, it is primarily linked to the fact that Albanians constitute a sizeable percentage of the country's population (officially 22.9 per cent but most likely above 30 per cent).[12] Relations during the past decade can be described as strained but largely peaceful. They certainly represent a relative success story compared with the situation between Serbs and Albanians in neighbouring Kosovo: there has been no armed conflict and relatively few acts of violence, while Albanian political elites have exhibited a willingness to participate fully and constructively in the political process. Nevertheless, substantial problems persist that are not unrelated to what can aptly be described as the 'Albanian Factor' in SEE. The Slav-Macedonian majority fears that the Albanians will eventually opt for autonomy or secession.

Today, ethnic co-existence in FYROM appears increasingly distant and based on suspicion. The views of the two communities diverge, especially on the future status of Kosovo. Albanians are overwhelmingly in favour of Kosovo breaking out of the Federal Yugoslav Republic. To quote the leader of the *DPA* Arben Xhaferi:

> We support independence for Kosovo. The most basic argument is

that only an independent Kosovo could help built stability in Albania and the region. Besides, why can a modern politician with the tolerance of Kostunica not follow the example of Havel, who was prompt to realize the signs of the times and permitted Slovakia to become independent?[13]

FYROM's national majority interprets such statements as a forerunner of arguments that could soon be directed against their country's constitutional order and territorial integrity.

Even more worrisome is the fact that on 22 January 2001, armed guerillas attacked a police station using automatic machine guns and grenades. As a result, one officer was killed and three were wounded. Many more such incidents occurred in the following months. The Albanian Liberation Army (*Ushtria Clirimtare Kombetare*) claimed responsibility, announcing in a proclamation:

> The uniform of the Macedonian conqueror will be under attack until the Albanian people are liberated ... We call [the Albanian] policemen to return to their families, so that they will not lose their lives without purpose on the altar of the Macedonian plans to dominate the Albanian majority.[14]

Furthermore, there have been indications that a perhaps different paramilitary group called the Albanian National Army (AKSH), has also begun to organize within FYROM. Although its existence has officially been denied, various reports and leaked documents suggest otherwise.[15] What is undisputed however is that large amounts of ammunition and weapons have entered the country and are in the possession of Albanians.[16] Later in the spring and summer of 2001, wide-spread clashes between armed Albanians and FYROM's security forces took place.

For the time being, FYROM's Albanians demand additional rights and their recognition not as a minority, but as a co-equal group to the Slav-Macedonians. Although it will prove impossible to satisfy this particular demand, a series of concessions could be offered in areas such as public employment, education and citizenship requirements.[17] Nevertheless, and regardless of the pursuit of such policies, FYROM's future will also be greatly influenced by developments in Kosovo. It is reasonable to expect that FYROM's Albanians will demand similar rights to the ones granted to Albanians in Kosovo. Thus, an independent Kosovo would prompt demands for autonomy or succession, causing FYROM's de-stabilization and perhaps disintegration.

The only attractive and viable alternative that the country's Slav-Macedonians can offer to the Albanian minority is that of a European future: the prospect of eventual European Union membership with its concomitant economic development, democratic stability, military security, employment opportunities and international prestige. This may indeed be viewed as a preferable outcome to the adventures of Albanian nationalism that would most likely entail violent struggles, war, deaths and perhaps a geographically enlarged, but certainly impoverished, isolated and backward Greater Albania.

In other words, FYROM's European path constitutes the best guarantee for a continued peaceful inter-ethnic co-existence and long-term territorial stability in this part of the western Balkans. However, as will be argued, FYROM's European future passes through Athens. Hence, relations with Greece become of paramount importance.

GREECE'S RAPPROCHEMENT WITH FYROM

Greece is the only member of the European Union in SEE, and subsequently capable to observe and influence decisions that affect the region's various countries. More specifically, Greece has the power to veto FYROM's accession or pose considerable hurdles to the young republic's efforts to secure funds and become increasingly more closely associated with the EU.

However, any such actions would prove counter-productive, since it is in Greece's national interest to assist FYROM's European perspective, and thus help maintain the country's existence and territorial integrity. To quote Greece's former Foreign Minister Antonis Samaras:

> It is in our interest to have a small, but truly independent state as a neighbor, than a big and powerful one. Such a state would serve our concern, and the concerns of the [European Union], for stability in the region.[18]

FYROM represents the perfect 'buffer state' that distances Greece from troubled areas and situations. For example, during the Kosovo Conflict FYROM 'absorbed' refugees and various other problems that would have probably come otherwise perilously close to Greece's borders. Furthermore, as the late Greek Prime Minister Andreas Papandreou had explained: 'we have every interest that [FYROM] does not disintegrate because this will mean a Balkan War'.[19]

According to Misha Glenny, Greeks fear that:

> The eventual outcome [of such a war] (after fighting more bloody than in Bosnia) would probably be the consolidation of a Greater Albania and a Greater Bulgaria on Greece's northern border and a

concomitant increase in Turkish influence (via Albania) in the region.[20]

In addition to FYROM's undisputed geo-strategic importance, it must be stressed that Athens and Skopje share similar views on Kosovo and the Albanian Factor. Both oppose the violent change of borders in SEE, and both consider an independent Kosovo as a major source of instability for the region.

Also, Greece's economic relations with FYROM are of particular importance. Greek products enjoy a comparative advantage because of factors such as geographic location and reduced transportation costs. This advantage is further strengthened from the considerable recognition and acceptance that Greek products have from FYROM's consumers.[21]

As a result, Greece is FYROM's second largest trading partner after Germany and the biggest foreign investor in the country.[22] Greek firms have bought the largest oil refinery, established supermarket chains, invested in the field of mining, meat processing, beer brewing and cement production. Furthermore, there are plans to construct an oil pipeline linking Skopje to Thessaloniki, while various joint ventures in the fields of electricity production, telecommunications and the expansion of railway lines between the two countries are being pursued.[23] FYROM's Foreign Minister Srgan Kerim has also stressed that 'both countries have a mutual interest to pursue common plans in sectors such as energy, ecology and tourism'.[24]

Having fully realized the importance of national interest considerations, common foreign policy preferences and significant economic opportunities, the government of Greece has cancelled almost all punitive policies against the new republic, as well as abandoned any rhetoric expressing animosity. Athens has been instrumental in securing that FYROM be the first western Balkan country to sign an Association and Stabilization Agreement with the EU.[25] Furthermore, a military agreement was signed in December 2000, covering increased cooperation in border patrolling, the safe exchange of confidential documents between the respective Chiefs of Staff, and collaboration in the areas of arms production.[26]

However, improvements in bilateral relations have met with some opposition in FYROM. For example, Greek investments have been denounced as a sellout of the country's national interest and the economy's best parts to an unfriendly and undeserving neighbour.[27] Particular criticism has been directed towards a Greek acquisition of FYROM's OKTA oil refineries.[28] Also, there seems to be considerable disagreement towards the resolution of the name-dispute on the basis of

'New Macedonia' or 'Northern Macedonia', in conjunction with substantial Greek aid and security guarantees.[29] FYROM's President Mr Boris Traijkovski has declared in no uncertain terms that 'our name, as an expression of our nation's identity is a matter of the highest national interest and dignity, [as well as] simultaneously an important issue for the country's stability'.[30] Opposition representatives have echoed these sentiments.[31]

Hence, it becomes evident from all of the above that an impressive and unexpected rapprochement between Greece and FYROM has occurred. However, the name issue remains unresolved, threatening to undermine gains, despite what appears to be an official desire to speedily settle this dispute. Improved bilateral relations could indeed create a partnership for stability in SEE, but they remain fragile. Ultimately, a series of policy-oriented recommendations, aided by specific action of international organizations, should be implemented in order to solidify and enhance the new positive situation.

TOWARDS A PARTNERSHIP FOR STABILITY

The following policy-oriented recommendations would strengthen relations between FYROM and Greece and contribute towards peace and prosperity in the region. More specifically:

1. Greece should pursue specific actions to guarantee the territorial integrity of FYROM, especially if Kosovo moves towards independence. In such an instance, Greece should submit proposals within the EU and NATO, explicitly asking that both organizations militarily guarantee FYROM's borders, even if that entails armed clashes against Albanian militant guerrilla groups.
2. Greece should coordinate joint actions with FYROM, aimed at postponing or averting Kosovo's independence. This can be pursued on the basis of joint statements and concerted actions within organizations to which both countries belong (UN, OCSE, and so on). Having the former adversaries Greece and FYROM declare common positions would attract international attention and underscore the seriousness with which regional actors perceive the future status of Kosovo. Greece could in addition present in common with FYROM views in NATO and the EU where it enjoys membership.
3. NATO must address the issue of border changes in SEE, making it absolutely clear that any attempt to violently alter FYROM's borders will be met with a determined response. In this manner, Albanian irredentist actions might be deterred to a considerable extent.

4. The United Nations Security Council should also pass a resolution warning against any irredentist plans against FYROM, declaring its willingness to support and guarantee the country's territorial integrity.

5. Greece should assist FYROM's efforts to eventually join the European Union by:

    • providing technical assistance and advice in order to assist FYROM harmonize with EU standards;
    • ensuring that funding for projects in FYROM through the Stability Pact for SEE remains considerable. Furthermore, Greece could help in the design, funding and implementation of additional FYROM-related projects within the Stability Pact framework;
    • advising FYROM's government on what kind of foreign policy-related actions and statements would be deemed unacceptable by the EU;
    • increasing the funding and number of FYROM-related projects that are included in Greece's Ministry of National Economy Plan for the Reconstruction of SEE;
    • speedily submitting for ratification to the National Parliament, FYROM's Association and Stabilization Agreement with the EU.

6. FYROM and Greece should settle the name issue in a manner that takes into consideration their recent rapprochement. Realities, sensitivities and international practices must be considered, though the fact remains that given Greece's efforts to aid FYROM, there must be no fear that a name acceptable to the sensitivities of the Greek people would imply territorial ambitions (future or present) of any sort. The Interim Agreement is supposed to expire in 2002,[32] and unless a solution is found soon, past passions and disputes may re-emerge threatening the gains in bilateral relations.

7. The EU must continuously and publicly endorse all reform efforts that bring FYROM closer to eventual membership. The impression should be created that the new republic is not fighting an uphill battle, but that the country's government and people are under constant aid and positive supervision by the Union. As a result, feelings of disappointment and efforts to pursue alternative and perhaps nationalistic policies will be weakened.

8. The EU must also contribute greatly in fighting corruption and crime in FYROM. The rise of illegal activities creates a weak state that cannot render adequate services to its citizens, and may thus lose legitimacy in the long run. Such a situation may be especially

dangerous for a country facing fragile inter-ethnic relations like FYROM. Thus, the EU must provide technical and legal assistance, as well as training in areas such as border control, anti-smuggling operations and the fight against drug trafficking.

9. The EU must make it clear that Bulgaria's prospects for membership require peaceful relations with FYROM and an abandonment of any irredentist or nationalistic aspirations against the smaller neighbouring country.[33] Pressure emanating from Brussels among these lines has persuaded Sofia to recognize the existence of a Slav-Macedonian language (though not of such a nation).

10. Finally, educational and cultural disputes between Greece and FYROM must also be addressed and resolved. Particularly problematic is the quality and accuracy of FYROM's textbooks.[34] It can only be judged as abysmal, and thus clearly does not contribute to a positive bilateral climate. For this reason, both governments should actively encourage efforts such as the 'Southeast European Joint History Project'.[35] In addition, committees of distinguished experts and academics should be appointed in order to discuss areas of disagreement and misunderstanding. Furthermore, funding should be made available to encourage travelling and exchange programmes for scholars, journalists, students and politicians. Perhaps the best way to maximize cultural understanding and tolerance would be through the establishment of the University of Southeastern Europe in Thessaloniki. The implementation of this proposal by the Greek government would provide an appropriate institutional umbrella framework that would encourage, organize and fund all of the aforementioned educational proposals and actions.

Greece and FYROM had an acrimonious dispute that defined their relations in the early part of the 1990s. However, the existence of significant common interests, the recent impressive rapprochement and the taking into account of the above policy recommendations, could create a strong partnership between the two states, supported by the international community, that would help ensure that Southeastern Europe will not be doomed to instability.

NOTES

1. Throughout this essay the term FYROM will be utilized. This approach has the advantage of conforming to the 1993 UN Security Council Resolution 813, according to which 'this state [will be] referred to for all purposes within the United Nations "the former Yugoslav Republic of Macedonia" pending settlement of the difference that has

arisen over the name of the state'. For the text of the resolution see Valinakis and Dales (1994), p.147 (in both Greek and English).

2. As a result of the almost exclusive attention that was paid to the dispute with FYROM, Greece's foreign policy was aptly described as having been 'skopjeanized' (Skopje being both the capital of FYROM and the term by which almost all Greeks referred to the new state).

3. For extensive accounts of events in Greece during this period see Kofos (1999); Skilakakis (1995) (in Greek); Tarkas (1995 and 1997) (in Greek); Tziampiris (2000); and Veremis (1995).

4. For an analysis (and the text) of the 1995 New York Interim Agreement see Rozakis (1996) (in Greek).

5. See Internet site: http://world.flash.gr/research/print_version_asp?articleid+2251

6. The main Slav-Macedonia party is *VMRO-DMPNE* headed by Ljubco Georgievski. Its major coalition party is the Albanian *DPA* which is led by Arben Xhaferi. Prior to coming into power following the November 1998 elections, both parties had tended to adopt the more extreme nationalist positions of their respective communities. However, as so often happens, the obligations of governing have had a moderating effect on their rhetoric and actions. For an analysis of the complicated and intricate partisan politics of FYROM's Albanians, see International Crisis Group, *Macedonia's Ethnic Albanians: Bridging the Gap* (2 August 2000) and Pettifer (1999).

7. International Monetary Fund, *The Economic Consequences of the Kosovo Crisis: An Updated Assessment.* The report was issued on 25 May 1999 and can be found at Internet site: http://www.imf.org/external/pubs/ft/kosovo/052599.htm

8. See Pierre J. Andrew, *De-Balkanizing the Balkans: Security and Stability in Southeastern Europe.* This is a special report released by the United States Institute of Peace (USIP) on 20 September 1999. See also BBC News, *Economic Crisis For Macedonia,* 6 May 1999. It can be found at Internet site: http://news.bbc.co.uk/hi/english/special_report/1999/kosovo/newsiiiid_3360000/336972.stm

9. See Internet site: http://www.nbrm.gov.mk/basic_economic_data.htm

10. For an official and succinct account of the efforts to privatize the economy see Internet site http://mpa.org.mk/privatization.htm

11. For a presentation and reliable discussion of FYROM's more recent economic situation, see International Monetary Fund, *FYROM: Recent Economic Developments,* Staff Country Report No. 00/72, June 2000. It can be found at Internet site: http://www.imf.org/external/pubs/ft/scr/2000/cr0072.pdf

12. For an objective discussion of the number of Albanians residing in FYROM (not necessarily citizens of the state), see International Crisis Group, op. cit., pp.4–6. Officially, Slav-Macedonians constitute some 66.6% of the population, Turks 4%, Roma 2.2% and Serb 2.1%. See CIA, *The World Factbook 2000: The Former Yugoslav Republic of Macedonia.* It can be found at Internet site: http://www.odci.gov/cia/publications/factbook/geos/mk.html

13. 'In FYROM We Are Living the Fable of the Fox and the Hawk', *E. Kathimerine,* 20 December 2000 (in English).

14. Eleftherotypia, *The Other 'UCK' Assumed Responsibility,* 26 January 2001 (in Greek). Note that the initials of the Albanian Liberation Army are UCK, and hence identical to those of the Kosovo Liberation Army (UCK in Albanian). Although the meaning of the words is different, the intended message is clear, since both groups espouse radical Albanian irredentist goals and welcome the use of violence. It is also of importance that FYROM's UCK proclamation indicated that it was the fourth in a series, thus raising suspicions that previous attacks to police stations were also perpetrated by them, the authorities possibly having suppressed publication of their literature. On this issue see also BBC News, *Albanian Militia Claims Macedonian Attack,* 26 January 2001 at Internet site: http://news.bbc.uk/hi/english/world/europe/newsid_1138000/1138980.stm

15. See International Crisis Group, op. cit., p.3.

16. See Sfetas (2000), p.337, (in Greek).

17. See especially the important recommendations contained in International Crisis Group, op. cit. An example of a working compromise between Albanians and Slav-Macedonians centres on the creation of an officially recognized Albanian-language University. An emotive issue that had even elicited violent protests during the 1990s, it was eventually resolved by law on 5 July 2000, following intense efforts by OSCE High Commissioner on National Minorities Max Van Der Stool. It will be funded by various Western governments, the Council of Europe and the Soros Foundation. See BBC News, *Macedonia Legalises Albanian-Language University*, 6 July 2000 at Internet site: http://news6.thdo.bbc.co.uk/hi/english/world/europe/europe/newsid%5F853000/8533 20.stm

18. Cited in Tziampiris (2000), p.51.

19. Ibid.

20. Glenny (1996), p.143.

21. Saritza (1996), p.239 (in Greek).

22. See Flash.gr, *FYROM: Only the Name Remains*, 4 December 2000 (in Greek) at Internet site; http://world.flash.gr//europe/balkan/2000/12/3/2251d/

23. See Tziampiris (2000), p.53.

24. Article by Mr. Kerim, titled 'Greek–Macedonian Relations As a Contribution to Cooperation and Security in the Balkans', published in *Ependytis*, 3–4 February 2001 (in Greek).

25. See BBC News, *EU Hails Triumph of Balkan Democracy*, 24 November 2000 at Internet   site: http://news.bbc.co.uk/hi/english/world/europe/newsid_1038000/1038639.stm

26. See *Eleftherotypia*, 'We Will Help Skopje Guard Their Borders', 12 December 2000 (in Greek).

27. On this point, see especially the interview of FYROM's Prime Minister Mr Georgievski in *E Kathimerini*, 22 October 2000 (in Greek).

28. See the furious comments of FYROM's Leader of the Opposition Mr Branko Cervenkovski published in *Eleftherotypia*, 9 July 2000 (in Greek).

29. See *To Vima*, 'They Are Reaching An Agreement On Skopje's Name', 26 January 2001 (in Greek); *Eleftherotypia*, 'Proposals With Offers For the Name', 9 February 2001 and *E Kathimerine*, 'The Name Issue At a Crucial Crossroad', 11 February 2001 (in Greek).

30. Cited in *Eleftherotypia*, 'Turmoil in Skopje As A Result of the Greek Proposal on the Name', 10 February 2001 (in Greek).

31. See ibid.

32. According to Article 23, any decision to withdraw from the Agreement after seven years will take effect only 12 months later. In other words, the 1995 Interim Agreement has a year-long, built-in extension.

33. In late 2000 Bulgaria's Ambassador in Skopje attended a meeting in which the represented Bulgarian views that were perceived as being against FYROM. His presence caused apprehension among the Slav-Macedonian elite, and was interpreted by many as a harbinger of a renewed Bulgarian nationalism in bilateral relations. See Flash. gr, *Skopje and Tirana* (in Greek) at Internet site: http://world.flash.gr/europe/balkan/2000/11/13/1882id.

34. See for example Kofos (1994).

35. See Internet site: http://www.cdsee.org.

REFERENCES

Glenny, Misha (1996): 'The Macedonian Question', in Danchev, Alex and Thomas, Helverson, eds, *International Perspectives On the Yugoslav Conflict*, London: Macmillan Press.

Kofos, Evangelos (1994): *The Vision of 'Greater Macedonia'*, Thessaloniki: The Friends of the Museum of the Macedonian Struggle.

Kofos, Evangelos (1999): 'Greek Policy Considerations Over FYROM Independence and

Recognition', in Pettifer, James, ed., *The New Macedonian Question*, London: Macmillan.

Pettifer, James (1999): 'The Albanians in Western Macedonia After FYROM Independence', in Pettifer, James, ed., *The New Macedonian Question*, London: Macmillan.

Rozakis, Christos (1996): *Political and Legal Dimensions of the New York Interim Agreement Between Greece and FYROM*, Athens: I. Sideris (in Greek).

Saritza, Mathildi (1996): 'FYROM's Economic Environment and Greece's Exports', in Tsardanidis, Charalambos, ed., *The Economic Relations Between Greece and the Former Yugoslav Republic of Macedonia*, Athens: I. Sideris, p.239 (in Greek).

Sfetas, Spyridon (2000): 'Skopje's Albanian Factor After the Dayton Agreement', in Karakostanoglou Veniamin, Kentrotis D. Kiriakos, Manta Eleftheria and Sfetas Spyridon, eds, *Kosovo and the Albanian Populations of the Balkan Peninsula*, Thessaloniki: Institute of Balkan Studies (in Greek).

Skilakakis, Theodoros (1995): *In the Name of Macedonia*, Athens: Elleneke Evroekdotike (in Greek).

Tarkas, Alexandros (1995 and 1997): *Athens Skopje. Behind Closed Doors, Volumes I and II*, Athens: Laverenthos (in Greek).

Tziampiris, Aristotle (2000): *Greece, European Political Cooperation and the Macedonian Question*, Aldershot: Ashgate Press.

Valinakis, Yannis and Sotires Dales (1995): *The Skopje Question*, Athens: I. Sideris.

Veremis, Thanos (1995): *Greece's Balkan Entanglement*, Athens: Hellenic Foundation for European and Foreign Policy and YALCO.

An Update and Conclusions

DIMITRI A. SOTIROPOULOS AND
THANOS VEREMIS

The events 11 September 2001 have contributed to a flight of Western attention from Southeastern Europe (SEE) towards western Asia and the Middle East. The extent and the pace with which US forces may withdraw from Bosnia-Herzegovina and Kosovo, in order to be deployed to regions closer to the heart of America's war against terrorism, is not known. Southeastern Europe, however, is still in the throes of political instability and economic decay.

Much of course will depend on the progress or lack of it in the economic sphere throughout the troubled Western Balkans. Progress will also depend on the willingness of the West to support the project of upgrading the region as a whole after the devastating decade of the 1990s. As several contributors to this volume have stressed (Bokova, Kondonis, Surroi, Vukadinovic, Tziampiris, Yannis), the long-term aim of this upgrading would be the integration of SEE with the European Union. There is of course a variety of opinions on how this integration is understood and how the integration can be effected. For instance, Bokova argues that the greatest challenge today is the integration of SEE into the European mainstream. First, there is a need to extend the European democratic space, with its liberal standards and procedures, into SEE. In this region there is a lack of institutions, lack of rule of law, and lack of competitive economies. In SEE, after the fall of communism, the 'withdrawal' of the state was negotiated in favour of a number of groups, which exist between in the public and the private sphere. Second, in terms of economic reforms, SEE countries need to combine strategies of integration into the EU with strategies of national development. However, it is difficult to count on endogenous factors to promote development. The Balkans need a new type of 'Marshall Plan'. They do *not* need new divisions, such as the division into 'Western' and 'Eastern' Balkans. However, most SEE countries are far from satisfying the Copenhagen criteria for economic competitiveness. To amend the situation, the Stability Pact and the EU integration effort should go hand in hand.

The idea that a 'Marshall Plan' is needed for SEE puts an emphasis on economic development. Another view is that, given the little economic interest of the West in SEE, security issues should come first. As Vukadinovic claims, due to wars in former Yugoslavia and to the problems of transition in the region as a whole, the international geo-economic interest in the Balkans has decreased. The incorporation of SEE into a wider security architecture is necessary in order to avert military and non-military threats to the region's stability. 'Security architecture' is a concept meaning a set of institutions which fulfil a security function and the arrangement of relations among those institutions. The international community has a sufficient military presence and interest in SEE. Non-military challenges are more difficult to meet. Among the latter, traditional Balkan disputes, new conflicts related to recently acquired national independence, potential points of crisis and new challenges to security, are included. After the future normalization of relations among SEE countries the current situation of 'unstable stability' could be overcome. One could envisage the inclusion of the SEE region as a whole into a new European Security Architecture.

A third view reminds us that we should not give up on regional cooperation because its past record has not been as slim as it may have appeared. Kut and ªirin explain that despite the legacy of the Balkan Wars early in the twentieth century and some deeply conflictual relations in the Balkans, examples of cooperation have not been scarce in the region. Without denying the existence of disputes, most Balkan states have managed to develop their bilateral relations and to participate in regional cooperation schemes. In the 1990s, Balkan countries have been involved in a number of initiatives, which can be classified in three categories: first, mostly economic cooperation schemes; second, political cooperation schemes; and third, military cooperation schemes. From 1996 to 1998, multilateral meetings of Balkan leaders took place. Currently, several schemes, initiated by the EU and the US, are still under way. The further success of cooperation schemes will depend on the full commitment of interested parties, on the non-exclusionary character of the schemes, and on good management of financial resources.

Others perceive such foreign affairs and security issues in a more focused manner and consider the fate of Kosovo, the integrity of FYROM and the evolution of relations of Serbia with Montenegro crucial for the stability of the region as a whole. What should be done with Kosovo? In his contribution, Surroi suggests that the decline of Serb rule over Kosovo is irreversible and that Kosovo eventually will become a state, even though it is debatable whether this state will have full sovereignty or not. Surroi claims that the future of Kosovo has been linked with two other processes, the ongoing disintegration of Yugoslavia and the process of European integration. Kosovo is undergoing three transitions: first, the transition from communism to democracy; second, the transition from minority to majority rule (from rule of Serbs over Albanians to self-rule of Albanians); and third, the transition from a multi-ethnic region to a nation-state. The United Nations Security Council Resolution 1244 implies a process, the endpoint of which will be that Kosovo becomes a state. Differences of opinion exist on the degree of sovereignty this state will have. The Albanian national movement has traditionally sprung up in different locations. It is a 'polycentric' movement, which may influence thinking over the future of Kosovo. Kosovo may be a unit with more flexible and permeable borders than typical ethnocentric nation-states. For Surroi, all of the above can decided upon in a two-step process. The first step would be to establish democratic self-rule in Kosovo, while the second step would be to reach a decision on its permanent status.

Kofos is of a different opinion. In his, he sees the need for a new interim status for Kosovo and puts forward the idea of a United Nations Trusteeship of Kosovo. His rationale is linked to the pivotal role of the situation in Kosovo for the stability of SEE as a whole. Kofos argues that as long as the status of Kosovo remains unclear, other Albanian groups outside of Kosovo, may increase their demands and escalate their political and military activities. In view of the above, placing Kosovo under the temporal 'trusteeship' of the United Nations could be a solution. This solution was applied after the Second World War to various colonies and territories formerly belonging to Western powers. The new status of Kosovo as a territory under United Nations trusteeship requires that FR Yugoslavia voluntarily agrees to this interim status and that one or more countries, perhaps including Yugoslavia, would constitute an Administering Authority to govern Kosovo while it prepares for self-government or independence.

A third answer to the question how to deal with Kosovo is to continue on the track set by the UN SC Resolution 1244. Yannis argues that the status of Kosovo may be 'frozen' because there is an absence of international and local consensus about its future. The more rigorous implementation of Resolution 1244 could prevent Kosovo from sliding back to open conflict. Democratic elections alone can not solve the problem. There is a need for a road map to meet the minimum demands of Kosovo Albanians and Serbs. However, it would be dangerous to meet the maximum demands of either. To that effect, a new 'agenda of coexisence' could be adopted which could ensure the functional autonomy of Serbs within the substantial autonomy of Albanians. There is also need for a long-term commitment from the international community to the development of the region. This does not necessary mean the indefinite perpetuation of an international military presence or undiminished financial aid, but substantive assistance to build effective democratic institutions. The democratic change in Serbia in 2000 and the victory of moderate political forces in the elections in Kosovo have opened a window of opportunity.

Simic shows in his essay how the situation in Kosovo is linked with the evolution of Serb–Montenegrin relations and with the domestic problems faced by FYROM. He argues that there are at least two different, but interlinked kinds of crisis the evolution of which should be closely monitored. First, a crisis has been provoked by Albanian extremists who have been active in Kosovo, Macedonia and southern Serbia; and second, the relations between Serbia and Montenegro remain unclear (a third problem which he analyses is the possible disintegration of Bosnia-Herzegovina). These problems have a common dynamic and one may influence the other. In concrete, since October 1997, there has been a 'cold war' between Podgorica and Belgrade, but open conflict has not erupted. Under Milosevic, repression by authorities in Belgrade has worked in favour of authorities in Podgorica. After the victory of democratic forces in Belgrade, periodic negotiations have taken place between Serbia and Montenegro. In 2001 in southern Serbia, the new Belgrade administration was able to contain the activities of the Albanian UCPBM, and the Yugoslav army has cooperated with NATO in the Ground Safety Zone. Simic is not in agreement with Yannis that the overall presence of the international community in Kosovo has been positive. For Simic, UNMIK and NATO have not confronted the remaining vestiges of UCK and have been unable to stop violence at the local level. The situation in Kosovo remains a long-term source of threats to regional security. Conversely, the break-up of the Yugoslav Federation might cause an escalation of the Kosovo crisis.

If, as all of the above authors claim, Yugoslavia and Kosovo are at the crossroads, FYROM has time and again faced parallel problems. Events in 2001 in FYROM were alarming. On 2 May 2001, FYROM President Boris Trajkovski appealed to US President Bush to resolve the conflict introduced in his state by the Albanian National Liberation Army – a new incarnation of Kosovo's UCK (Kosovo Liberation Army). On 3 May, the FYROM government unleashed helicopter and artillery fire against Albanian villages harbouring the rebels. On 11 May, Prime Minister Ljubco Georgievski announced the formation of a broad coalition by the country's four main political parties to address the crisis. On 13 August, representatives of the Macedonian Slav majority and the Macedonian

Albanian minority concluded an agreement in Ochrid which provided for significant constitutional amendments and reform to improve the status of Albanians in FYROM. The document was ratified by the parliament a few months later, but it is still unclear if this measure will restore peace in a badly divided country. There are those among the Albanians of FYROM who prefer to pursue a route of modernization and development within a multicultural state, rather than to submit to the irredentist sirens from the Kosovo Liberation Army and the NLA. But not all inhabitants of FYROM are of the same mind, be they Slav or Albanian Macedonians. Given the difficulty of FYROM' s army to maintain order in Albanian-dominated northwestern provinces and the escalation of violence that usually follows ethnic wars, the future appears to be in the balance.

The essay by Tziampiris addresses exactly some of these issues. He claims that in the past, relations between FYROM and Greece were problematic, but nowadays FYROM and Greece have an interest in maintaining good bilateral relations. FYROM has faced a difficult economic situation, which was aggravated by the economic burden of the Kosovo conflict in 1999. It has also faced challenges to its territorial integrity. Ethnic coexistence in FYROM remains a problem, because the views of the country's national majority and its Albanian minority diverge. Fortunately there has been an economic and diplomatic rapprochement between Greece and FYROM. It is important to secure FYROM's territorial integrity, an aim which can be achieved through the involvement of Greece, the European Union and other major international organizations.

The effects of involvement of the international community, of the EU and of international organization can be tested on the ground, that is, on specific societal levels and policy areas in which post-communist Southeastern Europe has made little progress. In this volume, several such levels and areas are singled out: civil society and non-governmental organizations (NGOs) in particular, mass media, school textbooks, public administration and, of course, corruption and organized crime. These are issues on which each country's institutions, interest groups and elites should be able to act effectively, while the influence of the West could be felt either through the Stability Pact or through other channels. But, at least in parts of the contributions to this volume, the verdict on the performance of domestic institutions and actors is rather negative, while the performance of the Stability Pact is debatable.

Kondonis, in his essay on the Stability Pact and NGOs, argues that it has taken the international community some time to realize that for the economic reform and democratization of SEE to succeed, different social actors in addition to governments must be involved. The Stability Pact was the result of the realization that economic development must be linked to a parallel democratic transition of society. Many NGOs in SEE are connected with government officials or with powerful international sponsors. Local NGOs look for such sponsors and, consequently, regional cooperation of civil society associations remains limited. The mobilization of NGOs is encouraged through the first Working Table of the Stability Pact. However, the implementation of the Pact in that particular field has met with problems. There is multi-collectivism, that is, too many members and partners, and this is reflected in a complex bureaucratic structure. There are conflicting interests and priorities and a lack of coordination. Member-states of the Pact have been reluctant to staff and financially support the Pact. States of SEE countries have been reluctant to cooperate with NGOs. Stability Pact projects have been approachable by a few NGOs and private companies. There is a need for direct action and political will to exploit the many positive aspects of the Stability Pact. Specific criteria for projects, such as 'added value' and 'regional transferability', may be applied with success and a more clear 'priority agenda' has to be set.

Another agenda of priorities is clearly required for the functioning of mass media and education, which are influential socializing agents. In regard to mass media, Lani and Cupi argue that in most countries of Southeastern Europe the transition to democracy has gone through a phase of a New Authoritarianism, evident, among other things, in the status of mass media. Such new authoritarian regimes were largely based on control of mass media (such as Serbia under Milosevic). Currently, there is consensus that regulation of print media would probably lead to censorship. On the other hand, most Southeast European countries have passed legislation on TV and radio broadcasting. A fair balance between necessary regulations and the freedom of the media has not yet been achieved. Some political leaders of post-communist Southeastern Europe are not open to accept intense criticism from the media. Some react strongly to criticism, while others have adopted a stance of indifference towards the media, which means that opinions voiced in and by the media are ineffective. Some mass media are controlled by political groups while other media have succumbed to economic interests. Since the transition from communism, partisan politics has penetrated the media, which have also been affected by economic difficulties and corruption. During the disintegration of Yugoslavia many media have promoted nationalist causes and have fuelled conflict. In the emerging democracies of Southeastern Europe, the spread of free press can be considered a major achievement; at the same time the image of the press in society is rather negative. There is a need for economic independence of the media and for the training of journalists. Support for reform of the media and for adoption of a code of ethics among journalists is highly recommended.

In regard to education, a crucial aspect is the type of ideas which are spread through the schooling system to the younger generations of Southeast Europeans. Murgescu suggests that despite common impressions, education systems and problems of identity formation in Southeastern Europe are far from homogeneous. The contents of school textbooks of geography and history are closely linked with the formation of national identities of Balkan peoples. But textbooks are not solely to blame for the spread of violent ethnic conflict. Mass media and the public discourse in general should also be taken into account. In view of the above, there are three categories of Southeast European states. The first category consists of states which have existed for several generations (Albania, Bulgaria, Greece, Romania and Turkey). Although violent conflicts have not erupted recently among these nation-states, textbooks used in their educational systems reflect a biased vision of the past. An even more biased vision is found in textbooks of a second category of states, which emerged from the disintegration of former Yugoslavia. None of these states seems prepared to offer a more balanced view of history. The third category consists of territories under the control of Western administration and military (Bosnia-Herzegovina and Kosovo). In these areas, values taught to pupils are at odds with ideas of reconciliation. There are possibilities for improving on textbooks and school curricula. An example is the EUSTORY network of history competitions for young people. Such specific efforts may be combined with support schemes for the educational systems in general and with training programmes in other subjects, beyond history and geography.

In discussing the mass media and education, the role of state administration and public institutions is obvious. However, this is perhaps the area where post-communist SEE countries encounter problems which for the moment seem insurmountable, if one judges from the spread of corruption and organized crime. In post-communist SEE, as Sotiropoulos argues, after 1989 the state has remained big and has become weak. It has been unable to counter organized crime and to provide better services to the people. A few small case studies illustrate these claims. The Bulgarian public administration used to be very politicized even before the rise of the Communist Party to power. Since the transition to democracy, administrative reform has been very slow, while extreme politicization has continued. However, in the late 1990s new laws reorganizing the administration were passed. The case of

Yugoslavia is different, particularly since this is a federal state. Under Milosevic, the administration as a whole became very rigid and, in many instances, corrupt. Kosovo has been administered partly by the local government and partly by UNMIK. The cases of Bulgaria, Yugoslavia and Kosovo share some common traits related to the problematic selection, compensation and training of civil servants. Administrative reform should primarily address the issue of corruption and should also be linked to the strengthening of democratic institutions, including the access of citizens to state services.

Today, this access seems often restrained by the informal and/or illegal patterns of behaviour imposed in parts of SEE societies by organized crime and by circles of corrupted officials. Krastev and Minchev both discuss this issue, offering different viewpoints. Krastev claims that in Southeastern Europe there is a general perception of public administration incompetence and of insecurity. A relevant case is that of Bulgaria, where there is a dilemma of fighting corruption or promoting economic reform. Attempting the former in the traditional fashion of increasing administrative controls, would require too many resources which are necessary for economic reform. Corruption is impossible to measure because the scope of the concept has changed over time, because it is rarely confirmed as such in the courts, and because there are no specific victims of corruption. In Bulgaria the probability of sentencing a corrupted official to a term in prison is nil. Various solutions, such as tightening institutional controls or offering pay increases to officials, do not work. Anti-corruption measures often lead to more state regulation and may also fuel populism as a strategy of political leaders. The Bulgarian government should proceed with deregulation and de-monopolization as well as with raising public awareness about corruption.

The viewpoint of Minchev is somewhat different. He sees that a major problem of the transition to democracy and the market in Southeast European countries is how these countries will adapt their institutions to the European model. The lack of foreign investment and a coherent legal framework have had the following effect: privatizations have been sidetracked into a route leading to a very large underground economy. This economy has fallen into the hands of members of the former nomenclature. Government failure and loss of public morale are related to the spread of corruption particularly since corruption has become a normal way of operation for private interests. In turn, people in SEE societies have fallen back to pre-modern forms of security (family or clan-based forms). Post-communist elites have mistakenly believed in the power of the 'invisible hand' of the market and the beneficial effects of 'civil society' and have not created adequate institutions to replace the dismantled totalitarian system. The way out is to change the abstract 'democratization' paradigm with the paradigm of development of effective representative and administrative institutions and of adaptation to the globalizing and multi-cultural world.

Most analysts would agree that SEE needs to develop towards that model. However, in the meantime, the region evolves in various directions, some of which are positive (the elections in Kosovo and the victory of moderate political forces) while others are ambiguous (the dispute between Fatos Nano and Ilir Meta in Albania and the resignation of Prime Minister Ilir Meta in the beginning of 2002), if not clearly detrimental to peace and development (the violent conflicts in Tetovo in spring and summer 2001). The economies of the region remain undeveloped, and the biggest problems are unemployment and lack of foreign investments. The West has not set a clear set of priorities in regard to the economic future of the region. The Stability Pact remains a complex set of processes although it bears a lot of potential to deliver substantive help to SEE. The quality of democracies in the region is very debatable. Despite holding regular elections, many SEE countries still do not possess effective democratic and administrative institutions. This is related to the flourishing corruption and organized crime. Possible solutions lie in a combination of regional and international initiatives, in which individual SEE countries and the international community will act together. On the side of the international community, there is a need for concrete actions in the context of a long-term commitment to the region. This will require political will on the part of important Western powers, and more concerted and coordinated efforts on the part of involved international organizations. On the side of individual SEE countries, there is a need for mobilization of their own economic and human resources and willingness to build institutions and processes which will allow these countries to adapt to the requirements of political and economic integration with Europe. This prospect allows the optimistic conclusion that Southeastern Europe is not doomed to instability.

Biographical Notes

Irina Bokova is Chairperson of the Board of Trustees at the European Policy Forum, Sofia, Bulgaria.

Frrok Cupi is Director of the Albanian Telegraphic Agency, at Tirana.

Evangelos Kofos is Historian and Balkan Area Advisor, ELIAMEP.

Haralambos Kondonis is an Advisor on International Development Cooperation in Southeast Europe in the Ministry of Foreign Affairs of Greece, and Special Advisor of the Chair of the Working Table 1 on Democratization and Human Rights of the Stability Pact. He is Research Fellow of ELIAMEP on Balkan Affairs.

Ivan Krastev is Director of the Centre for Liberal Strategies, Sofia.

Şule Kut is a Professor of International Relations at Istanbul Bilgi University.

Remzi Lani is Director of the Albanian Media Institute, at Tirana.

Ognyan Minchev is Director of the Institute for Regional and International Studies, Sofia.

Mirela-Luminiţa Murgescu is Assistant Professor at the Faculty of History, University of Bucharest.

Predrag Simic is Senior Research Fellow at the Institute of International Politics and Economics, Belgrade.

N. Asli Şirin is a teaching assistant and MA candidate at Istanbul Bilgi University.

Dimitri A. Sotiropoulos is Lecturer of Political Science at the Department of Political Science and Public Administration of the University of Athens, and Research Fellow of ELIAMEP.

Veton Surroi is the publisher of the newspaper *Koha ditore*, Prishtina.

Aristotle Tziampiris is a Lecturer at the International and European Studies Department of the University of Piraeus and Research Fellow of ELIAMEP.

Radovan Vukadinovic is a Professor of Political Science at the University of Zagreb.

Thanos Veremis is a Professor of History at the Fletcher School of Law and Diplomacy, Boston and a member of the Board of Trustees of ELIAMEP.

Alexandros Yannis is a Research Associate at the Programme for Strategic and International Security Studies of the Graduate Institute of International Studies, Geneva University, and a former Political Advisor to the Special Representative of the UN Secretary General in Kosovo.

Abstracts

Is Southeastern Europe Doomed to Instability? A Regional Perspective
DIMITRI A. SOTIROPOULOS and THANOS VEREMIS

The purpose of this volume is to offer local perspectives on Southeastern Europe, written by experts coming from this region, who aim to show that instability is not endemic in post-communist Southeastern Europe. The analysis tries to focus on the interplay of regional and international actors. At the regional level some enduring common traits, shared by post-communist states, are highlighted. These include: first, structural problems in the economy and society, as well as inflexible perceptions of identity which are the legacy of the region's past; second, difficulties in shaping new policies in view of the fact that the state mechanisms of Southeast European countries are weak; third, multiple social problems, aggravating the situation in the form of a negative spiral, because of the different phases of transition that the countries of SEE go through; and fourth, in view of the above, a crisis of legitimacy faced by states in the region as they try to deal with strife, underdevelopment and criminal networks. The West has underestimated the long-term dangers of structural economic underdevelopment and changes of borders in Southeastern Europe. The Stability Pact has been the major response of the West to the challenges facing the region but its assets have been inadequate.

The Bright Side of Balkan Politics: Cooperation in the Balkans
ŞULE KUT and N. ASLI ŞIRIN

Despite the legacy of Balkan Wars early in the twentieth century and some deeply conflictual relations in the Balkans, examples of cooperation have not been scarce in the region. Cooperation efforts started in 1930 and continued in the 1950s and the 1960s. However, post-war attempts at cooperation failed mostly due to the Cold War environment, which set apart Greece and Turkey on the other hand and their Balkan neighbours on the other. Such efforts were revived in the late 1980s, while in the 1990s the Yugoslav conflicts delayed cooperation initiatives but also proved their necessity. Without denying the existence of disputes, most Balkan states have managed to develop their bilateral relations and to participate in regional cooperation schemes. In the 1990s Balkan countries have been involved in a number of initiatives, which can be classified in three categories: first, mostly economic cooperation schemes; second, political cooperation schemes; and third, military cooperation schemes. From 1996 to 1998, multilateral meetings of Balkan leaders took place. Currently, several schemes, initiated by the EU and the US, are still under way. The further success of cooperation schemes will depend on the full commitment of interested parties, on the non-exclusionary character of the schemes, and on good management of financial resources.

Integrating Southeastern Europe into the European Mainstream
IRINA BOKOVA

In the past, the response of the West to the challenges of Southeastern Europe was a response of neglect or of contradictory signals. Today, the greatest challenge is the integration of SEE into the European mainstream. First, there is a need to extend the European democratic space, with its liberal standards and procedures, into SEE. In this region there is a lack of institutions, rule of law and competitive economies. In SEE, after the fall of communism, the 'withdrawal' of the state was negotiated in favour of a number of groups which exist between the public and private spheres. Second, in terms of economic reforms, SEE countries need to combine strategies of integration into the EU with strategies of national development. However, it is difficult to count on endogenous factors to promote development. The Balkans need a new type of 'Marshall Plan'. They do *not* need new divisions, such as the division into 'Western' and 'Eastern' Balkans. However, most SEE countries are far from satisfying the Copenhagen criteria for economic competitiveness. To amend the situation, the Stability Pact and the EU integration effort should go hand in hand.

Civil Society and Multilateral Cooperative Models: The Role of Non-Governmental Organizations in the Stability Pact for Southeastern Europe
HARALAMBOS KONDONIS

It has taken the international community some time to realize that for the economic reform and democratization of Southeastern Europe to succeed, different social actors in addition to governments must be involved. The Stability Pact was the result of the realization that economic development must be linked to a parallel democratic transition of society. Many non-governmental organizations (NGOs) in SEE are connected with government officials or with powerful international sponsors. Local NGOs look for such sponsors and, consequently, regional cooperation of civil society associations remains limited. The mobilization of NGOs is encouraged through the first Working Table of the Stability Pact. However, the implementation of the Pact in that particular field has met with problems. There is multi-collectivism, that is, too many members and partners, and this is reflected in a complex bureaucratic structure. There are conflicting interests and priorities and a lack of coordination. Member-states of the Pact have been reluctant to staff and financially support the Pact. SEE States have been reluctant to cooperate with NGOs. Stability Pact projects have been approachable by a few NGOs and private companies. There is a need for direct action and political will to exploit the many positive aspects of the Stability Pact. Specific criteria for projects, such as 'added value' and 'regional transferability', may be applied with success and a more clear 'priority agenda' has to be set.

From an Omnipresent and Strong to a Big and Weak State:
Democratization and State Reform in Southeastern Europe
DIMITRI A. SOTIROPOULOS

Traditionally, before the advent of socialist regimes, the state in Southeastern Europe was overpowering and distant, that is, aloof from the demands of certain social strata and social categories. Under socialism, the state became omnipresent, regulating many aspects of the life of its citizens, and thus ceased to be distant. After 1989, the state in SEE has remained big and has become weak. It has been unable to counter organized crime and to provide better services to the people. A few small case studies illustrate these claims. The Bulgarian public administration used to be very politicized even before the rise of the Communist Party to power. Since the transition to democracy, administrative reform has been very slow, while extreme politicization has continued. However, in the late 1990s new laws reorganizing the administration were passed. The case of Yugoslavia is different, particularly since this is a federal state. Under Milosevic, the administration as a whole became very rigid and, in many instances, corrupted. Kosovo has been administered partly by the local government and partly by UNMIK. The cases of Bulgaria, Yugoslavia and Kosovo share some common traits, related to the problematic selection, compensation and training of civil servants. Administrative reform should primarily address the issue of corruption and should also be linked to the strengthening of democratic institutions, including the access of citizens to state services.

The Difficult Road to the Independent Media: Is the Post-Communist Transition Over?
REMZI LANI and FRROK CUPI

In most countries of Southeastern Europe, the transition to democracy has gone through a phase of a New Authoritarianism. Such new authoritarian regimes were largely based on control of mass media (for example, Serbia under Milosevic). Currently, there is consensus that regulation of print media would probably lead to censorship. On the other hand, most Southeast European countries have passed legislation on TV and radio broadcasting. A fair balance between necessary regulations and the freedom of the media has not yet been achieved. Some political leaders of post-communist Southeastern Europe are not open to accept intense criticism from the media. Some react strongly to criticism, while others have adopted a stance of indifference towards the media, which means that opinions voiced in and by the media are ineffective. Some mass media are controlled by political groups, while other media have succumbed to economic interests. Since the transition from communism, partisan politics has penetrated the media, which have also been affected by economic difficulties and corruption. During the disintegration of Yugoslavia many media have promoted nationalist causes and have fuelled conflict. In the emerging democracies of Southeastern Europe, the spread of a free press can be considered a major achievement; at the same time the image of the press in society is rather negative. There is a need for economic independence of the media and for the training of journalists. Support for reform of the media and for adoption of a code of ethics among journalists is highly recommended.

Rewriting School Textbooks as a Tool of Understanding and Stability
MIRELA-LUMINIŢA MURGESCU

Despite common impressions, education systems and problems of identity formation in Southeastern Europe are far from homogeneous.

The contents of school textbooks of geography and history are closely linked to the formation of national identities of Balkan peoples. But textbooks are not solely to blame for the spread of violent ethnic conflict. Mass media and the public discourse in general should also be taken into account. In view of the above, there are three categories of Southeast European states. The first category consists of states which have existed for several generations (Albania, Bulgaria, Greece, Romania and Turkey). Although violent conflicts have not erupted recently among these nation-states, textbooks used in their educational systems reflect a biased vision of the past. An even more biased vision is found in textbooks of a second category of states, which emerged from the disintegration of former Yugoslavia. None of these states seems prepared to offer a more balanced view of history. The third category consists of territories under the control of Western administration and military (Bosnia-Herzegovina and Kosovo). In these areas, values taught to pupils are at odds with ideas of reconciliation. There are possibilities for improving on textbooks and school curricula. An example is the EUSTORY network of history competitions for young people. Such specific efforts may be combined with support schemes for the educational systems in general and with training programmes in other subjects, beyond history and geography.

Corruption and Organized Crime in Southeastern Europe: A Paradigm of Social Change Revisited
OGNYAN MINCHEV

A major problem of the transition to democracy and the market in Southeast European countries is how these countries will adapt their institutions to the European model. The lack of foreign investment and a coherent legal framework have had the following effect: privatizations have been sidetracked into a route leading to a very large underground economy. This economy has fallen into the hands of members of the former nomenclature. Government failure and loss of public morale are related to the spread of corruption, particularly since corruption has become a normal way of operation for private interests. In turn, people in SEE societies have fallen back to pre-modern forms of security (family or clan-based forms). Post-communist elites have mistakenly believed in the power of the 'invisible hand' of the market and the beneficial effects of 'civil society' and have not created adequate institutions to replace the dismantled totalitarian system. The way out is to change the abstract 'democratization' paradigm with the paradigm of development of effective representative and administrative institutions and of adaptation to the globalizing and multicultural world.

How to Control Corruption in Southeastern Europe: The Case of Bulgaria
IVAN KRASTEV

In Southeastern Europe there is a general perception of public administration incompetence and insecurity. A relevant case is that of Bulgaria, where there is a dilemma of fighting corruption or promoting economic reform. Attempting the former in the traditional fashion of increasing administrative controls would require too many resources which are necessary for economic reform. Corruption is impossible to measure because the scope of the concept has changed over time, because it is rarely confirmed as such in the courts, and because there are no specific victims of corruption. In Bulgaria the probability of sentencing a corrupted official to a term in prison is almost nil. Anti-corruption measures, such as tightening institutional controls or offering pay increases to officials, do not work. Anti-corruption measures often lead to more state regulation and may also fuel populism as a strategy of political leaders. The Bulgarian government should proceed with deregulation and de-monopolization as well as with raising public awareness about corruption.

Southeastern Europe and European Security Architecture
RADOVAN VUKADINOVIC

Traditionally the Balkans had no geopolitical centre of their own. Balkan states gravitated towards great powers outside their own geopolitical space. After the end of the Cold War, the disintegration of Yugoslavia, along with the preceding dissolution of the Warsaw Pact, created a security vacuum in the Balkans. Due to wars in former Yugoslavia and to the problems of transition in the region as a whole, the international geo-economic interest in the Balkans has decreased. The incorporation of SEE into a wider security architecture is necessary in order to avert military and non-military threats to the region's stability. 'Security architecture' is a concept meaning a set of institutions which fulfill a security function and the arrangement of relations among those institutions. The international community has a sufficient military presence and interest in SEE. Non-military challenges are more difficult to meet. Among the latter, traditional Balkan disputes, new conflicts related to recently acquired national independence, potential points of crisis, and new challenges to security, are included. After the future normalization of relations among SEE countries the current situation of 'unstable stability' could be overcome. One could envisage the inclusion of the SEE region as a whole into a new European Security Architecture.

The Albanian Question in the Aftermath of the War: A Proposal to Break the Status Deadlock
EVANGELOS KOFOS

The NATO intervention in Kosovo in 1999 resolved some problems but also fuelled wider Albanian nationalist aspirations. Albanian nationalist movements have spread outside the borders of the Albanian state, in Presevo and Tetovo, throughout 2001. There have been attempts to coordinate the cultural and economic integration of Albanian groups in an 'Albanian Space' in Southeastern Europe. There has also been an escalation of the domestic conflicts in FYROM. Albanian mobilization in all those areas may be attributed to the continuing nebulous international status of Kosovo. As long as the status of Kosovo remains unclear, other Albanian groups outside of Kosovo may increase their demands and escalate their political and military activities. In view of the above, placing Kosovo under the temporal 'trusteeship' of the United Nations could be a solution. This solution was applied after the Second World War to various colonies and territories formerly belonging to Western powers. The new status of Kosovo as a territory under United Nations trusteeship requires that FR Yugoslavia voluntarily agrees to this interim status and that one or more countries, perhaps including Yugoslavia, would constitute an Administering Authority to govern Kosovo while it prepares for self-government or independence.

The International Presence in Kosovo and Regional Security: The Deep Winter of UN Security Council Resolution 1244
ALEXANDROS YANNIS

Despite the fall of Milosevic in FR Yugoslavia and the victory of moderate political forces in the municipal and national elections in Kosovo, the situation in that area remains precarious. The representatives of the international community stationed in Kosovo enjoy today greater legitimacy among the Kosovar Albanian and Serbian communities than in the past. For the time being, the status of Kosovo may be 'frozen' because there is an absence of international and local consensus about its future. The more rigorous implementation of UN Security Council Resolution 1244 could prevent Kosovo from sliding back to open conflict. Democratic elections alone cannot solve the problem. There is a need for a road map to meet the minimum demands of Kosovo Albanians and Serbs. However, it would be dangerous to meet the maximum demands of either. To that effect, a new 'agenda of coexisence' could be adopted which could ensure the functional autonomy of Serbs within the substantial autonomy of Albanians. There is also need for a long-term commitment of the international community to the development of the region. This does not necessary mean the indefinite perpetuation of international military presence or undiminished financial aid, but substantive assistance to build effective democratic institutions. The democratic change in Serbia in 2000 and the victory of moderate political forces in the elections in Kosovo have opened a window of opportunity.

Ten Concepts That Will Define the Future of Kosovo (A Personal Note)
VETON SURROI

The events of 1999 showed that a reversal of political domination in Kosovo was possible. The decline of Serb rule over Kosovo is irreversible. All this has amounted to a revolution. However, there has been a lack of law and order. The feeling of liberation, sensed by Kosovo Albanians, has not been accompanied by a clearly determined future. This future of Kosovo has been linked with two other processes, the ongoing disintegration of Yugoslavia and the process of European integration. Kosovo is undergoing three transitions: first, the transition from communism to democracy; second, the transition from minority to majority rule (from rule of Serbs over Albanians to self-rule of Albanians); and third, the transition from a multi-ethnic region to nation-state. Resolution 1244 implies a process, the endpoint of which will be that Kosovo becomes a state. Differences of opinion exist on the degree of sovereignty this state will have. The Albanian national movement has traditionally sprung up in different locations. It is a 'polycentric' movement, which may influence thinking over the future of Kosovo. Kosovo may be a unit with more flexible and permeable borders than typical ethnocentric nation-states. All of the above can decided upon in a two-step process. The first step would be to establish democratic self-rule in Kosovo, while the second step would be to reach a decision on its permanent status.

Yugoslavia at the Crossroads: Reforms or Disintegration?
PREDRAG SIMIC

In 2000 the drama of former Yugoslavia ended, but several problems remained unsolved. First, a crisis has been provoked by Albanian extremists who have been active in Kosovo, Macedonia and southern Serbia; and second, the relations between Serbia and Montenegro remain unclear. The two problems have a common dynamic and one may influence the other. Since October 1997, there has been a 'cold war' between Podgorica and Belgrade, but open conflict has not erupted. Under Milosevic, repression by authorities in Belgrade has worked in favour of authorities in Podgorica. After the victory of democratic forces in Belgrade, periodic negotiations have taken place between Serbia and Montenegro. In southern Serbia the new Belgrade administration was able to contain the activities of the Albanian UCPBM and the Yugoslav army has cooperated with NATO in the Ground Safety Zone. In Bosnia, six years after the Dayton Peace Agreement, the joint organs remain weak while the international administration has obtained more competencies. In Kosovo, UNMIK and NATO have not confronted the remaining vestiges of UCK and have been unable to stop violence at the local level. The situation in Kosovo remains a long-term source of threats to regional security. Conversely, the break-up of the Yugoslav Federation might cause an escalation of the Kosovo crisis.

Greece and FYROM: A Partnership for Stability in Southeastern Europe?
ARISTOTLE TZIAMPIRIS

In the past, relations between FYROM and Greece were problematic, but nowadays FYROM and Greece have an interest in maintaining good bilateral relations. FYROM has faced a difficult economic situation, which was aggravated by the economic burden of the Kosovo conflict in 1999. It has also faced challenges to its territorial integrity. Ethnic co-existence in FYROM remains a problem, because the views of the country's national majority and its Albanian minority diverge. Fortunately there has been an economic and diplomatic rapprochement between Greece and FYROM. It is important to secure FYROM's territorial integrity, an aim which can be achieved through the involvement of Greece, the European Union and major international organizations.

An Update and Conclusions
DIMITRI A. SOTIROPOULOS and THANOS VEREMIS

The events of 11 September 2001 have shifted the attention of the international community away from Southeastern Europe. However, this region continues developing in various directions, some of which are positive (the elections in Kosovo and the victory of moderate political forces) while others are ambiguous (the dispute between Fatos Nano and Ilir Meta in Albania and the resignation of Prime Minister Ilir Meta in the beginning of 2002), if not clearly detrimental to peace and development (violent conflicts in FYROM in spring and summer 2001). The economies of the region remain undeveloped, and the biggest problems are unemployment and lack of foreign investments. The West has not set a clear set of priorities in regard to the economic future of the region. The Stability Pact remains a complex set of processes although it bears a lot of potential to deliver substantive help to SEE. The quality of democracies in the region is very debatable. Despite holding regular elections, many SEE countries still do not possess effective democratic and administrative institutions. This is related to flourishing corruption and organized crime. Possible solutions lie in a combination of regional and international initiatives, in which individual SEE countries and the international community will act together. On the side of the international community, there is a need for concrete actions in the context of a long-term commitment to the region. This will require political will on the part of important Western powers, and more concerted and coordinated efforts on the part of involved international organizations. On the side of individual SEE countries, there is a need for the mobilization of their own economic and human resources and a willingness to build institutions and processes which will allow these countries to adapt to the requirements of political and economic integration with Europe. This prospect allows the optimistic conclusion that Southeastern Europe is not doomed to instability.

Index

Books of Related Interest

The Kosovo Tragedy

Human Rights Dimensions

Ken Booth, *University of Wales, Aberystwyth* (Ed)

The 1999 conflict over Kosovo was described as being as significant for
international affairs as the pulling down of the Berlin wall, an
importance deriving from the centrality of human rights in the build–up,
conduct and aftermath of the war. This volume is the first
comprehensive attempt to explore the tragedy from the perspective of
human rights in all their dimensions. An international group of
specialists debate key human rights issues: the experiences from Bosnia,
the contentious concepts, the wrongs done to the victims, the manner of
the fighting, the current situation in Kosovo, and the lessons for
humanitarian intervention.

Contributors: *Ken Booth, Carrie Booth Walling, Daniela Kroslak, Tim
Dunne, Caroline Kennedy-Pipe, Penny Stanley, Marianne Hanson,
William Walker, Alex Bellamy, Nicholas J Wheeler, Jim Whitman,
Hilaire McCoubrey, Marc Weller, Eric Herring, Ian Mitchell, Jasmina
Husanovic, Tarak Barkaun, Chris Brown, Richard Falk, Colin Gray,
Melanie McDonagh and John Stremlau.*

408 pages 2001
0 7146 5085 4 cloth
0 7146 8126 1 paper
A special issue of the International Journal of Human Rights

FRANK CASS PUBLISHERS
Crown House, 47 Chase Side, Southgate, London N14 5BP
Tel: +44 (0)20 8920 2100 Fax: +44 (0)20 8447 8548 E-mail: info@frankcass.com
NORTH AMERICA
5824 NE Hassalo Street, Portland, OR 97213 3644, USA
Tel: 800 944 6190 Fax: 503 280 8832 E-mail: cass@isbs.com
Website: www.frankcass.com

Kosovo: The Politics of Delusion

Michael Waller, Kyril Drezov and **Bülent Gökay**,
all at *Keele University*

Why did Kosovo become the focal point of NATO's undeclared war
against Yugoslavia? The American-inspired 'international community',
with NATO as its military arm, is the next in a long succession of
outside powers –including The Roman Empire, the Ottoman Empire,
the Habsburg Empire and the Soviet Empire – to impose order on the
Balkans. In 1995 NATO acquired its first Balkan protectorate in Bosnia,
following a clash with Slobodan Milosevic and the forces of Serbian
nationalism under his control. Routine human rights violations,
escalating violence, irreconcilable claims and danger of a spill-over into
neighbouring states, made Kosovo the natural candidate for another
NATO involvement in the Balkans.

Part One deals with the background and history of the conflict, while
Part Two gives diverse opinions on NATO's attack on Yugoslavia and
the consequent occupation of Kosovo by KFOR. The editors combine a
dispassionate treatment of the key aspects of the conflict with highly
charged personal opinions about the rights and wrongs of NATO's
intervention.

200 pages 2001
0 7146 5157 5 cloth
0 7146 8176 8 paper

FRANK CASS PUBLISHERS
Crown House, 47 Chase Side, Southgate, London N14 5BP
Tel: +44 (0)20 8920 2100 Fax: +44 (0)20 8447 8548 E-mail: info@frankcass.com
NORTH AMERICA
5824 NE Hassalo Street, Portland, OR 97213 3644, USA
Tel: 800 944 6190 Fax: 503 280 8832 E-mail: cass@isbs.com
Website: www.frankcass.com

Peacebuilding and Police Reform

Tor Tanke Holm, *Police Advisor for the UN Programme at the NUPI* and **Espen Barth Eide**, *Director of the UN Programme, NUPI* (Eds)

The past decade has seen rapid growth in international efforts in the area of police reform assistance and civilian police (CIVPOL) operations. Experts in the fields of peacekeeping, civilian police activities and police reform, both academics and practitioners, discuss the issue of internationally assisted police reform in transitions from war to peace. Contributions include theoretical insights and informed case studies, from El Salvador and Guatemala, the Balkans, West Bank and Gaza, and Mozambique and South Africa. The concluding chapter discusses the trend towards internationally provided executive authority policing seen in the ongoing operations in Kosovo and in East Timor.

Contributors: *Espen Barth Eide, Tor Hanke Holm, Rama Mani, Halvor Hartz, Chuck Call, Michael Barnett, Francesca Marotta, Otwin Marenin, William Stanley, Brynar Lia, Mark Malan and Claudio Cordone.*

240 pages 2000
0 7146 4987 2 cloth
0 7146 8040 0 paper
A special issue of the journal International Peacekeeping
Cass Series on Peacekeeping No 7

FRANK CASS PUBLISHERS
Crown House, 47 Chase Side, Southgate, London N14 5BP
Tel: +44 (0)20 8920 2100 Fax: +44 (0)20 8447 8548 E-mail: info@frankcass.com
NORTH AMERICA
5824 NE Hassalo Street, Portland, OR 97213 3644, USA
Tel: 800 944 6190 Fax: 503 280 8832 E-mail: cass@isbs.com
Website: www.frankcass.com

Region, State and Identity in Central and Eastern Europe

Judy Batt and **Kataryna Wolczuk**, both at the
University of Birmingham (Eds)

Post-communist state transformations in Central and Eastern Europe
have been accompanied by an upsurge of identity politics as newly
independent peoples sought to redefine themselves and their place in
Europe. This book examines the role of competing identities – national,
ethnic, regional, European – and models of the state in debates over the
introduction of new regional levels of government in Central and
Eastern Europe, and in the often problematic relationships between
centres and regions as these countries adjust to democratization and
redefining their place in the 'new Europe'.

224 pages 2002
0 7146 5243 1 cloth
0 7146 8225 X paper
A special issue of the journal Regional and Federal Studies
Cass Series in Regional and Federal Studies

FRANK CASS PUBLISHERS
Crown House, 47 Chase Side, Southgate, London N14 5BP
Tel: +44 (0)20 8920 2100 Fax: +44 (0)20 8447 8548 E-mail: info@frankcass.com
NORTH AMERICA
5824 NE Hassalo Street, Portland, OR 97213 3644, USA
Tel: 800 944 6190 Fax: 503 280 8832 E-mail: cass@isbs.com
Website: www.frankcass.com